I dedicate this book
to my two special *keikis*,
Nicole and Roy Jr., with love.

Niihau

Kauai

Oahu

Molokai

Nicolina's

Maui

Hawaii

Lanai

Roy's Poipu
Bar & Grill

Roy's Hawaii Kai
Honolulu

Roy's Kahana
Bar & Grill

Roy's Waikoloa
Bar & Grill

Roy's

Feasts from Hawaii

ROY YAMAGUCHI

and John Harrisson

Hawaii Photography by Franco Salmoiraghi
Food Photography by Lois Ellen Frank

Ten Speed Press

Ten Speed Press

P.O. Box 7123, Berkeley, California 94707

Front cover photo by David Franzen, Honolulu, HI.

Cover and text design by Fifth Street Design, Berkeley, CA.

Food photography by Lois Ellen Frank, Santa Fe, NM.

Food photography styling by Janne Yamaguchi and Fifth Street Design.

Other photography copyright © Franco Salmoiraghi, Honolulu, HI.

Additional photo captions:
Pages 8–9: Taro fields in the Hanalei Valley, Kauai. Page 37: A selection of offerings from Roy's bar. Photo by Lois Ellen Frank. Pages 38–39: Lava from the active Kilauea volcano meets the sea, Volcanoes National Park, Big Island. Page 53: Garden waterfall, Kauai. Pages 54–55: Guava tree orchard, Kauai. Pages 76–77: Lava flowing past trees, Volcanoes National Park, Big Island. Pages 96–97: Harvesting prawns at the Hawaii Prawn Co., Kahuku, Oahu. Pages 124–25: Herding cattle beneath the slopes of Mauna Kea, Parker Ranch, Big Island. Page 139: Waterfall, Molokai. Pages 148–149: Leleiwi Fishpond, near Leleiwi Point, Big Island. Page 167: Guava harvesters, Kilauea Agronomics, Kauai, Pages 188–189: Port of Honolulu and the Aloha Tower, Oahu. Pages 210–211: Volcanoes of the Big Island—snowcapped Mauna Kea (foreground) and Mauna Loa (background).

Distributed in Australia by Simon & Schuster Australia, in Canada by Ten Speed Press Canada, in New Zealand by Southern Publishers Group, in South Africa by Real Books, and in the United Kingdom and Europe by Airlift Book Company.

Library of Congress Cataloging-in-Publication Data:

Yamaguchi, Roy, 1956–

Roy's feasts from hawaii

/Roy Yamaguchi and John Harrison

p. cm.

Includes index.

ISBN 0-89815-637-8

I. Cookery, Hawaiian. I. Harrisson, John II. Title.

TX724.5A3Y36 1995

641.59969—dc20   94-26690

    CIP

Printed in China

10 11 12 13 14 15 — 07 06 05 04 03

Contents

Appetizers

Soups

Salads

Roy's Antipasti Salad, 65

Seared Shrimp Salad with Feta Cheese and Candied Garlic, 66

Warm Spinach Salad with Spicy Shrimp and Scallops, 68

Smoked Ahi Salad with Cilantro Vinaigrette and Red Bell Pepper Coulis, 69

Curried Lemon Grass-Crusted Swordfish Salad with Red Ginger-Soy Vinaigrette, 70

Duck Pastrami with Molokai Greens and Balsamic Cabernet Sauce, 72

Crispy Scallop and Fresh Fruit Salad with Creamy Blue Cheese Dressing, 73

Mango and Papaya Salad with Crabmeat, Crispy Shiu Mai, and Orange-Chile Sauce, 74

Teriyaki Duck Salad with Candied Pecans and Papaya in a Raspberry Vinaigrette, 75

Pastas and Imu Pizzas

Roy's House Pasta with Chicken and Shrimp in Sun-Dried Tomato Sauce, 79

Ravioli of Lamb, Goat Cheese, and Pesto with Napoletana Sauce, 80

Thai-Style Pasta Aglio e Olio, 82

Grilled Shrimp and Clam Linguine, 83

Linguine alla Carbonara with Chicken and Asparagus, 84

Asian Pasta Primavera, 86

Basic Pizza Dough, 87

R.J.'s Keiki-Style Pizza with Straight Cheese, 88

Grilled Shrimp and Eggplant Pizza with Pesto, Feta, and Goat Cheese, 89

Puna Goat Cheese and Shiitake Mushroom Pizza with Wilted Baby Greens, 90

Mongolian Chicken Pizza, 92

Duck and Mushroom Pizza with Honey-Hoisin-Cilantro Sauce, 93

Mozzarella Pizza with Mizuna Lettuce and Pan-Roasted Tomatoes, 94

Fish and Shellfish

Seared Opakapaka and Scallops with Lobster-Passion Fruit-Ginger Sauce, 99

Garlic and Herb-Crusted Mahimahi with Cucumber-Tomato-Ginger Salsa, 100

Seared Lemon Grass-Crusted Salmon with Watercress-Ginger Sauce, 102

Ono and Pan-Fried Oysters with Lobster-Curry Sauce, 104

Hibachi Tuna with Maui Onion Salad and Ponzu Sauce, 106

Seared Lemon Grass-Crusted Swordfish with Thai Curry Sauce, 107

Broiled Hawaiian Swordfish in Miso, 108

Grilled Miso-Crusted Butterfish with Three Caviars and Avocado, 109

Ulua with Banana-Curry Sauce, 110

Asian-Style Ono with Spicy Shrimp and Bell Peppers, 112

Seared Ahi with Passion Fruit-Shrimp Salsa, 113

Cassoulet of Shrimp, Opakapaka, Scallops, Oysters, and Clams in Cioppino Broth, 114

Rustic Opakapaka with Tuscan-Style White Beans and Herb-Infused Olive Oil, 116

Mahimahi with Szechwan-Style Clams and Bell Peppers, 117

Shrimp Shiu Mai and Hawaiian Prawns with Sesame Butter Sauce, 118

Curried Shrimp with Enoki Mushroom-Cucumber Relish, 120

Kona Crab Cakes in Spicy Butter Sauce, 121

Grilled Spiny Lobster with Bean Thread Noodles and Macadamia Nuts, 122

Meat and Poultry

Lanai Venison in Red Currant-Cabernet Sauce with Pesto Potatoes, 127

Grilled Pork Medallions with Watercress Salad and Shoestring Potatoes, 129

Rack of Lamb with Bangkok Curry Sauce, 131

Parker Ranch Filet Mignon with Pan-Crisped Onions and Honey-Mustard Sauce, 132

Veal Chops with Mediterranean Vegetables and Madeira Tomato Sauce, 134

Venison with Grilled Vegetable Gratin and Cognac Peppercorn Sauce, 136

Braised Pork with Island-Style Applesauce, 137

Mongolian-Style Grilled Short Ribs with Leeks au Gratin and Mashed Potatoes, 138

Chicken Katsu with Crispy Eggplant Chips and Maui Onion Salad, 140

Crispy Lemon Grass Chicken with Red Wine Curry Sauce, 141

Grilled Chicken with Black Bean Mango Salsa and Crispy Taro, 142

Roy's Chinatown Duck with Plum-Peach Sauce, 144

Gratin of Corn-Fed Turkey with Johnny Apple Stuffing and Creamed Spinach, 146

Side Dishes and Salsas

Japanese White Rice, 151

Jasmine Rice, 152

Roy's Mashed Potatoes, 153

Thai Potato Croquettes, 153

Crispy Couscous, 154

Goat Cheese Hash, 155

Tuscan-Style White Beans, 156

Garlic Spinach, 157

Thai-Style Curried Vegetables, 157

Asian Ratatouille, 158

Creamed Corn, 160

Red Bell Pepper Mousse, 160

Island Mint Chutney, 161

Asian Salsa, 162

Shiitake Mushroom and Corn Salsa, 162

Cucumber Caper Relish, 163

Black Bean Papaya Relish, 163

Avocado Salsa, 164

Sun-Dried Tomato Relish, 165

Roasted Tomato Salsa, 166

Tropical Island Salsa, 166

Brunch

Hawaiian Sweet Bread, 171

French Toast with Caramelized Apples, Strawberries, Star Fruit, and Plums, 172

Johnny's Griddle-Top Bread Pudding with Fresh Fruit Coulis, 174

Banana Pancakes with Raspberry Coulis and Candied Pecans, 175

Japanese-Style Seafood Frittata with Sautéed Spinach and Shrimp Butter Sauce, 176

Fresh Mushroom Frittata with Potatoes, Onions, Cheese, and Pancetta, 178

Louisiana Crab Cakes Benedict with Andouille and Tarragon-Mustard Sauce, 179

Roy's Homemade Corned Beef Hash with Poached Eggs, 180

Oriental Gravlax, 181

Loco Moco Bistro-Style, 182

Shrimp Spring Rolls with Orange-Chile Sauce, 183

Shrimp Hash with Spicy Lobster Sesame Sauce, 184

Desserts

Basic Recipes

Acknowledgments

My special thanks are due to a number of people who made this book a reality.

First, Janne Yamaguchi, who shared my vision and helped conceptualize and develop the artistic layout of the book.

John Harrisson brought his sense of dedication to coordinating the many facets of this project, and even moved to Hawaii to learn the true meaning of the spirit of *ohana*.

Lois Ellen Frank and Franco Salmoiraghi brought their creativity and professionalism to the photography; it was a pleasure working with them. Walter Whitewater and Trez Harrisson worked tirelessly behind the scenes and did all that we asked to perfection.

Brent Beck worked with us all to translate our ideas and vision into the design of this book. Jackie Wan fine-tuned and tweaked the text as only she knows how.

To my partner Gordon Hopkins, to Casey Logsdon, and to David Abella, my special thanks and appreciation for your creativity and work on the recipes. Likewise, to my many friends in the kitchen at Roy's who have helped me in so many ways.

Last, but not least, my thanks to Mona Mento-Moore for her scheduling skill, and many *mahalos* to my other partners, Randy Caparoso, Christian Maldonado, and Philip Shaw for keeping things humming along in the meantime. My gratitude also goes to Myrtle, Freddie, and Terry Lee, Judy and Vince Sykes, and Mike McKenna for believing in Roy's.

Introduction

This book is more than a collection of recipes that reflect what I call my contemporary Euro-Asian cooking style. It is a celebration, in words and pictures, of the incomparable backdrop that Hawaii provides for my food, and the wealth of local resources that continually inspire me. It is also a tribute to the unique ethnic and culinary diversity of the Hawaiian islands that have shaped my repertoire.

Hawaii has witnessed a remarkable culinary revolution over the last few years, thanks in large part to the resurgence in local agriculture and the development of high-quality specialty produce right here on our islands. Hawaii has always enjoyed world-class local seafood as well as a wide array of tropical produce, but in the past, local chefs (especially those with a European background) were reluctant to showcase them. In fact, as often as not, they preferred to fly in fresh and frozen foods from the mainland (even fish!). In recent years, a number of like-minded chefs joined to form the Hawaiian Regional Cuisine movement, and one of our aims was to encourage local food growers and suppliers to work together with the restaurants. They would produce the goods, and we would provide the market. Of course, many of the growers and suppliers were already here, but there is now a much closer bond.

It has been exciting and rewarding to witness the growth of high-quality Hawaiian-grown produce, some examples of which are profiled throughout the book. The use of local foodstuffs is integral to my cooking, and you'll see references to many of them—Big Island macadamia nuts, Kona coffee, sweet Maui onions, freshwater shrimp from the large aquafarms at Kahuku, herbs and greens from Nalo Farms, Waimanalo corn, and the wonderful Puna goat cheese from Steve and Karin Sayre's Orchid Island farm—in the recipes. In most cases, you can find appropriate substitutes in your region.

In retrospect, it seems entirely logical that my upbringing and career brought me to Hawaii, the crossroads of the Pacific Rim. I used to visit Hawaii with my parents as a child and my grandparents lived on Maui (my father was born there), so I've always had warm memories of the islands. As soon as I came to live here and opened Roy's restaurant in 1988, I knew that this lush, tropical paradise was my spiritual home and that it would be a continual source of inspiration for my cooking.

When I'm asked how I got started in the restaurant business, I think back to when I was in high school. I came up with the brilliant plan to take a home economics course in order to meet girls (in those days, home economics was exclusively a female preserve). As it turned out, it didn't improve my social life much, but I did discover that I really liked cooking. In fact, I enjoyed it so much, I decided to repeat the class.

In my second year, the class held a special Thanksgiving dinner; each student was to prepare a special dish for it, and could invite a guest to the dinner. I decided to invite the school's career counselor, which turned out to be a fortuitous move. The event was a great success (I prepared turkey with a bread stuffing), and after dinner, my satisfied guest, now back in the role of counselor, leaned over toward me and asked what I wanted to do with the rest of my life. When I hesitated a moment, he added, "I'm telling you, I think you have a future in cooking." And that's how it all began. His comment made such an impression on me that I made up my mind

to go to school at the Culinary Institute of America in New York State after graduating from high school. It was a major decision on my part because, although I was an American citizen, I had grown up in Japan (my father worked at a U.S. Army base outside Tokyo), and had never even been to the mainland United States. Language was not a problem, because we spoke both English and Japanese at home, and I had been educated in American schools in Japan. Still, New York was a big unknown to me. My parents were supportive of my plans; after all, my grandparents had owned a restaurant and general store in Hawaii, so I was carrying on a family tradition. Besides, my dad was an excellent cook and prepared most of our family meals (we very rarely ate out—occasionally he'd take us for noodles at a Chinese restaurant after church on Sundays). And so, I set out for New York. I was only eighteen at the time, and I had a lot to learn.

In fact, one of the first things I learned was how little I knew about food. Sole, halibut, flounder, and crayfish were all new to me, as were such common vegetables as turnips and zucchini. I'll never forget the first time I encountered an artichoke. I was having dinner with some new friends from the Culinary Institute, and when faced with this strange delicacy, I pretended I knew how to eat it. I tackled it with a knife and fork and began chewing on the tough outer leaves. Studying at the CIA was a great learning experience for me and laid the foundation for the "Euro" part of my cooking style. We were taught that classic French cooking plus the so-called *nouvelle* cuisine were the epitome of fine food preparation. A major influence (and required reading) was Escoffier, the king of chefs. We also learned about Italian cooking and the cuisines of other Mediterranean countries. (Another thing I learned early on was to call the Institute the CIA. I still stop people in their tracks when I say I trained at the CIA.) I learned a lot outside of school, too. Since the school was just outside New York City, I got to try all kinds of foods, local and otherwise.

To help support myself while I was going to school, I worked in the kitchen at the Huguenot Manor Country Club in New Paltz, New York. The Perry family (Mike Sr., his wife Katherine, and son Mike Jr.) owned and ran the club. I still think of Katherine as my American mom. We worked together in the kitchen, and she took care of me—she'd fix me spaghetti and meatballs for breakfast and we'd share pretzels and Coke after work. She was an important and positive influence on me in those formative years.

Another individual who shaped my career—more than either of us could have known at the time—was LeRoi Folsom, a vice president of the CIA. He invited me to his house for Thanksgiving dinner, along with two other students from Japan who also had nowhere special to go for the holiday. One of our discussions turned to my future career, and when I mentioned I would probably begin my professional life in the kitchen of a classic French restaurant, LeRoi asked me why. I said, as if it were a silly question, "Because French cuisine is the *best* cuisine." LeRoi's next words set me thinking and planted seeds in my mind that were to change my outlook forever: "Everything's good if it's done well," he said, "not just French cuisine. Why not Italian cuisine, or Chinese or Japanese?"

Despite LeRoi's advice, the first job I accepted after graduating from the CIA in 1976 was in a French restaurant. I moved to Los Angeles (mainly because my brother was attending the University of Southern California at the time), and ended up at the Escoffier Room of the Beverly Hilton Hotel, one of the most prestigious formal dining rooms in the city. I started out as a prep cook and then

Roy's Feasts from Hawaii

graduated to line chef. On the way to work every day, the bus I rode passed a restaurant awning that read JAPANESE-FRENCH CUISINE. After a while, I started daydreaming about what that might mean exactly; the idea of mixing cuisines intrigued me.

The next turning point in my career occurred when I interviewed at the legendary L'Ermitage in West Hollywood, where Michel Blanchet was chef. During the interview, owner Jean Bertranou asked me point-blank if I could "really" cook. We discussed the premise that cooking was more than throwing ingredients into a pan or working with formulas, and he told me of his conviction that in order to "really" cook, I had to have a burning desire to do so. He equated it with the creative passions of a master artist or musician. I came away from the interview with a vague feeling of insecurity. The next day I watched Michel Blanchet cook on a television show, and his performance made me even more nervous. When L'Ermitage called me back, I thanked them and explained that I couldn't take the job right now. I just wasn't ready to *really* cook. Instead, I took a job at a small Scandinavian restaurant, where I polished my skills and gathered my thoughts for a while. Slowly, I developed a real hunger to meet a greater challenge, and the kind of intense desire that Bertranou had talked about. I reapplied to L'Ermitage, and was hired as a line cook there. I stayed for two years, and during that time I learned an incredible amount, especially from Michel and Jean. And there were others. John Sedlar, now at Abiquiu in Santa Monica, was in the L'Ermitage kitchen too, and I also worked alongside guest chefs such as Roger Jaloux (from Paul Bocuse's restaurant) and Alain Detourniers. And I cooked for Michel Guerard, Jean Blanchet, and the Troisgros brothers—experiences that took me to another level.

Ready for new challenges, I left L'Ermitage to open a new restaurant, Le Serene, in Burbank. There, for the first time, I had the freedom to develop my own style, and began to experiment with combinations drawn from Asian and French cuisines. Then, Michael McCarthy asked me to join his team at the acclaimed Michael's, where he had assembled an amazingly talented group of chefs—Jonathan Waxman, Mark Peel, Nancy Silverton, and Gordon Naccarato, among others. Michael ran a great operation, and I learned a great deal about running a restaurant from my short stay there.

Several months later, I was offered the position of head chef at Le Gourmet, the fine dining room in the Sheraton Plaza La Reina near the Los Angeles airport. There I had the luxury of experimenting with some very high-priced ingredients—truffles, foie gras, and fresh fish flown in from the Greenwich Fish Company in New York, for example—and I could indulge in creating the cross-cultural dishes that I loved, as I had full control of the kitchen. While at Le Gourmet, two of Wolfgang Puck's partners at Spago invited me to join them as executive chef and partner in their new restaurant venture, 385 North.

And so I moved on again. We opened the restaurant on North La Cienega Boulevard in 1984, and it was there, in my own place at last, that I really developed my Euro-Asian cuisine, fusing the knowledge and techniques I had learned along the way with wonderful ingredients and a growing confidence that this was the unique direction I really wanted to pursue. 385 North received rave reviews and I was proud to be nominated for California's Chef of the Year for 1986–1987, but somehow, it never clicked as a restaurant—I think the space was just too big and not intimate enough for the Los Angeles market. (We needed to fill most of our 250 seats for the atmosphere to be vibrant and exciting.) Still, it was a growth experience for me.

After four years, 385 North was sold and I decided to move on again, but this time to Hawaii. I took an offer on a restaurant space in the Honolulu suburb of Hawaii Kai, overlooking the wide, sandy Maunalua Bay beneath Koko Head. And so, in 1988, I opened Roy's, a 170-seat, two-level restaurant with an open kitchen. I was only too happy to renew my acquaintance with island life. But beyond that, Hawaii seemed like an ideal place to further develop my Euro-Asian style, not only because of its location at the crossroads of the Pacific Rim but also because of its unique and wonderful cultural mix. I was more interested in the resident population than the ephemeral tourist trade (although I wanted to appeal to that, too), and I recognized that people here were used to Asian flavors. Most of the hotels and a majority of the independent restaurants in Honolulu served French and European food, so I figured my style of cooking just might work. In addition, I believed my food represented a cutting-edge approach to Pacific Rim cuisine, which was one element lacking in Hawaii's restaurant food scene at the time.

My aim was to serve exciting, innovative, fun food of the highest quality in an elegant yet casual atmosphere, and at affordable prices. Fortunately, this approach struck a chord in Honolulu, and our local clientele became wonderfully loyal. In addition to winning numerous restaurant awards, I was honored to be named Best Chef for 1993 in the Pacific and Northwest by the James Beard Foundation. We have since opened several other restaurants: Roy's Kahana Bar and Grill and Roy's Nicolina (named after my daughter) on Maui; Roy's Poipu Bar and Grill on Kauai; Roy's Pebble Beach in the Inn at the Spanish Bay in California; Roy's in Tokyo; and Roy's on Guam in the Hilton Hotel. Soon to open is Roy's Waikoloa Bar and Grill on the Kona Coast of the Big Island.

The recipes in this book are representative of the selection of dishes we serve at the various Roy's restaurants. Some of the dishes are permanent fixtures on the menus, others are more seasonal. Some are my own favorites, or are very popular with our guests. There is even a pizza recipe, especially for the *keikis* (it's named after one of my own *keikis*, Roy Jr.). I hope you'll enjoy browsing through the book and giving the recipes a try.

A few words are in order about just what to expect. First of all, as you will see in the recipes that follow, my cooking is a blend of French, Italian, Thai, Japanese, Chinese, and Polynesian cuisines, with a few other influences thrown in for good measure. I like strong, assertive flavors and unusual combinations, and I insist on using absolutely fresh produce, meat, and fish, all preferably from local sources. I use a lot of Asian ingredients in my cooking, some of which may be new to the home cook. There's an extensive glossary in the back of the book to help you out on that score. Sometimes I indicate specific brands that I like to use, and some items are only available locally—like the Hawaiian spiny lobster and poi—but in most cases, substitutes are indicated. However, there's no need to follow the recipes to the letter. I recommend you use them as guides. *Real* cooking, as Jean Bertranou taught me, is more than following a formula. So, be sure to experiment, improvise, and take a few chances.

Cooking has been my life, and, before you head into your kitchen, I want to thank you for making it a part of yours, too.

Appetizers

Appetizers should be an exciting prelude to the food that follows, and should set the tone for the rest of the meal. They play an important role at Roy's, and we always have more than a dozen on the menu. We even encourage our guests to dine on a series of appetizers, instead of ordering a main course in the traditional way. I, for one, prefer this "grazing" style of eating; it allows you to explore the range of flavors and textures the menu offers.

I also love the Chinese tradition of dim sum (literally, "heart warmers"), and many of the appetizers in this chapter reflect that affection. In fact, the starter section of the menu at Roy's is titled "Dim Sum–Style Appetizers." Dim sum are simply snacks—spring rolls, dumplings, meatballs or pastries—stuffed with all kinds of fillings. They come in many different shapes and types. I especially enjoy going to a Chinese restaurant with my family on the weekend and ordering a variety of dim sum from the procession of carts that are loaded with appetizer-sized portions of food. It can also be fun to make four or five different dim sum or appetizers and share them as a meal with friends.

The Hawaiian pupu is an enduring tradition that lies somewhere between hors d'oeuvres and side dishes. Pupu platters usually feature morsels such as wontons, taro or coconut chips, or small cuts of grilled chicken, fish, or meat that can be shared by the whole table. Most of the recipes in this chapter can be served pupu style.

Roy's Kalua Pork Quesadillas with Smoked Mozzarella, Avocado, and Lomi Lomi Salmon

))) SERVES 4 (((

The Hawaiian word kalua refers to the traditional method of cooking food in a rock-lined underground oven called an imu. Kalua pig—a whole pig that has been baked in an imu—is the highlight of any luau. We don't have a real imu at the restaurant (I call our wood-burning pizza oven an imu because it produces the same smoky effect as the pit technique), but I've found that pork shoulder or pork butt can be cooked in a covered grill or smoker with a result that tastes just like the real thing. In this recipe, Hawaii meets the Southwest, by way of the Mediterranean.

Lomi Lomi Salmon:
1 salmon fillet, about 5 ounces
3 tablespoons sea salt
2 tablespoons thinly sliced scallions
1 Maui onion, finely diced

3 Roma tomatoes, peeled, seeded, and finely diced

. . .

2 pounds pork shoulder or pork butt
3 tablespoons sea salt or kosher salt
8 corn tortillas

8 ounces smoked mozzarella cheese, thinly sliced
½ cup Garlic Spinach (page 157)
2 avocados, peeled, pitted, and thinly sliced

*S*prinkle the salmon fillet with the sea salt, submerge in cold water, and refrigerate for 4 to 12 hours (overnight works well). Drain off the water and finely chop the salmon. At this point, the salmon can be held in the refrigerator for a day. Shortly before serving, combine the salmon with the scallions, onion, and tomatoes and reserve in the refrigerator.

Prepare the grill. Coat the pork heavily with the salt, place in a heavy all-metal pot or saucepan, and add enough water to come about one-third of the way up the sides (the meat should not be covered with water). Place the pot on the grill, cover the grill, and slowly cook over low heat for about 3 hours. (Replenish the coals by adding fresh dry coals periodically.) The meat should be pale in color, plump, and soft. (The meat can also be cooked in a smoker.) Remove the pork and, when cool enough, shred the meat in long strips.

To prepare the quesadillas, place 4 tortillas on a work surface, layer with the cheese, Garlic Spinach, avocado, and pork (about ½ cup pork per quesadilla), and top with another tortilla. Heat a cast-iron or nonstick skillet and cook the quesadillas over low heat for about 1½ minutes on each side, or until the cheese melts and everything is warmed through.

To serve, cut each quesadilla into quarters and arrange in the center of each serving plate. Garnish with the Lomi Lomi Salmon.

Napoleon of Hawaiian Swordfish with Beet Juice

If you don't want to go to the trouble of decorating the napoleon with vegetable "scales," you could top it with caviar, instead. Either way, this appetizer will be as much a visual treat as it is a taste delight.

Vegetable "Scales":
1 zucchini, unpeeled
1 Japanese eggplant, unpeeled
1 red bell pepper, seeded
1 yellow bell pepper, seeded
...

4 beets, peeled and quartered
3½ tablespoons olive oil
½ carrot, julienned
¼ red bell pepper, seeded and julienned
8 paper-thin slices eggplant
8 mild Hawaiian red chiles (or red jalapeño or Fiesta chiles), peeled, seeded, and cut in half

2 medium-sized tomatoes, peeled, seeded, and chopped
2 tablespoons plus ¼ teaspoon minced fresh basil
½ cup Roy's Mashed Potatoes (page 153)
¼ teaspoon minced fresh parsley
18 ounces swordfish steaks or *shutome*

To prepare the vegetable "scales," cut a ⅛-inch-thick lengthwise strip off the zucchini; do likewise with the eggplant. Using a metal decorating tip ¼-inch in diameter, cut small circles out of the yellow and red bell peppers, and the zucchini and eggplant strips. Set aside.

To make the beet juice, put the beets in a saucepan with water to cover. Bring to a boil, then simmer until the water is dark in color. Remove the beets (save them for another use) and reduce the liquid over high heat until the flavor is pronounced and you have about 2 to 3 tablespoons concentrated juice. Set aside.

Heat ½ tablespoon of the olive oil in a sauté pan and sauté the carrot and bell pepper over high heat until just tender. Remove and reserve. Add another ½ tablespoon of oil to the pan and sauté the eggplant over high heat until cooked through. Remove and reserve. Heat ½ tablespoon of the oil and sauté the chile halves over medium heat until soft. Remove and reserve. Cook the tomatoes and 2 tablespoons of the basil over medium heat for about 5 minutes. Remove from heat.

In a mixing bowl, combine the mashed potatoes with the remaining ¼ teaspoon of basil and the parsley.

Cut the swordfish into 12 slices, each about 2½ x 4 inches. (*Shutome*, a Hawaiian swordfish, is perfect for this; if you're working with swordfish steak, do the best you can to achieve this size, as this will determine the dimensions of the napoleon.) Heat the remaining 2 tablespoons of oil in a skillet, and sear the swordfish slices over medium-high heat for about 45 seconds per side, until just cooked.

To assemble each napoleon, place 1 slice of swordfish on a serving plate and cover with 4 of the sautéed red chile halves. Place a slice of eggplant on top of the chiles, cover with another portion of fish, and then add one-quarter of the sautéed carrot and bell pepper. Cover with another slice of eggplant and one-quarter of the mashed potato. Top with a third fish slice. Decorate the napoleon with vegetable "scales," using the circles of red and yellow bell peppers, zucchini, and eggplant with the skin side up. Spoon some of the beet juice around the napoleons.

Pictured on opposite page

Roy's Feasts from Hawaii

Eggplant and Goat Cheese Napoleon with Potato Flowers

⁂ SERVES 4 ⁂

This recipe gives a straightforward vegetarian dish an elegant presentation. I like to add the element of height to some of my dishes, and this is a good example of that vertical approach.

½ cup olive oil

4 potatoes (about 1 pound), peeled and thinly sliced

1 large eggplant, cut into 8 rounds, ½ inch thick

1 tablespoon minced garlic

1 tablespoon chopped fresh rosemary

1 tablespoon chopped fresh thyme

Salt and freshly ground pepper to taste

1 pound fresh goat cheese

½ cup Pesto (page 214)

2 cups Sun-Dried Tomato Sauce (page 218)

Garnish:

4 slices goat cheese

4 sprigs fresh thyme

Preheat the oven to 350 degrees and prepare the grill. Brush a baking sheet lightly with a little of the olive oil. Overlap the potato slices like petals to form 12 "flowers" on the baking sheet, each about 3½ inches in diameter (use more than one baking sheet if necessary, or cook in batches). Lightly brush the flowers with no more than ¼ cup of the olive oil and bake for 10 minutes, or until golden brown. Drain on paper towels and keep warm.

Season the eggplant slices with the garlic, the remaining olive oil, and the rosemary, thyme, salt, and pepper. Grill for 2 to 3 minutes per side, or until slightly charred. Mix the goat cheese and ¼ cup of the Pesto together in a bowl until well combined. Spread some of this mixture on one side of each slice of grilled eggplant.

Ladle ½ cup of the Sun-Dried Tomato Sauce onto each serving plate. Place one potato "flower" on top of the sauce, followed by a slice of eggplant and a little more sauce. Repeat, ending with a third potato "flower." Serve with a slice of goat cheese and a sprig of thyme. Surround with dabs of the remaining Pesto.

I may have missed my true calling: goatherding! Billy, Larry, and Wally soon made friends with me, or maybe it was my T-shirt they liked. Perhaps it was the tasty goat treats I slipped them discreetly when Karin and Steve Sayre (see opposite page) weren't looking.

14

Roy's Feasts from Hawaii

Puna Goat Cheese from Rural Hawaii

Edible art: a tray of goat cheese from the Sayres' farm in Puna.

South of Hilo, in the eastern corner of the Big Island, the Puna District features lush rain forests, rich agricultural land, and the occasional volcanic upheaval. In 1979, Steve and Karin Sayre bought six acres just outside Kurtistown in Puna. Their land was covered with bush, but they hacked a path through the forest and built a cabin. They tried growing vegetables at first, but there seemed to be more weeds than vegetables, and neither Steve nor Karin could get enthusiastic about weeding.

After a while, Steve and Karin decided to try goat farming. They began with a single goat, and built up their herd, which now numbers about sixty. More than half are Nubians, and the rest are Swiss Toggenbourg, Alpine, La Mancha, and Saanen breeds. This diversification results in rich and flavorful milk. The Sayres started pro-ducing goat cheese commercially in January 1991, and now their production is up to 150 pounds per week. The Sayres' Orchid Island Chevre Goat Milk Cheese is the product of the only licensed goat dairy in the state.

The goat milk production at the ranch tends to be seasonal; it peaks in summer, drops in the fall and rises again at the end of the year. Sometimes, it varies with the climate. On average, the yield will be 11 to 15 gallons per day; not all the goats produce milk at any one time. Each gallon of goat milk yields about 1½ pounds of cheese. The amazing thing about the Sayres' operation is that they achieve this prodigious output without utilities—they use a diesel-powered generator and batteries. Collected rainwater, rather than piped-in water, supplies all their needs.

The process of turning the milk into cheese takes five days. It begins with pasteurizing and then setting with a French culture and nonanimal rennet. After 24 hours, at room temperature, the curd is separated from the whey and ladled into molds to drain for 48 hours. Salt is then added to draw out more whey, and the cheese is placed on a rack to firm up. On the sixth day, the cheese is packed (presumably, Steve and Karin rest on the seventh day!).

Steve and Karin Sayre supply the goat cheese for all of Roy's restaurants, other chefs who make up the Hawaiian Regional Cuisine Group, and numerous resorts and hotels. The Sayres have also stocked a couple of the $QE2$'s world cruises with their cheese, and limited quantities find their way to the mainland.

It's no small wonder the kids on the farm like to hang around my young friend Aza Sayre.

Terrine of Local Vegetables with Red Bell Pepper Sauce

≫ S E R V E S 8 T O 10 ≪

Traditionally, terrines are molded layers of meat or vegetable pâtés. This recipe makes a colorful and spectacular way of serving layers of fresh vegetables.

2 large tomatoes

2 cups spinach leaves

2 large carrots

1 daikon, sliced

2 large heads broccoli, cut into florets

2 zucchini

2 large green bell peppers, roasted, peeled, and seeded (page 220)

...

2 large yellow bell peppers, roasted, peeled, and seeded (page 220)

2 large red bell peppers, roasted, peeled, and seeded (page 220)

2 cups Vegetable Stock (page 214)

3 packages unflavored gelatin

Red Bell Pepper Sauce:

3 red bell peppers, roasted, peeled, and seeded (page 220)

2 tablespoons olive oil

Salt and freshly ground pepper to taste

*B*lanch the tomatoes in boiling water for 20 to 35 seconds. Shock in ice water and peel off the skin. Cut into quarters, discard the seeds, and trim away enough of the pulp so that the pieces of tomato lie flat. Pat dry with paper towels.

Return the water to a boil, adding a little salt. Blanch the spinach for about 15 seconds. Shock in ice water, drain, and pat dry with paper towels.

Cut the carrots into 1/16-inch slices (a Japanese slicer or mandoline works best for this), and trim the slices to the width of the terrine mold. Blanch in the boiling salted water for about 30 seconds. Shock in ice water, drain, and pat dry.

Cut the daikon into 1/16-inch slices (again, a Japanese slicer or mandoline works best for this) and trim the slices to fit the width of the terrine mold. Blanch in the boiling salted water for about 20 seconds. Shock in ice water, drain, and pat dry.

Likewise, blanch the broccoli in the boiling salted water for about 1 minute, shock in ice water, drain, pat dry, and mince.

Peel the zucchini and cut the peel into 3-inch strips (save the zucchini itself for some other use). Blanch the peel in the boiling salted water for 10 seconds. Shock in ice water, drain, and pat dry.

Cut the roasted bell peppers in half, trim until they lie flat, and pat dry on paper towels.

To make an aspic, place 1 cup of warm Vegetable Stock in a mixing bowl and add the gelatin. Bring the remaining cup of Vegetable Stock to a boil in a saucepan, add to the bowl and stir until the gelatin dissolves.

To prepare the terrine, line a 3 x 6-inch terrine mold with plastic wrap, cut so that 1 inch of wrap extends over all the edges. Dip the spinach leaves in the aspic and line the bottom and sides of the mold with a single layer. The spinach should also extend over the edges of the mold by 1 inch. Dip the carrot slices in the aspic and arrange a layer of carrots in the bottom of the mold. Repeat with the daikon, each of the bell peppers, the broccoli, tomatoes, and zucchini, dipping each in aspic before layering them (with the broccoli it will be simpler to arrange a layer of it in the mold, then brush it with a thin layer of aspic). When you reach the top of the mold, add the remaining bell peppers, fold the spinach leaves over the top, and then fold over the plastic wrap. Cut out a piece of cardboard to fit inside the terrine and weight it down evenly (a few cans of tomatoes will work). Refrigerate overnight.

To prepare the sauce, purée the 3 red bell peppers in a blender or food processor. Strain into a bowl and add the olive oil. Mix thoroughly and season with salt and pepper.

To serve, unmold the terrine on a platter and cut it into ½-inch slices. Ladle about 2 tablespoons of sauce onto each serving plate and arrange 1 or 2 slices of the terrine on top of the sauce.

Harvey Sacarob and his daughter, Maile, tending the fields at Sun Bear Produce, Honaunau, Big Island.

Blackened Ahi with Soy-Mustard Sauce

⟫ SERVES 4 ⟪

It seems like a long time ago that Paul Prudhomme first captured national attention with his blackened redfish down in New Orleans. Once I tasted this classic, I was inspired to create a Pacific version. This is the result, and it has become one of my signature dishes. The sandalwood contained in the blackening spice is optional, but gives a reddish color and intriguing flavor. We grind our own but you can use Yogi brand sandalwood, available by calling the company in New Orleans (504-486-5538). If you prefer, you can use ¼ cup of any Cajun spice blend instead of making up your own blackening spice.

Soy-Mustard Sauce:
¼ cup Colman's mustard powder
2 tablespoons hot water
2 tablespoons unseasoned rice
    vinegar
¼ cup soy sauce
...

Beurre Blanc (page 216)

Blackening Spice:
1½ tablespoons paprika
½ tablespoon cayenne powder
½ tablespoon pure red chile powder
¼ teaspoon freshly ground white pepper
½ tablespoon ground sandalwood
    (optional)
...

1 ahi tuna fillet, about 2 inches thick
    and 5 inches long (about 8 ounces)

Garnish:
2 or 3 tablespoons red pickled ginger
½ teaspoon black sesame seeds
1 ounce Japanese spice sprouts or
    sunflower sprouts (top 2 inches
    only)
1 tablespoon seeded and diced yellow
    bell pepper (optional)
1 tablespoon cucumber, cut into
    matchsticks (optional)

To prepare the Soy-Mustard Sauce, mix the mustard powder and hot water together to form a paste. Let sit for a few minutes to allow the flavor and heat to develop. Add the vinegar and soy sauce, mix together, and strain through a fine sieve. Chill in the refrigerator.

Warm the *Beurre Blanc* in a double boiler.

Mix all the blackening spices together on a plate, and dredge the ahi on all sides. Heat a lightly oiled cast-iron skillet and sear the ahi over high heat to the desired doneness (about 15 seconds per side for rare, to 1 minute per side for medium-rare). Cut into 16 thin slices.

For each serving, arrange 4 slices of the ahi in a pinwheel or cross shape on the plate. Ladle a little of the Soy-Mustard Sauce in two opposing quadrants between the tuna, and ladle the *Beurre Blanc* in the other two quadrants. To garnish, put a small mound of the red pickled ginger on the *Beurre Blanc* on either side, and sprinkle the sesame seeds over the Soy-Mustard Sauce. Arrange the spice sprouts, bell pepper, and cucumber at the very center of this pinwheel.

Kahuku Shrimp on a Stick with Wasabi Cocktail Sauce and Papaya-Mint Relish

On the northern tip of Oahu, in the area called Kahuku, there are several commercial aquaculture farms that raise large quantities of fresh- and saltwater shrimp and prawns (see page 82). Soaking the wooden skewers in water before adding the shrimp prevents them from burning on the grill.

1 cup Papaya-Mint Relish (recipe follows)

1 pound extra-large shrimp (about 16 to 20), peeled and deveined

Salt and freshly ground pepper to taste

¼ cup peanut oil

Wasabi Cocktail Sauce:

2 tablespoons powdered wasabi

2 tablespoons water

¾ cup ketchup

2 tablespoons prepared horseradish

Prepare the Papaya-Mint Relish and set aside.

Prepare the grill and soak 16 to 20 short bamboo or wooden skewers in water. Skewer the shrimp, tail end first, and slide the shrimp down the skewers, with the head end toward the pointed end of the skewer. Season with salt and pepper, coat with the peanut oil, and keep refrigerated.

To prepare the sauce, combine the wasabi powder with the water to form a paste. Cover and let stand for 15 minutes. Combine the ketchup and horseradish in a separate dish and add the wasabi paste, and mix well.

Sear the shrimp on the grill for about 1 minute per side, or until cooked through. Place 2 table-spoons of the cocktail sauce on each plate and arrange 4 or 5 skewers on each plate. Serve with the Papaya-Mint Relish on the side.

Papaya-Mint Relish

1 large ripe papaya, peeled, seeded, and diced

1 tablespoon julienned fresh mint leaves

1 tablespoon julienned fresh cilantro

1 teaspoon seeded and minced jalapeño

1 to 2 teaspoons seeded and diced red bell pepper

1 teaspoon finely minced Maui onion

Juice of 1 lime

Salt and freshly ground pepper to taste

Thoroughly combine all the ingredients in a mixing bowl. Refrigerate for 1 hour.

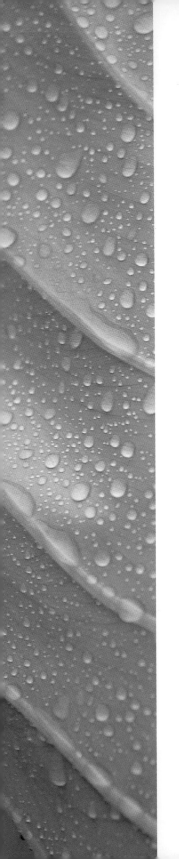

Crisp Vegetable Sushi with Thai Peanut Dip

I originally created this recipe as an appetizer for our prix fixe vegetarian menu, and it's been a popular starter with our guests who are looking for alternatives to meat dishes. To make the sushi, you need a bamboo sushi rolling mat—available at most Asian markets—and, of course, the sushi nori, flat sheets of seaweed, specially prepared for making sushi.

Thai Peanut Dip:

2 cups unsweetened coconut milk

½ cup smooth peanut butter

¼ cup brown sugar

¼ cup soy sauce

1 tablespoon unseasoned rice vinegar

2 kaffir lime leaves

¼ cup julienned fresh Thai basil

¼ cup red curry paste (preferably Mae Ploy brand Matsaman curry paste)

½ onion, chopped

2 tablespoons minced garlic

1 tablespoon minced shallot

1 tablespoon minced lemon grass

1½ cups chopped fresh cilantro

Sushi:

1½ cups finely julienned carrots

1½ cups finely julienned celery

1½ cups finely julienned fennel bulb

1½ cups finely julienned daikon

1 beet, peeled and julienned (about ½ cup)

¼ cup light soy sauce (preferably Yamasa brand)

Salt and freshly ground pepper to taste

6 sheets sushi nori, trimmed to 5 x 8 inches

Peanut oil, for frying

Japanese spice sprouts, for garnish (optional)

*C*ombine all the Thai Peanut Dip ingredients in a nonreactive saucepan. Bring to a simmer. Cook gently over low heat, taking care not to boil the mixture. When the sauce begins to thicken and the oils from the curry rise to the surface, adjust the sugar, soy sauce, and vinegar if necessary, and remove from the heat. Let cool and discard the lime leaves before serving.

Blanch the carrots for about 15 seconds; plunge into ice water, cool, drain, pat dry, and place in a bowl. Prepare the other vegetables in the same manner (the beets should be blanched slightly longer—about 1 minute), placing each in a separate bowl. Drizzle the vegetables with the soy sauce, and season with salt and pepper.

Place a sheet of nori on the bamboo sushi rolling mat, with the 5-inch edge along the bottom. Arrange the vegetables neatly along the lower edge. Roll up the nori tightly, and seal the edges with a little soy sauce or water. Each roll should be about 1 to 1½ inches in diameter.

Heat enough peanut oil in a large skillet to come ½ inch up the sides. Pan-fry the sushi over medium heat for about 1½ minutes per side, or until crisp. Remove and drain on paper towels. Cut two 1-inch pieces from each roll, then cut the remaining larger pieces in half on a diagonal. To serve, arrange 4 pieces on each plate (2 with a straight cut, 2 diagonal). Garnish with Japanese spice sprouts if desired, and serve with the Thai Peanut Dip on the side.

Pictured on opposite page (upper left)

Opakapaka Sashimi with Basil

⋙ SERVES 4 ⋘

I got the inspiration for this dish from Roger Jaloux, who represented Paul Bocuse at L'Ermitage for a while. When he was there, he composed a special menu that included a salmon sashimi that was out of this world. My recipe is quite similar to his, except that I use opakapaka instead of salmon. Pink snapper is the best substitute for this dish if opakapaka is unavailable.

1 fillet opakapaka (about 10 ounces), thinly sliced

8 fresh basil leaves

8 fresh opal basil leaves

2 teaspoons fresh lemon juice

4 teaspoons soy sauce

2 tablespoons olive oil

Garnish:

2 tablespoons tobiko caviar

2 tablespoons salmon caviar

½ teaspoon toasted white sesame seeds (page 220)

*A*lternate slices of opakapaka with the green basil and opal basil, arranging it as artfully as possible. Drizzle the lemon juice, soy sauce, and olive oil over each serving. Garnish with the caviars, and sprinkle with the sesame seeds.

Pictured on page 21 (lower right)

Now this is what I call basil! Dean Okimoto's herbs at Nalo Farms are the best (for more about Nalo Farms, see page 61).

Roy's Feasts from Hawaii

Crispy Duck Triangles with Orange-Chile Sauce

❧ SERVES 4 ❧

This appetizer is especially popular in our Tokyo restaurant. It's made with lumpia wrappers, which are the Philippine equivalent of Chinese egg roll wrappers. You can find fresh or frozen lumpia wrappers in most Asian markets, or use egg roll wrappers. Any leftover duck meat or filling can be frozen for future use.

Filling:
1 duck, about 4 to 5 pounds
Salt and freshly ground pepper to taste
2 tablespoons canola oil
½ onion, diced
¼ cup diced choy sum
2 tablespoons sliced scallions
1 tablespoon minced fresh cilantro
¼ cup sliced shiitake mushrooms
2 tablespoons diced kimchee
5 water chestnuts, diced

1 teaspoon minced garlic
1 teaspoon minced shallot
1 teaspoon minced ginger
½ teaspoon dried red chile flakes
8 fresh mint leaves
2 tablespoons julienned fresh basil
1 tablespoon oyster sauce
1 tablespoon sweet chile sauce
   (preferably Lingham's brand)
3 egg yolks
. . .

8 lumpia or egg roll wrappers, cut
   into 5-inch squares
1 egg, beaten
2 tablespoons cornstarch
1 cup peanut oil
1 cup Orange-Chile Sauce (page 217)

Garnish:
4 sprigs flat-leaf parsley
1 teaspoon black sesame seeds
2 teaspoons chopped toasted peanuts
   (page 220)

Preheat the oven to 400 degrees. Season the duck with salt and pepper and place in a roasting pan. Roast in the oven for 15 minutes, turn down the heat to 350 degrees, and roast for another 45 minutes. It's fine if the duck is a little undercooked. Let the duck rest for 30 minutes, and then separate the meat from the bones (use the bones for stock). Remove the skin and any remaining fat. Coarsely chop the duck meat (you need at least 1 cup).

In a wok or large sauté pan, heat the canola oil and stir-fry the onion, choy sum, scallions, cilantro, mushrooms, kimchee, water chestnuts, garlic, shallot, ginger, chile flakes, mint, and basil over medium heat for about 2 minutes. Add the oyster sauce and chile sauce and cook for 1 minute longer. Strain, and separately reserve both vegetables and liquid. Place the vegetables in a bowl with the duck meat.

In a clean pan, reduce the reserved liquid to a glaze and combine with the duck and vegetables. Add more oyster sauce or chile sauce for a stronger flavor, if desired. Add the egg yolks and mix well. Drain off any excess liquid: if the filling is too wet, it will be harder to work with and the wrappers may break.

Lay out the wrappers on a work surface and place 2 to 3 heaping tablespoons of the duck filling in the center of each. Fold each wrapper to form a triangle, brush the edges with the beaten egg, and press together to seal. Sprinkle the triangles with cornstarch to prevent them from sticking.

Heat the peanut oil in a large skillet and fry the triangles over medium heat for 45 seconds to 1 minute per side, or until golden brown. Drain on paper towels. To serve, spoon about ¼ cup of the Orange-Chile Sauce onto each serving plate. Cut the triangles in half, and arrange 4 halves on each plate. Garnish with the parsley, sesame seeds, and peanuts.

Pictured on opposite page

Smoked Duck Potstickers with Orange-Chile-Plum Sauce

❧ SERVES 4 ❧

This is a Pacific Rim pairing of the traditional duck and orange. Although this recipe was designed for smoked duck, you can substitute plain roasted duck (see the preceding recipe), or the Chinatown Duck (page 144). Whichever kind you use, you'll need about 1½ cups diced duck meat to make the potsticker filling.

Potsticker Filling:

1 whole boneless duck breast (about 4 ounces)

2 tablespoons canola oil

1 tablespoon minced garlic

1 tablespoon minced shallot

1 small Maui onion, minced

½ cup minced yellow onion

½ cup diced choy sum

½ cup minced fresh cilantro

¾ cup chopped gai choy, kimchee, or napa cabbage

½ cup diced water chestnuts

Pinch of dried red chile flakes

1 cup diced fresh shiitake mushrooms

1 tablespoon oyster sauce

20 fresh mint leaves

¼ cup julienned fresh basil

1 tablespoon sweet chile sauce (preferably Lingham's brand)

1 egg yolk

…

1 tablespoon cornstarch, plus additional for sprinkling

2 tablespoons water

20 potsticker wrappers

¼ cup canola oil

Orange-Chile-Plum Sauce (page 217)

Garnish:

2 tablespoons orange zest

4 sprigs fresh oregano

2 teaspoons black sesame seeds

Roast the duck breast over wood chips in a smoker for 10 to 15 minutes (place a pan of water under the duck to catch the drippings and prevent flareups). Alternatively, place over wood chips on a low fire in a covered grill for 8 to 10 minutes. Remove the skin and any remaining fat, and dice.

In a wok or large sauté pan, heat the canola oil and stir-fry the diced duckmeat, garlic, shallot, onions, choy sum, cilantro, gai choy (or kimchee or napa cabbage), water chestnuts, chile flakes, mushrooms, oyster sauce, mint, and basil for 5 minutes over high heat until well combined and cooked through. Drain off the liquid into a saucepan, and reduce to a syrupy consistency. Return the reduced liquid to the duck mixture, add the chile sauce and egg yolk, and mix well.

Mix 1 tablespoon of the cornstarch and the water together in a small bowl. To make the potstickers, lay out the wrappers on a work surface and place a heaping tablespoon of the filling in the center of each. Moisten the edges of the wrappers with the cornstarch mixture, fold in half, and seal the edges. Sprinkle with a little cornstarch to prevent them from sticking.

Heat the ¼ cup canola oil in a cast-iron skillet or heavy-bottomed sauté pan. When hot, fry the potstickers over medium-high heat for about 1½ minutes per side, or until browned.

To serve, ladle the Orange-Chile-Plum Sauce onto warm serving plates. Place 5 potstickers on each plate in a star shape and garnish with the plum slices from the sauce, if desired, placing 1 slice between each potsticker. To garnish, place ½ tablespoon of the orange zest and a sprig of oregano in the center of each potsticker "star," and sprinkle with the sesame seeds.

Shrimp-Stuffed Tofu with Daikon Sauce

Tofu, or soybean curd, is a remarkably healthful ingredient because it's low in calories and sodium, high in protein, and contains no cholesterol. I really enjoy it, especially when it's cooked with other tasty ingredients, because it takes on their flavors so readily. This dish is also one way of giving tofu an attractive presentation.

Daikon Sauce:

2½ tablespoons grated daikon

2 teaspoons grated ginger

1 teaspoon minced garlic

2 tablespoons minced scallions

½ cup fresh lemon juice

½ cup soy sauce

1 teaspoon *shichimi*

...

3 tablespoons sesame oil

½ tablespoon minced garlic

½ tablespoon minced ginger

2 tablespoons chopped water chestnuts

3 ounces choy sum or spinach, cut into 2-inch pieces (about 1½ cups)

½ teaspoon toasted white sesame seeds (page 220)

⅛ teaspoon chile paste with garlic (preferably Lan Chi brand)

2 tablespoons canola oil

1 pound extra-large shrimp (16 to 20), peeled and deveined

1 pound firm tofu, drained and patted dry

2 eggs, beaten

½ cup flour, sifted

1 cup canola oil

Garnish:

12 fresh chives

Julienned radicchio, sautéed in olive oil (optional)

Combine all the Daikon Sauce ingredients in a mixing bowl and refrigerate for 1 hour.

Heat the sesame oil in a wok or sauté pan and stir-fry the garlic, ginger, water chestnuts, and choy sum over medium-high heat for about 1 minute. Remove from the heat and with a slotted spoon, transfer to a bowl, leaving the oil in the wok or pan. Sprinkle the mixture with the toasted sesame seeds and set aside.

In a mixing bowl, combine the chile paste with the 2 tablespoons of canola oil and coat the shrimp with the mixture. Reheat the wok or sauté pan and sear the shrimp quickly over medium-high heat, about 30 seconds (the shrimp will be cooked further in the next step). Remove from the pan and reserve.

Cut the tofu into 8 pieces, each about 2 x 3 x ½ inch thick. Make 4 "sandwiches," using the tofu as the bread and the stir-fried vegetables and seared shrimp as the filling (a layer of vegetables plus 4 shrimp per sandwich).

Place the beaten eggs and flour in separate shallow bowls. Carefully dip the tofu sandwiches into the eggs, coating them thoroughly, then dredge in the flour. Heat the cup of canola oil in a clean skillet and fry the filled tofu over medium heat for about 1½ minutes per side, until the shrimp has cooked through and the tofu is golden brown.

To serve, cut each "sandwich" diagonally and pour the Daikon Sauce over. Garnish with the chives sticking from the top of the tofu. Scatter the sauteed radicchio around the tofu, if desired.

Pictured on opposite page (upper left)

Roy's Feasts from Hawaii

Hamachi Spring Rolls and Lime Chile Sauce

⁂ SERVES 4 ⁂

In these spring rolls the ingredients are all neatly layered, so that when cut, the finished product somewhat resembles a sushi roll. The accompanying Lime Chile Sauce perfectly accents the hamachi (yellowfin tuna).

1 cup Lime Chile Sauce (recipe follows)

6 tablespoons sesame oil

½ cup julienned carrots

2 tablespoons minced garlic

2 tablespoons minced ginger

4 ounces bean sprouts

4 ounces shiitake mushrooms, sliced

1 Japanese cucumber, seeded and cut into ¼-inch matchsticks

½ cup daikon or turnip, cut into ¼-inch matchsticks

2 ounces bean thread noodles

2 tablespoons light soy sauce (preferably Yamasa brand)

2 tablespoons fish sauce

1 cup chopped fresh cilantro

8 sheets round rice paper wrappers

8 ounces fresh hamachi (yellowfin tuna), cut into 8 strips

1 egg, beaten

1 tablespoon cornstarch

Peanut oil, for frying

12 fresh chives

1 teaspoon toasted white sesame seeds (page 220), for garnish

Prepare the Lime Chile Sauce and set aside.

Heat 2 tablespoons of the sesame oil in a wok or large sauté pan and stir-fry the carrots with one-third of the garlic and ginger over high heat for 30 seconds. Transfer to a bowl. Repeat for the bean sprouts and mushrooms, placing each in a separate bowl. Place the cucumber and daikon in separate bowls.

Bring a stockpot of water to a boil and cook the bean thread noodles until soft, about 10 to 15 minutes. Strain through a sieve, transfer to a mixing bowl, and toss with the soy sauce, fish sauce, and cilantro. Set aside.

Dip the rice paper in warm water for 10 seconds to soften (if you let them get too wet, they will start to break). Pat dry with a clean kitchen towel and lay out on a work surface. Place a strip of the hamachi on the rice paper and add a layer of each of the different vegetables. Brush the edges of the rice paper with the beaten egg, roll up, folding in the ends like a burrito, and dust with the cornstarch.

Heat enough peanut oil in a large skillet to come ½ inch up the sides. Using tongs, immerse the spring rolls in the hot oil and pan-fry over medium-low heat for about 1 minute per side, or until golden and crisp.

To serve, cut each spring roll in half. Spoon ¼ cup of the Lime Chile Sauce on each serving plate and stand 4 spring roll halves, cut side up, on the sauce. Garnish the rolls with the chives and the sesame seeds.

Pictured on page 27 (lower right)

Lime Chile Sauce

⁂ YIELD: ABOUT 1 CUP ⁂

½ cup mirin

¼ cup plum wine

¼ cup sake

¼ cup sweet chile sauce (preferably Lingham's brand)

1 or 2 ripe plums, pitted and chopped

Juice and zest of ½ orange

1 or 2 kaffir lime leaves, very finely julienned

In a heavy saucepan, combine all the ingredients, bring to a simmer over high heat, lower the heat and slowly reduce to about 1 cup. Strain and cool to room temperature.

Japanese Shrimp and Clam Miso Appetizer

❧ SERVES 4 ❧

Growing up in Japan, a bowl of healthful miso was often my breakfast, which is in keeping with the national tradition. As a result, it has always been one of my favorite foods.

1 cup white wine

1 teaspoon minced shallot

1 teaspoon minced garlic

12 fresh Manila clams

4 medium shrimp, peeled and deveined

2 teaspoons olive oil

Salt and freshly ground pepper to taste

Vinaigrette:

½ cup light soy sauce (preferably Yamasa brand)

¼ cup white miso (*shiro miso*)

¼ cup unseasoned rice vinegar

1 tablespoon finely diced onion

1 tablespoon finely sliced scallion

¾ teaspoon minced garlic

¾ teaspoon minced ginger

1½ tablespoons sugar

Vegetables:

1 cup fresh corn kernels

½ Japanese cucumber, seeded and julienned

2 ounces Japanese spice sprouts, tops only

Garnish:

1 teaspoon finely sliced scallion

1 teaspoon toasted white sesame seeds (page 220)

Place the wine, shallot, and garlic in a large stockpot, and bring to a boil. Add the clams, reduce the heat to a gentle boil, and steam for about 1 minute, until the clams open (discard any that remain closed). Remove the clams and when cool, extract the clam meat from the shells and reserve.

Prepare the grill. Brush the shrimp with olive oil and season with salt and pepper. Grill the shrimp for about 1 minute per side, or until cooked through. (Alternatively, sauté the shrimp in a skillet over medium-high heat.)

To prepare the vinaigrette, thoroughly whisk all the ingredients together in a mixing bowl.

Pan-roast the corn kernels in a dry skillet over medium-high heat until lightly browned, about 30 seconds. Transfer to a mixing bowl, add the cucumber, sprouts, and enough of the vinaigrette to lightly dress the ingredients, and toss together gently. Divide between serving plates.

In a mixing bowl, toss the reserved clams and shrimp together in enough of the vinaigrette to lightly dress, and place on top of the vegetables. To garnish, sprinkle each serving with the scallion and sesame seeds.

Lokowaka Fishpond, Keaukaha, Big Island.

Hawaiian Spiny Lobster Wrapped in Cabbage with Lobster-Nage Sauce

※ SERVES 4 ※

Borrowing on the French technique of wrapping foods in cabbage was one of my earliest experiments in Euro-Asian cuisine. It has withstood the test of time and remains one of my favorite presentations. Unfortunately, I can only guarantee the results of this dish if you begin with live lobsters. Once you get over the idea, the task itself is not that difficult. See page 215 for directions on preparing live lobsters.

¼ cup warm Nage (recipe follows)

2 Hawaiian spiny lobster tails or Maine lobster tails

⅓ cup vegetable oil

2 tablespoons julienned leek

1 teaspoon minced shallot

1 teaspoon minced garlic

1 teaspoon minced ginger

4 ounces shiitake mushrooms, julienned

4 tablespoons julienned fresh basil

4 teaspoons finely minced fresh tarragon

1 teaspoon mushroom soy sauce

1 teaspoon *rayu* (spicy sesame oil)

…

½ red bell pepper, seeded and finely diced

½ yellow bell pepper, seeded and finely diced

1 zucchini, finely diced

1 Japanese eggplant, finely diced

8 napa cabbage leaves, about 6 inches wide

Lobster-Nage Sauce:

2 tablespoons Lobster Paste (page 215)

1½ cups *Beurre Blanc* (page 216)

…

2 tablespoons salmon caviar, for garnish

1 tablespoon finely chopped fresh basil, for garnish

Prepare the Nage and set aside.

Slice the lobster tail meat thinly. Heat half of the vegetable oil in a sauté pan and sauté the lobster over medium-high heat for 15 to 20 seconds, until just cooked through. Remove 8 slices and reserve for garnish. Heat the remaining vegetable oil in a clean sauté pan and sauté the leek, shallot, garlic, ginger, and shiitake mushrooms over medium-high heat for about 1 minute. Remove from the heat, add the rest of the cooked lobster to the pan together with the basil and tarragon, and thoroughly combine. Season with the mushroom soy sauce and *rayu*.

Blanch the bell peppers, zucchini, and eggplant in boiling water for 5 seconds, and drain. Blanch the cabbage leaves in boiling water for 30 seconds, drain, and set aside.

To prepare the Lobster-Nage Sauce, combine the Lobster Paste and *Beurre Blanc* in a double boiler, stirring until well blended. Add the reserved Nage and stir to combine. Keep warm.

Lay out the cabbage leaves on a work surface. Divide the lobster mixture between the cabbage leaves; roll up the leaves, tucking the edges under as neatly as possible. To serve, place two rolls on each serving plate. Spoon the sauce around the rolls. Place 2 of the reserved lobster slices on top of each roll, topped by a little of the salmon caviar. Sprinkle the blanched vegetables and the basil garnish over the sauce and around the rolls.

Roy's Feasts from Hawaii

Nage

2 cups white wine

2 tablespoons white vinegar

3 cups water

1 clove garlic

½ cup finely diced onion

1 cup seeded and chopped tomato

3 ounces whole mushrooms

¼ cup chopped carrot

⅓ cup chopped celery

1 green bell pepper, seeded and chopped

1 red bell pepper, seeded and chopped

2 teaspoons chopped fresh basil

1 teaspoon chopped fresh chives

6 small bay leaves

5 peppercorns

Place all the ingredients in a saucepan and simmer for about 1 hour. Strain, and reduce the liquid in a clean saucepan over medium-high heat to about ⅔ cup.

Seafood Risotto with Fresh Asparagus and Wild Mushrooms

⋙ S E R V E S 8 ⋘

I started cooking risottos after trying them once at Locanda Veneta, a Los Angeles restaurant owned by Antonio Tomasi. I was so impressed, and I recognized their potential for expressing different flavors and textures. This particular risotto is very creamy, but surprisingly light.

4 cups uncooked short-grain (Calrose) rice

4 cups Shrimp Stock (page 214) or water

1 tablespoon canola oil

2 ounces spinach, chopped (about 1 cup)

2 to 4 ounces asparagus, diced

Shrimp Butter Sauce:

1½ cups *Beurre Blanc* (page 216)

2 to 3 tablespoons Shrimp Paste (page 214)

Salt and freshly ground pepper to taste

...

4½ cups Chicken Stock (page 213)

¼ teaspoon minced garlic

1½ tablespoons julienned fresh basil

1½ tablespoons minced fresh thyme

4 ounces mushrooms, stemmed and quartered

2 pounds extra-large shrimp (about 32), peeled, deveined, and diced

10 ounces scallops, quartered

2 tablespoons grated parmesan cheese, plus extra for garnish (optional)

Salt and freshly ground pepper to taste

$\mathcal{S}$oak the rice in water for 1 hour and drain. Place the rice and Shrimp Stock in a large saucepan and bring to a boil. Lower the heat and simmer for 15 to 20 minutes or until just tender; the liquid should be just evaporated.

Heat the canola oil in a sauté pan or skillet, and wilt the spinach over medium-high heat for 10 to 15 seconds. Set aside. Blanch the asparagus in boiling water for 30 seconds, drain, and set aside.

To make the Shrimp Butter Sauce, warm the *Beurre Blanc* in a double boiler. Whisk in the Shrimp Paste until well blended, and season with salt and pepper. Keep warm.

Bring the Chicken Stock to a boil in a large stockpot, add the garlic, basil, thyme, and mushrooms, and cook over high heat for 1½ minutes, or until the mushrooms are tender. Add the shrimp, scallops, spinach, and asparagus. Stir in the cooked rice, and cook for 1½ minutes, or until the rice is heated through. The rice should absorb most of the stock; add more stock if the rice seems too dry. Add the parmesan cheese and the Shrimp Butter Sauce and mix thoroughly. Adjust the seasonings if necessary.

Serve the risotto in soup bowls. Sprinkle with additional parmesan cheese, if desired.

Pan-Fried Crispy Calamari with Pancetta and Pesto

» SERVES 4 «

Calamari, or squid, as it is more commonly known, is one of my favorite foods. For this dish, I use very tiny squid that are no more than 2 inches long, as they are the most tender.

1 pound tiny calamari

2 teaspoons olive oil

2 tablespoons finely diced pancetta

5 mushrooms, quartered

2 teaspoons capers

2 tablespoons julienned pepperoncini (sweet peppers)

2 kalamata black olives, pitted and quartered

2 teaspoons fresh lemon juice

2 teaspoons chopped fresh basil

2 teaspoons chopped fresh thyme

1 cup Basic Tomato Sauce (page 215)

Salt and freshly ground white pepper to taste

1 cup flour

1 cup cornstarch

2 tablespoons finely sliced scallions

2 tablespoons minced garlic

1½ cups canola oil

Garnish:

2 teaspoons Pesto (page 214)

2 teaspoons chopped fresh parsley

Cut the calamari in half lengthwise, leaving the head and tentacles attached. Rinse under cold water to clean away the innards; drain and set aside.

Heat the olive oil in a small saucepan, and sauté the pancetta over high heat for 30 seconds, or until it begins to crackle. Turn the heat down to medium, add the mushrooms, capers, pepperoncini, and olives, and sauté for about 1½ minutes. Add the lemon juice, herbs, tomato sauce, salt, and pepper and cook for about 15 to 20 seconds, stirring to incorporate. Remove from the heat and set aside.

Combine the flour, cornstarch, scallions, and garlic in a mixing bowl and dredge the calamari in the mixture, coating thoroughly. In a large sauté pan, heat the canola oil until very hot but not at smoking point. Fry the calamari until crisp, about 45 seconds. Remove with a slotted spoon and drain on paper towels.

To serve, ladle the pancetta sauce into serving bowls. Place the calamari on top of the sauce, drizzle a little of the Pesto around the edge of the sauce, and sprinkle with the parsley.

Ahi Tartare with Crispy Polenta and Tartar Sauce

As a kid, I loved sashimi (sliced raw fish) dipped in soy sauce and served with hot rice. This appetizer is my Hawaiian alternative to the traditional beef tartare. Make sure the tuna is extremely fresh (sashimi quality).

Ahi Tartare:

5 ounces ahi tuna, finely diced

1 large tomato, seeded and finely diced

Tartar Sauce:

4 anchovy fillets, finely minced

1½ tablespoons finely minced garlic

1 tablespoon finely minced capers

2 egg yolks

1½ tablespoons finely diced red onion

1½ tablespoons crisply cooked bacon, crumbled

3 tablespoons finely grated parmesan cheese

1 teaspoon Dijon mustard

1 tablespoon fresh lemon juice

½ teaspoon minced fresh thyme

¼ teaspoon Tabasco sauce

¼ teaspoon Worcestershire sauce

1 tablespoon red wine vinegar

3 tablespoons extra virgin olive oil

Salt and freshly ground pepper to taste

…

4 squares of Crispy Polenta (recipe follows)

1 teaspoon chopped fresh parsley, for garnish

Combine the ahi and tomato in a bowl and reserve in the refrigerator.

To prepare the Tartar Sauce, thoroughly mash together the anchovies, garlic, and capers in a large mixing bowl. Whisk in the egg yolks, and stir in the red onion, bacon, parmesan, mustard, lemon juice, thyme, Tabasco sauce, and Worcestershire sauce. Whisk in the vinegar and olive oil until the sauce is well blended. Season with salt and pepper.

Prepare the Crispy Polenta. To serve, lightly spread the Tartar Sauce on each piece of polenta, and top with about 1 to 2 tablespoons of the ahi mixture. Spoon on a little more Tartar Sauce and garnish with the parsley.

Keawa Nui Fishpond, Molokai (the island of Lanai is in the background).

Roy's Feasts from Hawaii

Crispy Polenta

This recipe makes more than you will need for the Ahi Tartare, but the leftovers can be served with other dishes. For instance, serve it with eggs for a nice brunch, or try it with meat or poultry. Store it in the refrigerator, and crisp it up just before serving. As a variation, stir in a little grated parmesan cheese, instead of (or in addition to) the herbs called for.

3 cups milk	¼ teaspoon finely minced garlic	1½ cups yellow cornmeal
¼ cup julienned fresh basil	½ teaspoon salt	¼ cup canola oil or corn oil
1 teaspoon chopped fresh thyme	½ teaspoon freshly ground pepper	

*C*ombine the milk, basil, thyme, garlic, salt, and pepper in a heavy-bottomed saucepan, and bring to a boil. Gradually add the cornmeal, and cook over low heat, stirring, for 5 minutes, until thick and no longer grainy. Transfer the mixture to a baking sheet and spread out to a ½-inch thickness using a spatula coated with oil to prevent the polenta from sticking to it. Cut into triangles or squares, or whatever shapes take your fancy. (The polenta can be prepared ahead up to this point and fried later.)

Heat the oil in a sauté pan and when it is very hot, add the polenta. Sauté over medium-high heat until the polenta is crispy on both sides.

TAMASHIRO MARKET HAS BEEN an institution in downtown Honolulu for more than 40 years. The Tamashiro family was originally from the Big Island, but after a tsunami (tidal wave) hit Hilo in 1946, Walter Tamashiro brought the family business to Honolulu (this was an excellent move—Hilo was devastated again in 1960).

Tamashiro's business card proudly states "Largest Selection of Seafoods in the 50th State!" This is a legitimate boast—three-quarters of the store's sales come from fresh fish, seafood, and *poké* (seasoned raw fish salads). Tamashiro's also sells Hawaiian specialties such as poi, fish jerky, edible seaweeds and sea vegetables, as well as tropical fruits, vegetables and herbs, and a wide array of groceries. I still have fond memories of my Uncle Walt taking us to Tamashiro's when I was a kid to buy crabs, or sashimi-grade tuna. Little did I imagine then that one day I'd return to pick up some fish for my own restaurant and family!

Roy's Wood-Smoked Szechwan-Style Baby Back Pork Ribs

❯❯ SERVES 4 ❮❮

Several years ago, Bon Appétit *magazine ran a feature article on Roy's Restaurant. It included this recipe for smoked ribs; you might call it one of my signature dishes.*

Szechwan Marinade:
5 tablespoons white miso (*shiro miso*)
⅔ cup hoisin sauce
1½ tablespoons minced ginger
1½ tablespoons minced garlic
1½ tablespoons sake

1½ tablespoons soy sauce
2 teaspoons sugar
1 tablespoon chile paste with garlic
   (preferably Lan Chi brand)
…

2½ pounds baby back pork ribs
3 quarts Chicken Stock (page 213)
1 tablespoon minced ginger
2 teaspoons minced garlic
2 tablespoons minced fresh parsley
2 tablespoons minced fresh cilantro

*C*ombine the marinade ingredients together in a bowl and refrigerate overnight.

Place the pork ribs in a large saucepan with the Chicken Stock, ginger, garlic, parsley, and cilantro, and simmer for about 30 minutes, or until tender. Remove the ribs, and reserve the broth for soup or freeze for another time. Immediately brush the ribs with the Szechwan marinade, and let cool. Meanwhile, prepare the grill and soak some *kiawe* or mesquite wood chips in water in preparation for smoking the ribs.

Brush the ribs again with the marinade before roasting, and slowly cook the ribs over the wood chips on a covered grill until nicely browned and smoky (about 15 to 20 minutes). Serve with extra Szechwan marinade on the side.

IF YOU SHOULD FIND yourself sitting on our *lanai* (outdoor patio) around about dusk, you're in the ideal spot to watch the sun slip behind Diamond Head and into the tropic sea. In the other direction, the majestic, volcanic Koko Head drops into the gentle waters of the palm-fringed Maunalua Bay. Not a bad place to sip one of our refreshing cocktails and relax island-style.

Our guests love the laid-back festive atmosphere out here, and on weekend evenings they can soak in the live jazz or Phil Greek's melodic calypso music. Early evening dining is popular on the *lanai*, and nothing beats eating and drinking outside under the stars, warmed by the soothing summer trade winds.

Soups

Given the tropical climate of the islands, you might expect to find that soups are not very popular in Hawaii. However, people here accept the heat and humidity as a given, and don't let it influence their choice of first courses. In fact, although the demand for soups on the islands will never match that of colder regions in the United States, cream soups are particularly popular here. At Roy's, we always have a hot soup on the menu.

As with most of my other recipes, the soups at Roy's and in this chapter reflect a marriage between European techniques and Pacific Rim styles and ingredients. Indeed, this chapter takes us on a lightning culinary tour of France (chowders are derived from the French chaudières, or seafood stews, and the lightly sweetened and whipped Chantilly Cream is also French) by way of Italy, to Japan (kabocha squash and miso), China (duck noodle soup and shrimp dumplings), and Thailand (hot-and-sour soup and coconut curry).

Soups have long been popular throughout Europe as well as Asia, where they're a common, almost compulsory, feature of lunches and dinners; soups are sometimes even served at breakfast. Other soups (such as Peking duck soup) are traditionally served at the end of the meal. In Japan, it's common to serve a clear soup (shirumono) at the beginning of a meal and a miso-based broth at the end.

Don't be intimidated by the look of these recipes. Once you grasp the principles involved, they're actually very easy.

Roasted Corn and Sweet Potato Chowder

This soup recipe was inspired by the very sweet, pale yellow Waimanalo corn that is grown just a few miles from the restaurant. In the summer it's sold at roadside stands and from flatbed trucks. We make this soup whenever we can locate our favorite truck in a nearby cul-de-sac! You can make it with any sweet variety of corn.

5 ears of corn, husks left on
1 large red bell pepper
1 small yellow bell pepper
1 small green bell pepper
4 to 5 sweet potatoes (about 1½ pounds), cut into 2-inch chunks
¼ cup olive oil

½ onion, chopped
5 large cloves garlic, minced
¼ cup sliced leeks
½ stalk celery, chopped
3 quarts Vegetable Stock (page 214)
½ tablespoon minced fresh thyme
½ tablespoon minced fresh basil

1 bay leaf
½ tablespoon minced fresh chives
2 quarts heavy cream
Salt and freshly ground pepper to taste
½ tablespoon minced fresh parsley, for garnish

Preheat the oven to 350 degrees. Place the corn and bell peppers on baking sheets; roast the peppers in the oven for 20 minutes and the corn for 30 minutes. Remove the bell peppers and place them in a paper or plastic bag to "steam." When cool, peel, seed, and dice. Set aside. Shuck the ears of roasted corn and cut the kernels from the cobs, using a sharp knife (cut downwards along the cob, behind the kernels). Set the roasted corn aside. Cut the cobs into 2-inch pieces and set aside.

Meanwhile, boil the sweet potatoes until soft, about 20 minutes. Drain and cool; then peel and dice into the same size as the bell peppers. Set aside.

Heat the olive oil in a large saucepan or stockpot, and sauté the onion, garlic, leeks, celery, and corn cobs for about 5 minutes over medium heat, until the vegetables are translucent and lightly caramelized. Add the stock and herbs, and bring to a boil. Reduce the heat and simmer, uncovered, until the liquid is reduced to about 1 quart. Add the cream, and simmer for 30 minutes over low heat to reduce the liquid (once the cream has been added, be careful not to boil the chowder). Strain through a fine sieve into a clean pan. Return the chowder to the heat and simmer for about 5 to 10 minutes, watching it closely, until it thickens and reaches the desired consistency. Season with salt and pepper.

When ready to serve, add the sweet potato, corn, and bell peppers, and warm through. Ladle the chowder into serving bowls. Garnish with the chopped parsley.

Roasted Kabocha Squash Soup
with Chantilly Cream and Candied Pecans

Kabocha is a turban-shaped winter squash with an attractive light and dark green skin and a sweet orange-yellow flesh. Originally from Japan, it's now widely grown in the United States. I ate a lot of baked kabocha as a kid, sprinkled with soy sauce and sugar. In the process of creating a squash soup, I borrowed on those flavors from my childhood and matched the kabocha with a sweet garnish. You can substitute acorn squash or pumpkin if kabocha is not available.

5 pounds kabocha squash	1 small onion, chopped	2 cups heavy cream
4 tablespoons unsalted butter	4 quarts Chicken Stock (page 213)	Salt and freshly ground pepper to taste
1 stalk celery, chopped	½ tablespoon ground cinnamon	Chantilly Cream (recipe follows)
1 leek, white part only, chopped	½ tablespoon fresh thyme	2 tablepoons Candied Pecans (page 219)

Preheat the oven to 350 degrees. Place the whole squash on a baking sheet and roast in the oven for 45 minutes, or until it can be pierced easily with a toothpick. Remove and allow to cool. When cool, cut it in half. Scoop out the seeds, rinse and drain them, and set aside. Scoop out the flesh and reserve separately.

In a large saucepan or stockpot, melt the butter and sauté the celery, leek, and onion until transparent, about 2 to 3 minutes over medium-high heat. Add the Chicken Stock, cinnamon, and thyme, and reduce by half. Add the squash and heavy cream; bring to a light simmer and continue to cook for 15 minutes.

Meanwhile, spread the squash seeds out on a baking sheet and toast in a 350-degree oven for about 15 minutes. Remove and set aside.

Blend the soup with a hand-held electric blender until smooth, and continue to reduce over medium-high heat for about 5 minutes, or until the soup reaches the desired thickness. Strain into a clean pan, and season to taste with salt and pepper.

Prepare the Chantilly Cream.

To serve, ladle the soup into bowls, add a dollop of the Chantilly Cream to each serving, and sprinkle with the toasted squash seeds and Candied Pecans.

Chantilly Cream

1 cup heavy cream	Ground cinnamon to taste	Salt and freshly ground pepper to taste

In a mixing bowl, whisk the cream to soft peaks. Fold in the cinnamon, salt, and pepper.

Oyster Miso Soup

⫸ SERVES 4 ⫷

Celebrating the cherry blossom season in the spring is an important Japanese tradition, and oyster soup is a part of the celebration. This recipe bows to honor that custom. I prefer small oysters, such as Skookums, Fanny Bays, or Kumamotos, for this soup, as they have a particularly light, clean taste. Avoid the large Pacific oysters as they are too strongly flavored.

1 tablespoon sesame oil
3 ounces pork butt, cut into
⅛ x 1-inch strips
½ teaspoon minced garlic

½ teaspoon julienned ginger
4½ cups water
1 small leek, white part only, julienned
2 ounces bamboo shoots, sliced

¼ cup red miso
16 small fresh oysters, shucked
⅛ teaspoon *shichimi*
½ teaspoon *rayu* (spicy sesame oil)

*H*eat the sesame oil in a saucepan and sauté the pork, garlic, and ginger for about 1 minute over high heat. Add the water and cook for about 2 minutes longer. Add the leek and bamboo shoots and continue cooking for 2 minutes. Put the miso into a small sieve and dip the bottom of the sieve into the saucepan so that the miso dissolves without becoming lumpy. When the miso has completely dissolved, add the oysters and cook for 1 minute.

To serve, ladle the soup into bowls, putting 4 oysters into each one. Sprinkle the *shichimi* over the top and add a few drops of *rayu* to each bowl of soup.

Pristine Beach, Niihau.

Duck Noodle Soup with Shrimp

⇒ SERVES 4 ⇐

Probably my favorite soup of all is Chinese duck noodle, and this variation is a substantial soup that could actually be served as an entrée. I like to use precooked fresh Japanese udon noodles in this recipe (look for them in the refrigerator section of Asian markets). If you can't find them, ramen noodles will do. Just boil them ahead of time, following the directions on the package, taking care not to overcook them. Rinse well under cold water, and drain.

1 quart Chicken Stock (page 213)

3 tablespoons light soy sauce (preferably Yamasa brand)

4 duck legs

¼ cup canola oil

8 ounces extra-large shrimp (about 8 to 10), peeled and deveined

3 scallions, sliced

1 cup bok choy, cut on the bias

1 cup sliced gai choy or napa cabbage, or 1 additional cup bok choy

4 ounces shiitake mushrooms, sliced

1 cup bean sprouts

1 pound precooked udon noodles

Garnish:

1 red bell pepper, seeded and julienned

1 yellow bell pepper, seeded and julienned

½ bunch fresh chives, 2 to 3 inches long

Heat the stock and soy sauce in a large saucepan and braise the duck legs over low to medium heat until the meat is tender, about 45 minutes to 1 hour. Set the duck legs aside and strain the broth into a clean saucepan.

Heat the canola oil in a skillet and sauté the duck legs over medium-high heat until brown and crispy. Meanwhile, bring the broth to a boil and add the shrimp, scallions, bok choy, gai choy, mushrooms, and bean sprouts. Reduce the heat and simmer until the mushrooms are tender, about 3 minutes. Add the noodles and reheat briefly.

To serve, ladle the soup into bowls, distributing the noodles, seafood, and vegetables evenly, and put a duck leg in each bowl. Garnish with the julienned bell peppers and chives.

Pictured on opposite page

Thai Hot and Sour Miso Soup with Shrimp Dumplings

Thai cuisine has a long tradition of hot and sour soups. Sometimes, I enjoy a bowl at my favorite Thai restaurant after a busy evening in the kitchen. Here, I combine those flavors with Japanese miso.

12 Shrimp Dumplings
   (recipe follows)
6 cups Chicken Stock (page 213)
¼ cup red miso
4 ounces enoki mushrooms
1 leek, white part only, julienned
½ teaspoon minced ginger

½ teaspoon minced garlic
3 kaffir lime leaves
2 teaspoons finely minced lemon grass
½ teaspoon *rayu* (spicy sesame oil)
1 teaspoon fish sauce
⅛ teaspoon *shichimi*
Juice of 1 lime

Garnish:
2 tablespoons diced red bell pepper
2 tablespoons diced yellow bell pepper
3 tablespoons fresh cilantro
4 stalks lemon grass (optional)
1 teaspoon *furikake* (optional)

Prepare the dumplings, cook, and set aside.

Place the stock, miso, mushrooms, leek, ginger, garlic, lime leaves, lemon grass, *rayu*, and fish sauce in a large stockpot, and bring to a boil. Lower the heat and simmer for 15 minutes. Add the *shichimi* and lime juice, and strain into soup bowls.

To serve, add 3 shrimp dumplings to each bowl. Sprinkle the diced bell peppers around the edge of the soup bowls, and place some cilantro in the center. If desired, also garnish with the shrimp heads from the dumpling recipe and a stalk of lemon grass. Sprinkle *furikake* around the edge of the soup bowl.

Pictured on opposite page

Shrimp Dumplings

Filling:
1 pound medium shrimp, peeled and
   deveined (reserve 8 heads for
   garnish, if desired)
2 tablespoons heavy cream
1 small egg

½ teaspoon minced ginger
⅛ teaspoon minced garlic
½ tablespoon fish sauce
¼ cup finely diced water chestnuts
¼ teaspoon minced fresh basil
Salt and freshly ground pepper to taste

...
1½ tablespoons cornstarch
¼ cup water
12 wonton wrappers

In a food processor or blender, purée the shrimp, cream, egg, ginger, garlic, fish sauce, water chestnuts, and basil. Transfer to a bowl and season with salt and pepper. Cover with plastic wrap and refrigerate for 1 hour. Combine the cornstarch and water in a small bowl. Lay out the wrappers on a work surface and place ½ tablespoon of the filling in the center of each. Brush the edges of the wrappers with the cornstarch mixture, gather the edges together, and twist to close. Place the dumplings on a baking sheet lined with parchment paper, cover with plastic wrap, and refrigerate for 1 hour. (The dumplings can be stored in the refrigerator for up to 2 days.) Just before serving, bring a large saucepan of water to a boil and cook the dumplings for about 5 minutes, or until they float to the surface.

Hawaiian Prawns in Coconut-Curry Soup

⟫ SERVES 4 TO 6 ⟪

I never tire of the Thai-influenced combination of curry and coconut milk. In this soup, it is mellowed by the addition of palm sugar, which is readily available in Asian markets. Palm sugar has a pastelike consistency and should be yellowish brown in color, rather like peanut butter. (The paler it is, the fresher it is.) In an emergency, you can use brown sugar, but the flavor won't be the same.

2 quarts unsweetened coconut milk

½ cup palm sugar

3 stalks lemon grass, peeled and chopped

¼ cup fish sauce

½ tablespoon minced garlic

½ tablespoon minced ginger

½ cup fresh basil leaves

1½ pounds Hawaiian prawns or jumbo shrimp

4 tablespoons peanut oil

1 to 2 tablespoons red curry paste (preferably Mae Ploy brand Matsaman curry paste)

Salt and freshly ground pepper to taste

24 Hawaiian red chiles (or Thai or Fiesta chiles), for garnish

Place the coconut milk, palm sugar, lemon grass, fish sauce, garlic, ginger, and basil in a large stockpot, and bring to a boil. Lower the heat to a simmer and reduce the liquid by about one-quarter.

Remove the heads and shells of the prawns or shrimp, reserving all parts. Heat 2 tablespoons of the peanut oil in a sauté pan, and sauté the heads and shells until slightly browned. Add to the soup together with the curry paste, and continue to simmer until the soup thickens, about 15 minutes. Strain the soup, discarding the solids, and keep warm.

Lightly season the prawns or shrimp with salt and pepper. Heat the remaining 2 tablespoons of peanut oil in the sauté pan, and sauté the prawns or shrimp for 30 seconds on each side over medium-high heat, or until done.

To serve, divide the prawns between the soup bowls and ladle in the soup. Arrange the chiles in a pinwheel design to garnish each serving.

HERE I AM WITH my friend Neal Aoki, sales manager of Tropic Fish—we've known each other for years. Tropic was established in 1951 by Kiyoshi and Katherine Tanoue as a grocery store, and although it's still a family business, it's grown into the state's largest seafood wholesaler. The original store, named the Tropic Fish and Vegetable Center, is still a retail outlet.

Tropic supplies fine restaurants (including Roy's), supermarket chains, hotels, schools, and even the ubiquitous Hawaiian small lunch stands. The company also ships fish by air to Japan and the mainland United States. Tropic's single biggest selling product? Tuna.

Roy's Feasts from Hawaii

Red Chile Lentil Stew

This spicy recipe is highly versatile; in addition to making a hearty, warming soup, it can also be used as a side dish or condiment to accompany lamb or a hearty-flavored fish such as salmon or tuna—especially smoked tuna (see special directions below). As a soup, it should be served hot, but as a condiment or side dish, serve it warm or cold, and it will take on a quite different flavor.

1 cup red or brown lentils
2 tablespoons olive oil
4 ounces pancetta, finely diced
1 onion, finely diced
1½ tablespoons minced garlic
2 tablespoons finely diced carrot
2 tablespoons finely diced celery
3 bay leaves

1 teaspoon dried red chile flakes, crushed
1 pound tomatoes, peeled, seeded, and diced
2 cups Veal Stock or Chicken Stock (page 213)
1½ cups canned tomato juice
2 teaspoons julienned fresh basil
1 teaspoon minced fresh thyme

1 teaspoon minced fresh tarragon
1 tablespoon salt
½ teaspoon sugar
½ teaspoon freshly ground pepper

Vinaigrette:
½ tablespoon sherry vinegar
1½ tablespoons olive oil

Wash the lentils in a sieve under running cold water. Soak in a bowl of water for 30 minutes, drain, and set aside.

In a large stockpot, heat the olive oil and sauté the pancetta, onion, garlic, carrot, and celery over high heat until lightly browned, about 1 to 2 minutes. Stir in all the remaining ingredients except the lentils and vinaigrette. Continue stirring for about 1 minute, and then add the lentils. Cook over medium heat for about 30 minutes, until the lentils are barely tender but not mushy.

Just before serving, whisk together the vinaigrette and stir it into the lentils.

Variation: To prepare the lentils as a condiment or side dish, cut the quantities in half and omit the vinaigrette. Cook as described above, then strain the lentils, reserving the liquid for soup or stock. Cool the lentils by spreading on a baking sheet, then refrigerate. Serve cold, or warm the lentils in a saucepan with a little of the reserved cooking liquid.

Seafood Chowder with Asian Pesto Crostini

❧ SERVES 4 ❧

This recipe is my version of Manhattan clam chowder by way of Southeast Asia and the Mediterranean. It's proof that chowders do not have to be thick and heavy; this one's light, with clear, crisp flavors.

2½ tablespoons olive oil

5 cloves garlic, minced

¼ cup white wine

¼ cup fresh cilantro

1 bottle (32 ounces) clam juice

4 littleneck clams, thoroughly scrubbed

12 scallops

12 mussels, debearded

16 small shrimp (about 6 ounces), peeled and deveined (reserve 4 shrimp heads for garnish, if desired)

6 ounces ono (wahoo), cut into 12 pieces

3 ounces pancetta

1 large onion, finely diced

3 carrots, diced

2 stalks celery, diced

2 cups Vegetable Stock (page 214)

Asian Pesto Crostini:

¼ cup sesame oil

¼ cup shelled peanuts

¼ cup fresh cilantro

1 teaspoon fermented black beans

1 teaspoon finely diced kaffir lime leaf

4 slices French baguette bread, cut about ¼ inch thick

12 thin strips red bell pepper, about 1½ inches long

4 fresh Italian parsley leaves

...

8 to 12 fresh chives, for garnish

Heat 2 tablespoons of the olive oil in a stockpot and sauté the garlic over high heat so that it browns quickly. Add the white wine, cilantro, and clam juice, and bring to a simmer. Reduce the heat to low, and add the shellfish and ono to the broth. Cover and steam until the clams and mussels open slightly, about 45 seconds to 1 minute. The shellfish should be just barely cooked. Remove the shellfish and ono from the broth and set aside. Strain the broth through a fine sieve into a bowl and reserve.

Heat the remaining ½ tablespoon of olive oil in the stockpot, and brown the pancetta quickly over medium-high heat, about 30 seconds. Add the onion, carrots, and celery, and sauté for 1 minute. Add the Vegetable Stock and reserved clam broth, and bring to a boil. Reduce the heat and simmer until the vegetables are just tender, about 15 minutes. Remove from the heat, strain the soup through a sieve into a clean pan and discard the vegetables. Reduce the strained soup by half over high heat.

To prepare the Asian Pesto Crostini, blend together the sesame oil, peanuts, cilantro, black beans, and lime leaf in a blender. Toast the bread rounds on one side under a broiler. Spread the untoasted side with the pesto, and broil until bubbly. Decorate each crostini with 3 strips of the red bell pepper and a parsley leaf.

To serve, place 1 clam, 3 scallops, 3 mussels, 4 shrimp, and 3 pieces of ono in each bowl, keeping each kind of seafood together, if possible. Reheat the chowder and ladle into the serving bowls. Arrange 2 or 3 chives in each bowl, and garnish with a shrimp head, if desired. Serve with the crostini on the side.

Pictured on opposite page

Chilled Thai Melon Soup

⋙ SERVES 6 ⋘

I generally prefer hot soups, but this is an intensely refreshing summer soup. The most important thing is to use several different melons for their unique flavors, even if they're not the exact varieties called for here.

2 cups seeded and diced cantaloupe

2 cups seeded and diced Crenshaw or honeydew melon

2 cups seeded and diced watermelon

1 tablespoon *sriracha* chile sauce

1 tablespoon sweet chile sauce (preferably Lingham's brand)

1 cup unsweetened coconut milk

Juice of 3 limes

1 tablespoon minced ginger

2 tablespoons chopped fresh cilantro

1 tablespoon chopped fresh opal basil

3 tablespoons finely minced fresh mint

1 tablespoon chopped toasted peanuts (page 220), for garnish

In a food processor or blender, purée the melons, *sriracha* and sweet chile sauces, coconut milk, lime juice, ginger, cilantro, basil, and 2 tablespoons of the mint. Strain and chill.

Serve in chilled soup bowls, garnished with the remaining mint and the peanuts.

HAWAII BOASTS THE highest per capita watermelon consumption of any state in the country, and almost all of Hawaii's watermelons are grown by Larry Jefts at his 1,600-acre farm on Molokai. This adds up to more than 15 million pounds of watermelons every year!

Larry's farm also produces tomatoes (shown here being harvested), onions, snap beans, and greens. Jefts Farms is the state's main bell pepper supplier. Larry currently employs more than 100 farm workers on Molokai and has just begun planting 3,000 acres on Oahu, where he is expanding his operations. This land was previously occupied by sugar plantations, and Larry's business is a great example of how diversified agriculture can successfully replace the once-mighty sugar and pineapple production.

Salads

*B*elieve it or not, I never ate a salad until I was eighteen! Salad is not an element of Japanese cuisine, although greens in some form are a part of many other dishes. Now I prefer hearty salads, with items such as fish, seafood, chicken, or shiu mai, in addition to the lettuce or other greens. The salads in this chapter are substantial appetizers and, in some cases, can become main courses.

This is in keeping with the way salads are composed in many Asian countries. In places such as Thailand, Indonesia, and Malaysia (and in western India), salads tend to contain a variety of vegetables and fruits as well as greens. Aesthetic appeal and orderly presentation are common traits of Asian salads.

Most of the salads in this chapter are composed of a mixture of greens, which provide a delicate complexity of flavors. I recommend that you use the freshest vegetables you can find; don't worry too much about tracking down the exact greens called for. It's fine to use just two or three types of greens, or even just one kind.

In keeping with the Euro-Asian style of my cooking, the salad recipes that follow combine European-style vinaigrettes and Asian ingredients. You'll also notice that I like to create warm dressings and warm or wilted salads. Most of the dressings can be used with plain salads, if you prefer, and many of the salads can be prepared with a simpler dressing, or even with none at all.

Asparagus with Passion Fruit Vinaigrette

You'll often see asparagus served with an orange hollandaise sauce or an orange vinaigrette in French restaurants, so I adapted the pairing to give this salad a tropical, Hawaiian touch. Growing up in Japan, I remember eating lots of canned asparagus as a snack food. It was only when I arrived at the Culinary Institute of America in New York, at the age of eighteen, that I tasted fresh asparagus for the first time. I couldn't believe the difference!

Vinaigrette:

¾ cup unseasoned rice vinegar

¼ cup olive oil

2 tablespoons minced shallots

Juice of 5 passion fruit, strained (about 5 tablespoons)

2 tablespoons grated ginger

Salt and freshly ground pepper to taste

…

1¼ pounds fresh asparagus

2 tablespoons olive oil

Salt and freshly ground pepper to taste

Prepare the grill.

Whisk together all the vinaigrette ingredients in a bowl and set aside. Coat the asparagus with the olive oil and season with salt and pepper. Grill for 2 or 3 minutes. (Or, if you prefer, blanch the asparagus for 2 to 3 minutes in boiling water, shock in ice water, and drain.)

Stack the asparagus in an upright triangle on each plate (or arrange it as you wish), and spoon the vinaigrette over.

Harvesting baby lettuce at Nalo Farms, Oahu.

Grilled Eggplant Salad with Nalo Farms Greens and Goat Cheese Crostini

I created this salad for a special dinner I prepared in 1992 at the James Beard House in New York. It was an honor to have been invited to cook at the late great master's former residence. His home is now headquarters for the James Beard Foundation, an organization that does much to promote American cuisine.

Goat Cheese Crostini:
½ recipe Basic Pizza Dough (page 87), or 20 thin slices French baguette bread, toasted
¼ cup Basic Tomato Sauce (page 215)
5 tablespoons fresh goat cheese
2 teaspoons Pesto (page 214)
…
1 large eggplant
3 tablespoons olive oil

1 teaspoon minced garlic
1 teaspoon minced fresh rosemary
1 teaspoon minced fresh basil

Balsamic Vinaigrette:
2½ teaspoons balsamic vinegar
½ teaspoon red wine vinegar
1 tablespoon olive oil
1 tablespoon finely minced fresh basil

¼ teaspoon minced shallot
¼ teaspoon minced garlic
…
1 cup Basic Tomato Sauce (page 000), warmed
4 to 5 cups washed and torn mixed greens, such as mizuna, arugula, and radicchio (about 5 to 6 ounces)
10 yellow pear tomatoes, cut in half

Preheat the oven to 400 degrees.

To make the crostini with pizza dough, divide the dough into 20 pieces. Roll each piece into a ball about 1 inch in diameter and gently press into a football shape. Place on a pizza pan or baking sheet and bake in the oven for about 5 minutes, until golden brown. Let cool. Spread about ½ teaspoon of the tomato sauce over each crostini or slice of toast, and top with the goat cheese and a dab of the Pesto. Just before assembling the salad, place the crostini under the broiler to melt the cheese.

Cut 4 crosswise slices of eggplant, each about ¼ inch thick. Place the olive oil on a large serving platter and sprinkle the garlic and herbs over. Dip the eggplant in the oil mixture, turning to make sure the slices are evenly coated with oil, garlic, and herbs. Sear on a very hot griddle or grill, about 2 to 3 minutes per side.

Whisk together all the ingredients for the Balsamic Vinaigrette in a bowl and set aside.

To serve, ladle ¼ cup of the warmed Basic Tomato Sauce in a neat circle on each serving plate and place a slice of the eggplant in the center. In a mixing bowl, toss the greens with the vinaigrette and place on top of the eggplant. Arrange 5 crostini around each salad, with a pear tomato half between each crostini.

Pictured on opposite page

Maui Onions and Kula Tomatoes with Pancetta and Basil Balsamic Vinaigrette

※ SERVES 6 ※

This salad was created to highlight Maui's onions and tomatoes, both of which are sweet enough to rival those from any other place on earth. The Kula region, which lies on the lower slopes of Mount Haleakala, is Maui's salad bowl; from that area comes some of Hawaii's finest fresh produce.

Maui Onion Salad:
¼ cup extra virgin olive oil
1 ounce pancetta, diced
¼ teaspoon finely minced garlic
¼ teaspoon finely minced shallot

¼ cup balsamic vinegar
6 large fresh basil leaves, julienned
3 Maui onions, julienned
6 large ripe Kula beefsteak tomatoes

6 cups washed and torn baby mixed greens, such as arugula, mizuna, spinach, and red leaf lettuce, (about 5 ounces)
6 sprigs fresh basil, for garnish

To prepare the vinaigrette, heat the olive oil in a large sauté pan and sauté the pancetta, garlic, and shallot over medium-high heat for 1 minute. Remove from the heat and stir in the vinegar and half of the basil. Add the onions and return to the heat for about 30 seconds. Remove from the heat and stir in the remaining basil.

Core the tomatoes; cut a slice off the tops and bottoms and discard. Cut each tomato into 3 thick slices. Putting the salad together involves reassembling the tomatoes, so try to keep the slices in order.

To assemble, place a bottom tomato slice on each serving plate. Place a layer of the greens on top of the tomato, using up about half the greens. Place a layer of onions and a little vinaigrette over the greens, and then the center tomato slice. Add another layer of greens (use them all up), onions (save some for garnish), and top with the last slice of tomato. Garnish with a little more onion salad and a basil sprig. Pour a little of the remaining vinaigrette around the salad.

SWEET MAUI ONIONS are another major success story in the history of Hawaiian agriculture. Here's one grower who's part of that story, Silvestre Tumbaga, with some of his crop of deliciously sweet Maui onions. When I lived and worked in Los Angeles, I'd fly over to Maui to visit my grandparents in Wailuku. (I helped stock shelves and worked in the store while visiting from Tokyo when I was a kid. I'd be the one with a hand in the dried abalone and crack seed!) They'd usually send me back to California with a 100-pound bag of Maui onions. My fellow passengers would be carrying modest cartons of pineapple or macadamia nuts, or beautiful bouquets of local nursery-grown flowers—such as proteas, orchids, or dendrobriums—and there I'd be, struggling with my sack of onions.

Roy's Feasts from Hawaii

Nalo Farms: A Unique Source for Quality Produce

Talking herbs with Dean Okimoto beneath the Koolau mountains at Nalo Farms.

Dean Okimoto's Nalo Farms nestles beneath the wrinkled green *pali* (cliffs) of the Koolau mountain range in Waimanalo on the eastern, windward shore of Oahu. Just a few miles along the coastal road from Roy's, semi-rural upcountry Waimanalo is the location for a number of small-scale farms that grow vegetables, fruits, and flowers, and raise poultry and dairy cows. Waimanalo sweet corn is a specialty of the area, and Dean's produce is another.

Dean is a specialty grower who started out in 1985. He identified a niche market and is one of only two or three herb growers that specifically supplies restaurants. Dean grows most of the herbs we use at Roy's in Honolulu, as well as edible flowers, greens, and chiles. He farms two acres here on fertile soil, and because this is the cloudier, wetter side of Oahu, his land receives an ideal 50 or 60 inches of rain a year.

Dean's herbs are the best I have ever tasted, and they couldn't be any fresher. His main crop is basil, and he grows several types, including sweet Italian basil, Thai basil, and the purple opal basil. He also grows marjoram, sage, pineapple sage, oregano, rosemary, tarragon, chives, parsley, dill, sorrel, and spearmint, among other herbs, which he grows from seed in his hydroponic greenhouse. His plants are constantly picked and have a life span of about 1½ years, after which he plows the patch and replants with young herbs from home-grown seedlings.

Dean also grows the mesclun mix of lettuce we use at Roy's in our salads, which includes arugula, watercress, and mizuna lettuce. His beautiful edible flowers are mostly grown during the winter season. Dean is beginning production of red mustard greens and bok choy. I enjoy giving Dean seedlings from my travels whenever I encounter something new and different that I hope he'll grow—and I'm lucky that Dean is very receptive to new ideas. To be an innovative restaurant chef, you need a fertile imagination, the temperament to experiment, and a willing grower like Dean. It is suppliers like him that have helped the new style of Hawaiian Regional Cuisine evolve.

Roy's Caesar Salad with Crabmeat, Avocado, and Parmesan Pizza Balls

I prefer my Caesar salads hearty, creamy, and chunky rather than dainty and delicate. The sweetness and richness of crab is perfect for this salad, but you can substitute other types of seafood for the crab, or omit it altogether if you wish. The dressing also makes a great dipping sauce for deep-fried calamari.

Caesar Dressing:
6 anchovy fillets
4 cloves garlic
2 egg yolks
2 teaspoons Dijon mustard
1 tablespoon red wine vinegar
Juice of ½ lemon
½ teaspoon Worcestershire sauce

Dash of Tabasco sauce
½ teaspoon freshly ground pepper
2 tablespoons grated parmesan cheese
½ cup extra virgin olive oil
...
Basic Pizza Dough (page 87)
¼ cup grated parmesan cheese
1 large head romaine lettuce

1 large avocado, peeled, pitted, and sliced
12 ounces lump crabmeat (blue crab or Dungeness crab)

Garnish:
2 tablespoons shaved parmesan cheese
1 teaspoon *shichimi*

To prepare the dressing, place the anchovies, garlic, egg yolks, mustard, vinegar, lemon juice, Worcestershire sauce, Tabasco sauce, pepper, and parmesan cheese in a blender or food processor and purée. With the machine running, add the oil in a steady stream and blend until the mixture no longer separates when allowed to stand for several minutes.

Preheat the oven to 450 degrees. To prepare the pizza balls, roll the pizza dough out into 2 dozen 1-inch balls. Roll them in the grated parmesan cheese and place on a pizza pan or baking sheet. Bake for about 5 minutes, until golden brown, and let cool.

Place a mound of whole romaine leaves in the middle of each serving plate and arrange 6 pizza balls around each salad. Place a slice of avocado between the pizza balls, and top each avocado slice with about a tablespoon of crabmeat. Drizzle some of the dressing over the salad, and put the remainder in a ramekin or small pitcher to serve on the side. To garnish, sprinkle the shaved parmesan and *shichimi* over the salad.

Pictured on opposite page (upper left)

Asian Grilled Chicken Salad

⸎ SERVES 4 ⸎

This is a recipe that was created at Roy's Kahana Bar and Grill on Maui. In this one, a little Indian tandoori sauce is added to the marinade, giving the chicken a unique and intriguing flavor. Tandoori sauce is available at Indian or Asian markets.

Marinade:

½ cup sesame oil

¼ cup unseasoned rice vinegar

¼ cup Chicken Stock (page 213)

3 tablespoons soy sauce

½ teaspoon fish sauce

2 tablespoons tandoori sauce

Juice of ½ lime

2 cloves garlic, minced

2 tablespoons minced ginger

1 tablespoon minced shallot

1 Hawaiian red chile or red jalapeño chile, seeded and minced

Salt and freshly ground pepper to taste

...

4 boneless half chicken breasts, with skin on

2 tablespoons canola oil

12 wonton wrappers, julienned

Dressing:

¼ cup olive oil

1 teaspoon soy sauce

Juice of 1 lemon

Salt and freshly ground white pepper to taste

...

4 or 5 cups washed and torn mixed greens, such as red leaf lettuce, arugula, baby spinach, radicchio, and escarole (about 5 to 6 ounces)

Garnish:

8 Hawaiian red chiles or red jalapeño chiles

1 teaspoon toasted white sesame seeds (page 220)

1 teaspoon black sesame seeds

In a mixing bowl, whisk together the marinade ingredients until the mixture no longer separates when allowed to stand for several minutes. Marinate the chicken breasts for about 30 minutes.

Prepare the grill. Remove the chicken from the marinade and grill for 2 to 3 minutes per side, or until cooked through. Set aside.

Heat the canola oil in a skillet and fry the wonton wrappers until crispy. Remove and drain on paper towels.

Whisk together the dressing ingredients until the mixture no longer separates when allowed to stand for several minutes. Toss the greens with the dressing in a mixing bowl, and transfer to one side of each serving plate. Arrange the wonton strips on top and garnish with the chiles. Cut each chicken breast into 6 slices, fan out, and place to the side of the greens on each plate. Sprinkle with the sesame seeds.

Pictured on page 63 (lower right)

Roy's Antipasti Salad

The inspiration for this Mediterranean-style salad came to me after tasting an antipasti salad at Soho Touloilouwu's Italian Dinette in Tokyo (Soho is also a partner in the Roy's restaurant in Tokyo). Although you won't use all of the vinaigrette for this salad, you can refrigerate the amount left over and use it for any kind of green salad.

Vinaigrette:

1 cup extra virgin olive oil
2 tablespoons red wine vinegar
2 tablespoons champagne vinegar
1 tablespoon balsamic vinegar
2 tablespoons Dijon mustard
½ tablespoon Worcestershire sauce
½ tablespoon minced onion
½ teaspoon minced shallot
½ teaspoon minced garlic
½ teaspoon minced fresh parsley
½ teaspoon minced fresh thyme
½ teaspoon capers
Pinch of minced fresh dill

Pinch of minced fresh rosemary
Pinch of minced fresh tarragon
½ tablespoon salt
½ tablespoon freshly ground white pepper

...

1 red bell pepper, roasted, peeled, and seeded (page 220)
1 green bell pepper, roasted, peeled, and seeded
4 cups washed and torn mixed baby greens, such as arugula, radicchio, mizuna, and baby spinach (about 5 to 6 ounces)
8 slices prosciutto
8 slices salami

8 slices provolone
3½ ounces (1 ball) fresh Buffalo mozzarella cheese, cut into 4 slices
3 ounces grilled chicken breast, cut into 4 slices
1 cup Tuscan-Style White Beans (page 156), cooled
1 cup cooked and cooled green beans, angle-cut
¼ cup finely julienned zucchini
¼ cup finely julienned yellow squash

Garnish:

4 pepperoncini, cut in half
4 Kalamata black olives

Whisk together all the vinaigrette ingredients in a mixing bowl. Julienne the roasted bell peppers, transfer to a separate bowl and marinate briefly in ¼ cup of the vinaigrette.

Toss the greens with another ¼ cup of the vinaigrette, and arrange in the center of four large salad plates. Roll up the slices of prosciutto, salami, provolone, and mozzarella, and place them, along with the chicken slices, around the greens. On each plate, place two mounds of white beans opposite each other, and two mounds of green beans in the same way. Combine the zucchini and squash, place them on the greens, and top with the marinated bell peppers. Garnish with the pepperoncini and olives. Serve with the remaining vinaigrette on the side.

Seared Shrimp Salad with Feta Cheese and Candied Garlic

This recipe, which I created for 385 North, my former restaurant in Los Angeles, was published by Bon Appétit magazine in 1987. The inspiration for it came from Alain Dutournier, who was guest chef at L'Ermitage for a week or so when I worked there, and who impressed me with his confit of garlic. Alain owns a wonderful bistro in Paris called Au Trou Gascon.

Candied Garlic:
⅓ cup garlic cloves
1 cup white wine
½ cup sugar
2 tablespoons unsalted butter

Dressing:
1 teaspoon sherry vinegar

2 tablespoons olive oil
1 teaspoon salt
½ teaspoon freshly ground white pepper
...
16 extra-large shrimp (about 1 pound), peeled and deveined
Salt and freshly ground white pepper to taste

2 tablespoons canola oil
4 cups washed and torn mixed baby greens, such as romaine lettuce hearts, mizuna, and radicchio, (about 5 ounces)
2 ounces feta cheese, crumbled
16 Niçoise or Kalamata black olives
12 yellow pear tomatoes, cut in half

To prepare the candied garlic, place the garlic, wine, sugar, and butter in a small saucepan and cook slowly over low heat until the liquid becomes syrupy, about 10 minutes. The garlic should be tender without being mushy; if necessary, remove the garlic while finishing the reduction of the liquid. Keep warm in a double boiler.

Combine all the dressing ingredients in a small bowl and whisk until the mixture no longer separates when allowed to stand for several minutes.

Season the shrimp with salt and pepper and coat with the canola oil. Sear in a sauté pan over medium-high heat for about 1 minute per side.

Gently toss the greens with the dressing and feta cheese in a mixing bowl. Divide between serving plates, and arrange 4 shrimp, 4 olives, and 6 tomato halves around the edges of each salad. Scatter the candied garlic over the greens, and drizzle the warm syrup over all.

Pictured on opposite page (lower left)

Warm Spinach Salad with Spicy Shrimp and Scallops

❧ SERVES 4 ❧

This popular version of a wilted spinach salad comes from Roy's Kahana Bar and Grill, on Maui. You'll have some dressing left over, but it doesn't really work if you make it in a smaller quantity. Just refrigerate the remaining dressing for later use.

Dressing:
2 teaspoons canola oil
3 tablespoons minced lemon grass
1 teaspoon *shichimi*
½ teaspoon minced garlic
3 tablespoons fish sauce
3 tablespoons unseasoned rice vinegar
3 tablespoons Chicken Stock
   (page 213)
1 teaspoon sesame oil
½ teaspoon soy sauce
Juice of 1 lime
Salt and freshly ground white pepper
   to taste

Spicy Crust:
1 tablespoon finely minced lemon grass
1 red onion, finely julienned
2 tablespoons minced fresh mint
2 tablespoons minced fresh basil
2 tablespoons minced fresh cilantro
2 cloves garlic, minced
2 tablespoons minced ginger
1 Hawaiian chile (or red jalapeño or
   Fiesta chile), seeded and minced
...

12 extra-large shrimp (about 12
   ounces), peeled and deveined
8 scallops, each sliced into 3 rounds
2 tablespoons sesame oil
1 tablespoon olive oil
1 bunch spinach, washed and
   stemmed

Garnish:
1 red bell pepper, seeded
   and julienned
1 yellow bell pepper, seeded and
   julienned
1 teaspoon *shichimi*

To prepare the dressing, heat the canola oil in a saucepan, and sauté the lemon grass, *shichimi*, and garlic over medium heat for about 15 seconds. Remove from the heat and add the fish sauce, vinegar, stock, sesame oil, soy sauce, lime juice, salt, and pepper. Set aside.

Combine all the ingredients for the Spicy Crust in a bowl and coat the shrimp and scallops with this mixture. Heat the sesame oil and the olive oil in a sauté pan or skillet, and sear the shrimp and scallops over medium-high heat for 1 minute. Remove and reserve.

Heat ⅓ cup of the reserved dressing in a large sauté pan, and wilt the spinach over low heat for about 15 seconds. Transfer to serving plates. Top each salad with 3 shrimp and arrange 6 scallop slices around the edges. Garnish with the julienned bell peppers and sprinkle the *shichimi* over each salad.

Pictured on page 67 (upper right)

Smoked Ahi Salad with Cilantro Vinaigrette and Red Bell Pepper Coulis

This recipe was created by David Abella when he was executive chef at Roy's Kahana Bar and Grill on Maui. Although it was designed for ahi tuna, you can make it with other dense-fleshed fish such as marlin, swordfish, or ono (wahoo), if you prefer.

12 ounces ahi tuna

Cilantro Vinaigrette:
⅔ cup pineapple juice
Juice of 4 or 5 limes
¾ cup olive oil
2 tablespoons balsamic vinegar
½ cup roughly chopped fresh cilantro
Salt and freshly ground pepper to taste

Red Bell Pepper Coulis:
3 red bell peppers, roasted, peeled, and seeded (page 220)
½ tablespoon olive oil
1 teaspoon balsamic vinegar
¼ teaspoon ground cumin
Salt and freshly ground pepper to taste
...

1 tablespoon canola oil
Salt and freshly ground pepper to taste
1 large Maui onion, finely diced
2 tomatoes, finely diced
4 to 5 cups washed and torn mixed greens such as radicchio, escarole, red leaf lettuce, baby spinach, and arugula (about 5 to 6 ounces)

If you are using a smoker, cold-smoke the tuna for about 40 minutes over mesquite wood. If you want to smoke the tuna on a grill, you need a covered grill, soaked wood chips, and a means of controlling the temperature, as the fire should be no hotter than 65 to 75 degrees. For regular grilling, simply cook to medium-rare or rare over normal fire.

To prepare the vinaigrette, whisk together the pineapple juice, lime juice, olive oil, and vinegar in a bowl until the mixture no longer separates when allowed to stand for several minutes. Add the cilantro and season with salt and pepper.

To prepare the coulis, purée all the ingredients in a blender or food processor. Set aside.

Just before serving, coat the smoked tuna with the canola oil and season with salt and pepper. Heat a sauté pan or skillet until hot, and sear the tuna for about 15 seconds per side over high heat. Dice the tuna, transfer to a mixing bowl, and combine with the onion and tomatoes. In a mixing bowl, toss the greens with the vinaigrette and divide between 4 serving plates. Place the tuna mixture on top of the greens and drizzle with the coulis.

Curried Lemon Grass-Crusted Swordfish Salad with Red Ginger-Soy Vinaigrette

≫ SERVES 4 ≪

¼ teaspoon curry powder
¼ teaspoon minced lemon grass
¼ teaspoon *shichimi*
¼ teaspoon black sesame seeds
18 ounces swordfish, thinly sliced into 12 fillets
5 tablespoons sesame oil

¼ cup julienned leeks
8 wonton wrappers, julienned
Red Ginger-Soy Vinaigrette (recipe follows)
4 to 5 cups washed and torn mixed baby lettuce, such as arugula, mizuna, radicchio, and romaine (about 5 to 6 ounces)

¼ cup julienned red bell pepper
¼ cup julienned yellow bell pepper
¼ cup scallions, angle-cut
2 tablespoons Japanese spice sprouts
¼ cup minced Pink Pickled Ginger (page 219)

In a bowl, combine the curry powder, lemon grass, shichimi, and sesame seeds. Sprinkle over the swordfish fillets. Place 3 tablespoons of the sesame oil on a plate and gently coat the swordfish with the oil. Heat a sauté pan and sear the crusted fillets for 30 seconds per side over high heat for medium-rare. Let cool to room temperature.

Heat 1 tablespoon of the sesame oil in a clean sauté pan and sauté the leeks over medium-high heat until crispy. Remove with a slotted spoon and drain on paper towels. Add the remaining tablespoon of sesame oil to the pan, heat well, and fry the wonton strips until crispy. Remove and drain on paper towels.

Prepare the Red Ginger-Soy Vinaigrette.

Arrange a "nest" of the mixed greens in the middle of each serving plate. In a mixing bowl, gently toss the leeks, wonton strips, bell peppers, scallions, and sprouts with about 2 tablespoons of Red Ginger-Soy Vinaigrette (do not overmix or crush the ingredients, or let them become too soggy). Place the tossed salad inside the "nests" of lettuce, and arrange 3 slices of the swordfish around the salad on each plate. Drizzle the remaining vinaigrette around the fish and place a little of the pickled ginger between each fillet.

Pictured on opposite page

Red Ginger-Soy Vinaigrette

≫ YIELD: ABOUT 2 CUPS ≪

¼ cup sesame oil
⅓ cup unseasoned rice vinegar
3 tablespoons mirin
½ cup soy sauce
½ cup red pickled ginger
2 tablespoons sugar

1 teaspoon finely minced garlic
1 tablespoon minced onion
½ tablespoon minced shallot
1 teaspoon minced fresh cilantro
1 teaspoon minced fresh basil
⅛ teaspoon salt

⅛ teaspoon freshly ground white pepper
½ teaspoon black sesame seeds
½ teaspoon toasted white sesame seeds (page 220)
½ tablespoon scallions, angle-cut

Place the sesame oil, vinegar, mirin, soy sauce, ginger, sugar, garlic, onion, shallot, cilantro, basil, salt, and pepper in a blender or food processor and blend until smooth. Whisk in the sesame seeds and scallions, cover, and refrigerate. Whisk again before using.

Duck Pastrami with Molokai Greens and Balsamic Cabernet Sauce

*Traditional pastrami is made with beef, but duck can be cured and smoked with equally good results.
To prepare this salad, allow 3 days to make the duck pastrami.*

Curing Spice:
3 tablespoons coriander seed
2 tablespoons black peppercorns
2 tablespoons Szechwan peppercorns
2 tablespoons fennel seed
5 bay leaves
1 tablespoon kosher salt
1 tablespoon onion powder
1 tablespoon garlic powder
1 tablespoon anise seed

1 teaspoon dried red chile flakes
…
4 boneless half duck breasts,
   with skin on

Balsamic Cabernet Sauce:
1 cup Cabernet Sauce (page 216)
¼ cup balsamic vinegar

Vinaigrette:
1 teaspoon olive oil
1 small clove garlic, minced

½ teaspoon red wine vinegar
⅛ teaspoon fresh lemon juice
Pinch of salt
…
1½ cups julienned radicchio
12 leaves mizuna lettuce
4 red jalapeño, Fiesta, or serrano
   chiles, seeded and thinly sliced
   into rings, for garnish

Cut four 7-inch squares of cheesecloth; have them ready at hand, along with some butcher's twine. Place all the curing spice ingredients in a blender and pulse until uniformly ground. Spread the spices out on a small plate. Wash and pat the duck breasts dry, then roll them in the spices, making sure they are well covered. Wrap each breast in cheesecloth, and secure with butcher's twine. Arrange the duck on a plate, and cover with a second plate weighted down with a brick or any heavy object that weighs about 5 pounds. Refrigerate for 3 days.

Remove the cheesecloth and lightly cold-smoke the duck breasts with apple wood or apple wood chips for about 20 minutes, keeping the temperature below 75 degrees, or grill over a very low fire. Refrigerate until ready to serve.

Meanwhile, combine the Cabernet Sauce and balsamic vinegar in a saucepan and bring to a simmer. Turn down the heat to low and reduce for 5 to 10 minutes. You should end up with about ¾ cup of sauce thick enough to coat the back of a spoon.

To prepare the vinaigrette, heat the olive oil in a skillet and sauté the garlic over medium heat until translucent. Transfer to a small bowl, and whisk in the vinegar, lemon juice, and salt.

Just before serving, toss the radicchio in a bowl with the vinaigrette. Strain the Balsamic Cabernet Sauce through a fine strainer and spoon it onto one side of each serving plate. Slice the duck breasts as thinly as possible, and arrange them in a fan shape on top of the sauce. Place the mizuna at the apex of the fan, along with a mound of radicchio. Garnish with the red chile rings.

Crispy Scallop and Fresh Fruit Salad with Creamy Blue Cheese Dressing

≫ SERVES 4 ≪

Sometimes there's nothing as delicious as eating fried scallops with a blue cheese dip. That's why I created this recipe. Diced fresh mango or papaya make a rich tropical alternative for the garnish.

Creamy Blue Cheese Dressing:
¼ cup crumbled Maytag blue cheese
½ cup buttermilk
1 tablespoon unseasoned rice vinegar
½ teaspoon minced garlic
Pinch of *shichimi*
Salt and freshly ground pepper to taste
1 teaspoon minced fresh basil
1 teaspoon Worcestershire sauce
...

1 teaspoon *shichimi*
1 teaspoon minced garlic
1 teaspoon minced ginger
16 scallops (about 1 pound)
2 tablespoons cornstarch
½ cup olive oil
2 heads romaine lettuce, washed and torn, or 6 cups mixed baby greens, such as arugula, mizuna, and radicchio

Garnish:
16 fresh raspberries
16 orange sections (from 2 oranges)
16 fresh blueberries
2 tablespoons crumbled Maytag blue cheese

Place all the dressing ingredients in a bowl and mash together. Set aside.

Combine the *shichimi*, garlic, and ginger together on a plate. Roll the scallops in the mixture to coat thoroughly, then dredge in the cornstarch. Heat the oil in a skillet and sauté the scallops over medium-high heat for about 30 seconds per side, or until crisp and medium-rare.

Toss the greens with the dressing in a mixing bowl and arrange in the center of each serving plate; or, if you prefer, ladle the dressing directly on the plates and place the greens on top. For each serving, arrange 4 scallops around the greens, along with 4 pieces of each fruit. Sprinkle the blue cheese garnish over the greens.

Note: You can substitute other seasonal fruit for the berries and oranges.

You can't beat a slice of local papaya with a spritz of lime juice first thing in the morning. These are Kauai Sunrise papayas (Sunrise Packing Co.).

Mango and Papaya Salad with Crabmeat, Crispy Shiu Mai, and Orange-Chile Sauce

⇨ SERVES 4 ⇦

Driving around the Hawaiian islands, you'll see plenty of mango and papaya trees growing along the roadside and in backyards. They are also grown extensively on commercial plantations. This salad offers an intriguing contrast of temperatures as well as textures.

Shiu Mai Filling:

6 ounces shrimp, peeled and deveined

1 small egg

2 ounces lump crabmeat

¼ Maui onion, finely diced

½ teaspoon minced garlic

1 teaspoon finely minced ginger

½ teaspoon minced shallot

½ cup coarsely chopped shiitake mushrooms

4 water chestnuts, finely diced

1 scallion, minced

1 tablespoon minced fresh cilantro

¾ teaspoon kosher salt

¼ teaspoon dried red chile flakes

1 teaspoon oyster sauce

2 teaspoons teriyaki sauce

…

1 teaspoon cornstarch

2 tablespoons water

8 wonton wrappers

1 cup canola oil

3 cups mizuna lettuce

1 tablespoon olive oil

Salt and freshly ground white pepper to taste

1 papaya, peeled, seeded, and julienned

1 mango, peeled, pitted, and julienned

½ cup seeded, julienned cucumber

6 ounces lump crabmeat

½ to ¾ cup Orange-Chile Sauce (page 217)

To prepare the shiu mai filling, place the shrimp and egg in a food processor and blend to a thick paste. Transfer to a mixing bowl, add the remaining filling ingredients, and mix thoroughly. In a separate small bowl, mix together the cornstarch and water.

To make the shiu mai, lay out the wonton wrappers on a work surface. Place a heaping teaspoon of filling in the center of each. Moisten the edges of the wrappers with the cornstarch mixture, and bring 2 opposite corners together. Pinch the top ½ inch together to close. Bring the other 2 edges together to the center and pinch to close; the shiu mai should look like an "X." Gently pinch and twist the top to secure, and push downward to form a swirl. Sprinkle with a little cornstarch to prevent the shiu mai from sticking.

Bring a saucepan of water to a rapid boil. Boil the shiu mai for about 1½ minutes, stirring so they do not stick to the pan; they will rise to the surface when they are done. Remove and drain. Heat the canola oil in a saucepan or deep-fryer, and fry the shiu mai over medium-high heat for about 1 minute, or until crispy.

In a mixing bowl, toss the mizuna lettuce with the olive oil, and season with salt and pepper.

Arrange the mizuna in one corner of the serving plates, with the leafy parts at the edges of the plate. At the stem end, pile the papaya, mango, and cucumber in layers, and place the crabmeat on top. Place 2 shiu mai at the side of each salad. Ladle 2 or 3 tablespoons of Orange-Chile Sauce on each plate. For an optional garnish, use a Kona (or other variety) crab claw.

Roy's Feasts from Hawaii

Teriyaki Duck Salad with Candied Pecans and Papaya in a Raspberry Vinaigrette

I have a soft spot for this old friend and trusty standby—it was one of the first salads I created for the menu at 385 North, my former restaurant in Los Angeles.

Teriyaki Marinade:

1 cup soy sauce

1 tablespoon chopped garlic

1 tablespoon grated ginger

1 cup sugar

1 teaspoon toasted white sesame seeds (page 220)

...

1 duck, about 4 to 4½ pounds

¾ cup red leaf lettuce

¾ cup arugula

¾ cup baby spinach leaves, torn

¾ cup radicchio, torn

¾ escarole, torn

2 tablespoons olive oil

3 ounces fresh shiitake mushrooms

Raspberry Vinaigrette:

¼ cup olive oil

½ teaspoon minced shallot

½ teaspoon minced garlic

½ teaspoon grated ginger

¼ cup raspberry vinegar

10 leaves fresh opal basil or regular basil

Salt and freshly ground pepper to taste

Garnish:

2 or 3 tablespoons diced papaya or mango

24 raspberries

4 sprigs fresh mint

¼ cup Candied Pecans, chopped (page 219)

$\mathcal{C}$ombine the marinade ingredients in a mixing bowl. Cut the duck breast away from the carcass, and remove the skin. Cut off the legs, keeping the thigh and drumstick in one piece, and remove the skin. Slit the meat from one end of the leg to the other so that you can remove the bone, leaving the meat in one piece. Marinate for 30 minutes.

Meanwhile, prepare the hibachi or grill. Remove the duck from the marinade and pat dry. Grill to the desired doneness. Cut each breast and leg in half, giving 4 portions of each (or julienne the duck meat if you prefer). Keep warm.

Mix the greens in a large salad bowl. Heat 2 tablespoons of olive oil in a sauté pan or skillet, and lightly brown the mushrooms for about 1 minute over medium heat. Add them to the greens. To prepare the vinaigrette, heat the remaining ¼ cup of olive oil in the pan and sauté the shallot, garlic, and ginger over high heat for 5 seconds. Deglaze with the vinegar; add the basil, salt, and pepper. Add to the greens while the vinaigrette is still warm, and toss together.

Place the warm salad on serving plates and lay the duck on top. Garnish by sprinkling the papaya or mango and raspberries around the salad. Place a mint sprig on the duck and sprinkle the Candied Pecans over the top.

Pastas and Imu Pizzas

Pizza holds a very special place in my heart—a cheese and pepperoni pizza was the very first thing I cooked, in home economics class at high school when I was in the ninth grade. The pizzas and pastas in this chapter, as well as those we serve at the restaurants, reflect my partiality for Italian cuisine. After all, the myriad pastas of Italy are not that far removed from the variety of noodles I grew up with in Japan; in fact, some of them are identical. We always have several pizza and pasta items on our menu, in a section all their own.

Imu refers to the pit oven used by the ancient Hawaiians for slow-roasting or steaming underground; it was their common cooking method. This practice is still used today in authentic luaus. The traditional imu is prepared by digging a hole, adding plenty of wood, and then placing porous stones on top. The wood is lit and when the stones become red-hot, they are spread out and covered first with a layer of chopped banana wood and then with some greenery such as ti leaves or grass. The food is typically wrapped in banana or ti leaves and then cloth or sacking. Finally, the imu is covered with some of the excavated earth to form an oven, and the food is left to cook slowly for several hours.

Traditionally, food such as chicken, wild fowl, pig, and dog (a status symbol among ancient Hawaiians) was cooked in the imu. Nowadays, whole pigs are the usual fare at authentic luaus. At Roy's we use a wood-burning oven in the corner of our kitchen to prepare our imu pizzas—no holes in the ground for us! All of the following pizza recipes can be cooked in a regular oven at home.

These pizza recipes make four small pizzas. They are perfect as appetizers for one or two people. Of course, you can make two larger main-course pizzas, or bake the whole recipe in a single large sheet pan and cut it into slices or small squares for a cocktail party.

Roy's House Pasta with Chicken and Shrimp in Sun-Dried Tomato Sauce

))) SERVES 4 (((

I first created this dish in Los Angeles for my good friend Derek Foy, who supplied me with a wonderful pasta machine that became much used. This is a recipe that has remained on my menus by popular request.

1 cup olive oil

2 tablespoons minced garlic

2 tablespoons minced shallots

2 teaspoons dried red chile flakes

1 pound boneless chicken breast, skin removed and julienned

8 ounces medium shrimp (about 15), peeled and deveined

20 broccoli florets

1 large red bell pepper, seeded and julienned

8 ounces shiitake mushrooms, julienned

12 ounces fresh spinach leaves

4 oil-packed sun-dried tomatoes, drained and julienned

1 teaspoon salt

1 teaspoon freshly ground pepper

1 pound fresh ramen noodles or other Asian noodles, cooked al dente

2 tablespoons minced fresh mixed herbs (such as basil, tarragon, and thyme)

Sun-Dried Tomato Sauce (page 218)

4 sprigs fresh basil, for garnish

Heat the olive oil in a large sauté pan or skillet, and sauté the garlic, shallots, and red chile flakes over medium-high heat for about 30 seconds. Add the chicken and sauté until the chicken starts to turn color, about 30 seconds. Add the shrimp, broccoli, red bell pepper, mushrooms, spinach, and sun-dried tomatoes, and season with salt and pepper. Toss well to mix, and sauté briefly until the chicken and shrimp are cooked through. Add the warm cooked noodles, fresh mixed herbs, and Sun-Dried Tomato Sauce, and mix thoroughly. Serve garnished with the basil.

Waikiki sunset, Oahu. Time to fire up the grill and get cooking.

Ravioli of Lamb, Goat Cheese, and Pesto with Napoletana Sauce

※ S E R V E S 4 ※

One theory has it that the concept of Chinese dumplings was carried back to Italy from China by thirteenth-century explorer Marco Polo and became the forerunner of ravioli—a true Euro-Asian hybrid. In any event, this recipe uses potsticker wrappers to make the Italian-style ravioli.

Filling:

2 tablespoons canola oil

1 pound lamb loin, finely diced

1 tablespoon olive oil

½ teaspoon minced garlic

6 ounces fresh spinach leaves

12 ounces Puna goat cheese, or Montrachet-type goat cheese

3 tablespoons julienned fresh basil

⅓ cup Pesto plus ¼ cup for garnish (page 214)

Salt and freshly ground pepper to taste

…

2 tablespoons cornstarch

¼ cup water

32 wonton wrappers

4 cups Napoletana Sauce (page 218)

1 to 2 cups cooked Tuscan-Style White Beans (page 156)

2 cups washed and torn mixed greens, such as mizuna, radicchio, romaine, and red-leaf lettuce (about 2 ½ ounces)

For the ravioli filling, heat the canola oil in a heavy skillet or saucepan, and sear the lamb for about 1 minute over high heat, stirring occasionally, until browned and medium-rare.

Heat the olive oil in a large sauté pan and sauté the garlic and spinach over high heat for 15 seconds, until the spinach is wilted. Transfer to a large mixing bowl, along with the goat cheese, lamb, basil, ⅓ cup Pesto, salt, and pepper, and mix well. Mix the water and cornstarch together in a small mixing bowl.

To make the ravioli, lay out the wonton wrappers on a work surface and place about 1½ tablespoons of the filling mixture in the middle of each. Moisten the edges of the wrappers with the cornstarch mixture, fold in half, and press to seal the edges together.

Reheat both the Napoletana Sauce and the beans. Bring a saucepan of water to a boil, and cook the wonton ravioli for about 2 minutes, or until completely heated through.

Place ¼ to ½ cup of the beans on each serving plate and arrange the raviolis in a pinwheel shape on top of the beans. Ladle the heated Napoletana Sauce over the raviolis and place the greens at the center of the pinwheel. Drizzle 1 tablespoon of the Pesto per serving around the raviolis as garnish.

Pictured on opposite page

Thai-Style Pasta Aglio e Olio

⋙ SERVES 4 ⋘

It only takes a few minutes to toss this "garlic and oil" pasta dish together.

¼ cup peanut oil

¼ cup sesame oil

3 cloves garlic, finely minced

1 small fresh Hawaiian red chile, or red jalapeño, with seeds, minced

2 tablespoons chopped toasted peanuts (page 220)

1 pound fresh Chinese egg noodles, somen, or spaghetti, cooked al dente

1 tablespoon chopped fresh opal basil

20 fresh mint leaves, julienned

1 tablespoon minced fresh cilantro leaves

Zest and juice of 1 lime

1 tablespoon fish sauce

4 sprigs fresh cilantro, for garnish

Heat the peanut and sesame oils together in a sauté pan or skillet, and sauté the garlic, chile, and peanuts over medium heat for about 30 seconds, until the garlic just turns golden. Remove from the heat and set aside.

Place the warm noodles in a bowl and toss with the oil and garlic mixture. Add the basil, mint, minced cilantro, lime zest and juice, and fish sauce and toss again. Serve on warm plates, garnished with the sprigs of cilantro.

KAHUKU, LOCATED ON THE FERTILE northern tip of Oahu, is renowned statewide for its thriving small-scale aquaculture enterprises. Kahuku used to be a sugar mill town until the early 1970s, but the former swampland in the area has proved perfect for raising saltwater shrimp, freshwater prawns, tilapia, carp, and catfish, to name just a few. State-wide, there are more than eighty aquaculture operations raising more than thirty different types of fish and seafood.

Aquaculture is nothing new in Hawaii. The ancient Hawaiians developed it into a fine art with their *loko i'a*, or fishponds. These were used mainly to rear and fatten fish for the chiefs and *kahuna* (religious leaders). It is estimated that at the time of Captain Cook's arrival in the late 1700s, there were 350 fishponds covering 6,000 acres spread across the Hawaiian islands. The fishponds adjoined the ocean or streams, and were enclosed by man-made walls with sluice gates through which small fish and nutrients could flow in and out. On Oahu, an 88-acre fishpond occupied part of Kaneohe Bay; another can still be seen a few miles along the coast at Heeia. The 123-acre fishpond at Huili has been working continuously since the beginning of the century.

Grilled Shrimp and Clam Linguine

» SERVES 4 «

I virtually lived on clam linguine with white sauce when I discovered Italian restaurants while in cooking school. It's still a favorite of mine, but since a lot of people prefer shrimp, this is my compromise.

3 tablespoons olive oil

2 cups water

24 fresh Manila clams

2 tablespoons canola oil

16 to 20 extra-large shrimp (about 1 pound), peeled and deveined, with tails left on

3 cups Basic Tomato Sauce (page 215)

1 pound fine linguine, cooked al dente

Salt and freshly ground white pepper to taste

2 tablespoons Pesto (page 214)

4 fresh sprigs basil, for garnish

Heat the olive oil and water in a heavy skillet. When it comes to a boil, add the clams, cover, and steam for about 1 minute over high heat, or until the clams just open. Extract the clam meat from the shells and keep warm.

Heat the canola oil in a heavy sauté pan and sear the shrimp on both sides for 1 minute over medium-high heat. Remove and keep warm.

Heat the Basic Tomato Sauce in a saucepan. Toss the warm pasta with the sauce, and season to taste with salt and pepper. Transfer to serving plates and top with the clams and shrimp. Drizzle with the Pesto and garnish with the sprigs of basil.

Prawn-farm harvesting at the Hawaiian Prawn Co., Kahuku, Oahu.

Linguine alla Carbonara with Chicken and Asparagus

⫸ SERVES 4 ⫷

I created this menu item by popular request for our regular customers who wanted a pasta with a rich, tasty cream sauce. The classic Italian carbonara sauce contains eggs, heavy cream, cheese, and pancetta. My version has everything but the eggs, but it's still very rich, because the sauce is so highly reduced.

Chicken Cream Sauce:

½ tablespoon canola oil

1 tablespoon minced garlic

¼ cup finely diced onion

4 ounces mushrooms, diced

2 quarts Chicken Stock (page 213)

2 tablespoons minced fresh basil

2 tablespoons minced fresh thyme

1 quart heavy cream

Salt and freshly ground white pepper to taste

…

4 boneless half chicken breasts, skin removed

Salt and freshly ground white pepper to taste

1 to 2 tablespoons canola oil

1½ tablespoons olive oil

1½ tablespoons minced garlic

1½ tablespoons minced shallots

1½ tablespoons diced pancetta

3 tablespoons seeded and julienned green bell pepper

3 tablespoons seeded and julienned red bell pepper

3 tablespoons seeded and julienned yellow bell pepper

4 ounces mushrooms, quartered

¼ cup oil-packed sun-dried tomatoes, drained and julienned, plus 4 whole ones for garnish

4 ounces asparagus, angle-cut

1 tablespoon mixed fresh herbs (such as basil, thyme, and rosemary)

1 pound linguine, cooked al dente

¼ cup grated parmesan cheese

4 sprigs fresh rosemary, for garnish

To prepare the sauce, heat the canola oil in a large saucepan and sauté the garlic, onion, and mushrooms over medium-high heat for about 2 minutes. Add the Chicken Stock and herbs and reduce by three-quarters, about 30 minutes. Meanwhile, prepare the grill. Add the cream to the saucepan and reduce again by one-half. Strain through a fine sieve and season the sauce with salt and pepper. Transfer to a blender or food processor and purée. Keep warm.

Season the chicken breasts with salt and pepper and brush with the canola oil. Grill the chicken, cut into thin slices, and keep warm.

Heat the olive oil in a sauté pan or skillet, and sauté the garlic, shallots, pancetta, bell peppers, mushrooms, julienned sun-dried tomatoes, and asparagus over medium-high heat for about 1 minute, or until tender and the pancetta is just browned.

Add the Chicken Cream Sauce and the mixed herbs, and cook until thickened, about 1 minute. Add the warm pasta and parmesan cheese, toss together, and adjust the seasonings.

Transfer the pasta to serving plates and pour the sauce from the pan around each bed of pasta. Place the sliced chicken breasts and the vegetables attractively on top of the pasta, and garnish each serving with a sun-dried tomato pierced with an upright rosemary sprig.

Pictured on opposite page (upper left)

Asian Pasta Primavera

This vegetarian pasta is another good example of my Euro-Asian style of cooking. Not only are the vegetables drawn from both sides of the world, but you can use linguine just as well as the Japanese ramen noodles.

2 tablespoons olive oil

2 tablespoons sesame or peanut oil

2 teaspoons minced ginger

2 teaspoons chopped garlic

2 teaspoons minced lemon grass

½ teaspoon minced kaffir lime leaves

2 cups julienned shiitake mushrooms

1 cup julienned carrots

1 cup bean sprouts

½ cup yellow bell pepper, seeded and finely julienned

½ cup red bell pepper, seeded and finely julienned

20 asparagus tips

Salt and freshly ground pepper to taste

1 pound fresh ramen noodles or linguine, cooked al dente

¼ cup light soy sauce (preferably Yamasa brand)

Juice of 1 lemon

Garnish:

4 ounces fresh goat cheese, crumbled

2 tablespoons Japanese plum paste

4 sprigs fresh basil

1 teaspoon black sesame seeds

1 sheet nori, julienned (optional)

*H*eat the olive and sesame oils together in a large heavy sauté pan, and sauté the ginger, garlic, lemon grass, and lime leaves for 30 seconds over high heat, or until lightly browned. Add the mushrooms, carrots, bean sprouts, bell peppers, and asparagus, and sauté for about 2 minutes longer. Season with salt and pepper, and remove from the heat.

Add the warm noodles or pasta to the vegetables in the pan. Toss well and season with soy sauce and lemon juice.

Serve on warm plates, and garnish with the goat cheese sprinkled around the noodles, a dollop of the plum paste on top, and a sprig of basil. Sprinkle with the sesame seeds and nori, if desired.

Pictured on page 85 (lower right)

Basic Pizza Dough

❊ ENOUGH FOR FOUR 7-INCH PIZZAS ❊

¼ teaspoon active dry yeast
  (½ package)
¾ cup lukewarm water (105 to 110
  degrees)

1 tablespoon honey
2 to 2½ cups flour (preferably bread
  flour, but all-purpose flour will do)

Pinch of salt
2 tablespoons olive oil

*S*prinkle the yeast over the water in a bowl, add the honey, whisk, and let sit for 5 minutes. Lightly oil the bowl of an electric mixer and fit the mixer with the dough hook. Put 2 cups of the flour and the salt in the bowl, and turn the mixer on at a very low speed. With the mixer running, slowly pour in the water and yeast mixture. Continue beating until the dough is well mixed. Increase the mixer speed slightly and beat in the olive oil. Beat at medium-high speed for about 4 to 5 minutes, until the dough looks smooth and satiny and gathers into a ball. Add more flour if necessary. (Note: the dough can be mixed by hand, but it is much easier to use a mixer.)

Transfer the dough to a lightly oiled bowl, cover with a damp towel or plastic wrap, and let rise in a warm place for about 45 minutes, or until doubled in bulk. Place on a lightly floured work surface, and divide into 4 portions. Knead each portion for 1 or 2 minutes and form into balls. Place on a baking sheet, and cover again with a damp towel or plastic wrap. Allow the dough to rise for another 15 minutes.

Roll each ball of dough out into a 6- to 7-inch circle, about ⅛ inch thick, sprinkling the dough, the work surface, and the rolling pin with extra flour to keep them from becoming sticky. Using your fingers, pinch the dough to create a raised edge all the way around the pizza. Now you're ready to add the toppings.

PELE IS THE LEGENDARY red-headed volcano goddess who inhabits the active Kilauea volcano on the Big Island. Myth relates how Pele traveled from a distant homeland to the Hawaiian islands, where she sought a home deep enough inside the earth to accommodate and enable her family to manifest themselves in volcanic eruptions—as lava, fire, smoke, and ash. Numerous Hawaiian legends feature the unpredictable Pele; many describe her curse, a destructive force that afflicts any who dare offend her. A modern version of Pele's curse holds that removing lava rock from Volcanoes National Park on the Big Island will bring bad luck, a legend vehemently believed by many—it seems like I know a few of these devotees!

R.J.'s Keiki-Style Pizza with Straight Cheese

❧ MAKES FOUR 7-INCH PIZZAS ❧

This is our basic pizza, and it's named after a very special keiki, my son, Roy Jr. At our restaurants, the only topping that goes on this pizza is mozzarella cheese, which almost all children like. There's no tomato sauce, which many kids dislike (I hated it when I was growing up!). For less fussy children (and most adults), I've added the tomato sauce option below, and, of course, you can add any other toppings you like.

1 recipe Basic Pizza Dough (page 87)   Basic Tomato Sauce (page 215), optional   1 cup shredded mozzarella cheese

Preheat the oven to 425 degrees. Roll the dough out into four 7-inch circles. If desired, spread about ½ cup of the Basic Tomato Sauce over each round of dough, leaving a ½-inch border all around. Sprinkle ¼ cup of the cheese on top. Place on a pizza brick or pizza pan and bake in the oven for about 15 minutes, or until the crusts are light golden brown.

PICTURES CARVED IN ROCK, or petroglyphs, are common forms of expression in many ancient cultures, but one of the densest concentrations of petroglyphs anywhere in the world is on the Big Island of Hawaii (they can also be found on all the other major Hawaiian islands). Many Hawaiian petroglyphs are hundreds of years old. They are found mostly on lava rock in open or barren country on the dry sides of the islands, where the largest communities of ancient Hawaiians were established. The petroglyphs are basic in design, yet enigmatic, and contain several levels of meaning. To interpret them fully, one must have a deep understanding of ancient Hawaiian society and culture.

The most common images are representations of human figures and family groups, canoes, paddles and sails, supernatural or protective spirits, and shapes such as circles or dots. None of the designs are without meaning; there are several theories about what the petroglyphs represent. Some are thought to be records of ocean trips or boundary markers. Others are believed to depict rituals and legends, or are symbols that promote long life and well-being.

Grilled Shrimp and Eggplant Pizza with Pesto, Feta, and Goat Cheese

This pizza is easy to make and light to eat. The mixture of cheeses gives the pizza a more satisfying, complex flavor than just a single type—a principle that applies to all kinds of pizza. If grilling is inconvenient, you can pan-sear or broil the shrimp and eggplant instead.

1 pound extra-large shrimp (about 16 to 20), peeled and deveined

3 tablespoons olive oil

32 slices Japanese eggplant, cut 1 x 2 x ⅛ inch thick

Salt and freshly ground pepper to taste

1 recipe Basic Pizza Dough (page 87)

½ cup grated fontina cheese

½ cup grated mozzarella cheese

1 cup Napoletana Sauce (page 218)

4 heaping tablespoons Puna goat cheese

2 heaping tablespoons crumbled feta cheese

4 teaspoons Pesto (page 214)

Garnish:

4 teaspoons minced fresh parsley

20 fresh chives

Prepare the grill and preheat the oven to 425 degrees. Lightly brush the shrimp with about 1 tablespoon of the olive oil and grill for about 1 minute on each side, or broil or pan-sear for 1 minute per side over medium-high heat. Slice the shrimp lengthwise and reserve. Season the eggplant slices with salt and pepper, and lightly brush with the remaining olive oil. Grill, broil, or pan-sear until browned on both sides.

Roll the dough out into four 7-inch circles. Mix the fontina and mozzarella cheeses together, and sprinkle ¼ cup of the mixture over each circle of dough, leaving a ½-inch border all around. Spoon the Napoletana Sauce over the cheese. Place the pizzas on a pizza brick or pizza pan and bake for about 15 minutes, or until the crusts are light golden brown.

Lay 8 strips of the eggplant across each pizza. Then lay 4 shrimp halves on top of the eggplant. Sprinkle a little goat cheese and feta around the shrimp on each pizza. Top with a teaspoon of the pesto and garnish with the parsley. Arrange the chives vertically between shrimp slices.

Pictured on page 91 (center, left)

Roy's restaurant logo designed in coral on black lava rock—a popular local art form, created here on the Kona Coast, Big Island.

Puna Goat Cheese and Shiitake Mushroom Pizza with Wilted Baby Greens

We find any excuse to use Karin and Steve Sayres' Puna goat cheese from their Big Island farm, but a Montrachet-style goat cheese can be substituted. Shiitakes are the mushroom of choice for this recipe, but any variety of wild mushroom would make a suitable alternative.

3 tablespoons canola or peanut oil
28 fresh shiitake mushrooms, caps only
1 recipe Basic Pizza Dough (page 87)
1 cup Basic Tomato Sauce (page 215)

Vinaigrette:
2½ teaspoons balsamic vinegar
1 tablespoon olive oil

1 tablespoon finely minced fresh basil
¼ teaspoon minced shallot
¼ teaspoon minced garlic
…
4 cups washed and torn mizuna or other baby lettuce (about 4 ounces)

10 ounces Puna goat cheese or Montrachet-type goat cheese, cut into 20 slices
10 yellow pear tomatoes, cut in half

Garnish:
2 teaspoons diced red bell pepper
2 teaspoons diced yellow bell pepper

Preheat the oven to 425 degrees. Heat the oil in a sauté pan and sauté the mushrooms over medium heat for about 1 minute. Set aside.

Roll the dough out into four 7-inch circles. Spread ¼ cup of the Basic Tomato Sauce over each round of dough, leaving a ½-inch border all around. Place on a pizza brick or pizza pan and bake in the oven for about 15 minutes, or until the crusts are light golden brown.

Whisk together the vinaigrette ingredients and toss with the mizuna in a mixing bowl. Arrange 7 sautéed mushroom caps in a circle in the center of each pizza. Place a mound of mizuna over the shiitakes and arrange 5 slices of goat cheese around the mizuna on each pizza. Place a pear tomato half, cut side down, between each slice of cheese. Combine the diced bell peppers and sprinkle over the mizuna to garnish.

Pictured on page 91 (upper right)

Mongolian Chicken Pizza

≫ MAKES FOUR 7-INCH PIZZAS ≪

When I lived in Tokyo, I loved to go to the Mongolian restaurants and savor their spicy cuisine. The sauce in this recipe can also be used as a barbecue sauce or glaze, or as a marinade or dip.

Mongolian Pizza Sauce:

1 cup hoisin sauce

2 tablespoons chile paste with garlic
  (preferably Lan Chi brand)

1 tablespoon teriyaki sauce

1 teaspoon grated ginger

1 teaspoon minced garlic

. . .

1 pound boneless chicken breast,
  with skin on

1 recipe Basic Pizza Dough (page 87)

¼ cup grated mozzarella cheese

2 tablespoons grated fontina cheese

2 tablespoons grated parmesan cheese

2 tablespoons canola oil

4 wonton wrappers, julienned

3 cups washed and torn mizuna
  lettuce (about 3 to 4 ounces)

Vegetable Mix:

¼ red bell pepper, seeded and
  julienned

¼ yellow bell pepper, seeded and
  julienned

1 tablespoon red pickled ginger

½ ounce Japanese spice sprouts

Garnish:

½ teaspoon toasted white sesame
  seeds (page 220)

½ teaspoon black sesame seeds

Prepare the grill. Put all the Mongolian Pizza Sauce ingredients in a mixing bowl, and mix well. Add the chicken and marinate for 15 minutes. Remove the chicken from the marinade and reserve the marinade. Grill the chicken (skin side down first), until cooked through, about 2 to 3 minutes per side. Cut the chicken into 16 slices.

Preheat the oven to 425 degrees. Roll the dough out into four 7-inch circles. Spread each with about 1 tablespoon or more of the reserved Mongolian Pizza Sauce, leaving a ½-inch border all around. Combine the cheeses and sprinkle them over the sauce. Place on a pizza brick or pizza pan and bake in the oven for about 15 minutes, or until the crusts are light golden brown.

Meanwhile, heat the canola oil in a skillet and fry the wonton strips until crispy. Remove, drain on paper towels, and set aside.

When the pizzas are done, place the mizuna on top of the pizzas, and lay 4 slices of chicken per pizza on top of the mizuna. In a bowl, toss the vegetable mix ingredients and wonton together. Place on top of the chicken, and garnish with the sesame seeds.

Pictured on page 91 (lower right)

Duck and Mushroom Pizza with Honey-Hoisin-Cilantro Sauce

You can prepare the duck yourself, using the Chinatown Duck recipe (page 144), or if you're lucky enough to live in a city with a Chinatown, you can purchase a roast duck there.

1 tablespoon olive oil
1 teaspoon minced garlic
28 shiitake mushrooms, caps only
2 tablespoons honey
¼ cup hoisin sauce
1 tablespoon chopped fresh cilantro
1 recipe Basic Pizza Dough (page 87)
1 cup grated mozzarella cheese

1 cup grated fontina cheese
1 cup diced roast duck (page 23)

Garnish:

1½ tablespoons julienned carrots
1½ tablespoons Japanese spice sprouts
1½ tablespoons very finely julienned
   Maui onion
1½ tablespoons red pickled ginger

1½ tablespoons Pink Pickled Ginger
   (page 219)
3 tablespoons unseasoned rice vinegar
1 teaspoon light soy sauce
   (preferably Yamasa brand)
½ teaspoon *furikake*
1 teaspoon black sesame seeds

In a sauté pan or skillet, heat the olive oil and sauté the garlic and mushrooms over high heat for 1 minute. Remove from the heat and set aside.

Put the honey, hoisin sauce, and cilantro in a small heavy saucepan and heat for 15 seconds, stirring to combine. Remove from the heat and cool to room temperature.

Preheat the oven to 425 degrees. Roll the dough out into four 7-inch circles. Spread some of the honey-hoisin mixture onto each, leaving a ½-inch border all around. Sprinkle the cheeses over, then the duck and sautéed shiitake mushrooms. Place on a pizza brick or pizza pan and bake in the oven for about 15 minutes, or until the crusts are light golden brown.

Meanwhile, toss all the garnish ingredients together in a mixing bowl. Remove the pizzas from the oven, top with the garnish and serve.

Mozzarella Pizza with Mizuna Lettuce and Pan-Roasted Tomatoes

≫ MAKES FOUR 7-INCH PIZZAS ≪

Greens may be an unusual pizza topping, but the mustardy flavor of the refreshing mizuna lettuce is what makes this straightforward pizza. You can substitute mustard greens.

1 recipe Basic Pizza Dough (page 87)

½ cup Napoletana Sauce (page 218)

4 Roma tomatoes, each cut into 5 slices lengthwise

Salt and freshly ground pepper

2 tablespoons olive oil

10 ounces mozzarella cheese, cut into 20 slices

1 cup washed and torn mizuna lettuce

Preheat the oven to 425 degrees. Roll the dough out into four 7-inch circles. Spread the Napoletana Sauce over each, leaving a ½-inch border all around. Place on a pizza brick or pizza pan and bake in the oven for about 15 minutes, or until the crusts are light golden brown.

Meanwhile, season the tomato slices with salt and pepper, and heat the olive oil in a heavy skillet or sauté pan. Pan-roast the tomatoes over medium-high heat until they are partly blackened on each side.

Remove the pizzas and arrange alternate slices of mozzarella and tomato in a circle on the pizzas (5 slices of each per pizza). Place ¼ cup of the mizuna upright in the center of each pizza.

Pictured on opposite page

A spectacular reminder that the Big Island of Hawaii is the most active volcanic region on the planet.

Fish and Shellfish

The ocean harvest—the rich bounty of fish and seafood—is one of the main elements that distinguishes Hawaiian cuisine from other regional cuisines. This precious resource is now appearing more than ever before on menus in restaurants and hotel dining rooms across the islands, but this was not always so. Until quite recently, with the development of Hawaiian Regional Cuisine by a group of a dozen or so young island chefs, most of the seafood consumed locally was imported from the West Coast and even further afield. A surprising amount was bought frozen. Today, this trend is changing, thank goodness, even though more seafood is still imported than is caught locally.

In ancient Hawaiian society, fishing and agriculture were the main sources of food. Fish supplied most of the protein in the Hawaiians' diet, although it was eaten mainly as a side dish rather than as a main course. There are no major rivers or natural freshwater lakes in Hawaii, but man-made saltwater and freshwater fishponds have always been cultivated and a few are still farmed. The open ocean and reefs surrounding the Hawaiian islands also have provided a rich variety of seafood.

Many ancient Hawaiian fishing legends celebrate the most successful of the fishermen and their exploits, and have been handed down through the generations. These tales echo traditional cultural values, including the importance of conserving and sharing the supply of fish and seafood.

Seared Opakapaka and Scallops with Lobster-Passion Fruit-Ginger Sauce

SERVES 4

I created this dish for an article and photo shoot that appeared in Art Culinaire, *a beautifully photographed recipe book published every other month or so. It tastes as good as it looks, so it has stayed on the menu. You can buy lobster heads at fish markets, or buy the whole lobster and use the rest for another recipe. Serve with Jasmine Rice (page 152) or Roy's Mashed Potatoes (page 153), if desired.*

8 opakapaka fillets, about 3½ ounces each

6 scallops, quartered

6 tablespoons peanut oil

Salt and freshly ground white pepper to taste

Lobster-Passion Fruit-Ginger Sauce:

1 tablespoon canola oil

2 Maine lobster heads

1 tablespoon chopped onion

1½ teaspoons chopped carrot

1½ teaspoons chopped celery

2 tablespoons minced fresh parsley

2 cloves garlic, minced

½ teaspoon chopped fresh tarragon

1 tomato, seeded and chopped

¼ cup brandy

1 cup white wine

2 cups water

1 tablespoon grated ginger

1½ tablespoons strained fresh passion fruit juice

1 tablespoon Lobster Paste (page 215)

...

1 cup *Beurre Blanc* (page 216)

Coat the opakapaka and scallops with the peanut oil. Season with salt and pepper, and refrigerate while preparing the sauce.

To prepare the sauce, heat the canola oil in a large saucepan and sauté the lobster heads, onion, carrot, and celery over medium heat for about 5 minutes . When the vegetables are semi-soft, add the parsley, garlic, tarragon, and tomato. Deglaze the pan with the brandy and then add the white wine. Reduce the liquid by two-thirds over medium heat, about 4 or 5 minutes. Add the water, lower the heat, and simmer for about 40 minutes. Transfer to a blender or food processor and blend until liquified. Force through a fine sieve into a clean saucepan, pushing down on the ingredients to extract the juices.

Squeeze the grated ginger in a garlic press, and add the ginger juice to the saucepan (there should be about 1 teaspoon). Discard the ginger pulp. Stir in the passion fruit juice and Lobster Paste, and further reduce the liquid over low heat until it becomes syrupy, about 10 minutes. Keep warm.

Gently warm the *Beurre Blanc* in a double boiler and keep warm.

Heat a dry cast-iron skillet until it is hot. Sear the opakapaka over medium-high heat for about 1 to 1½ minutes per side for medium doneness. Remove the fish and sear the scallops for 30 seconds, shaking the pan to cook them evenly.

Ladle the Lobster-Passion Fruit-Ginger Sauce on half of each serving plate, and ladle the *Beurre Blanc* over the other half. Place 2 opakapaka fillets in the middle, and place the scallops all around.

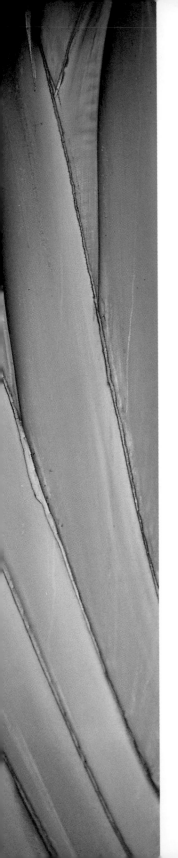

Garlic and Herb-Crusted Mahimahi with Cucumber-Tomato-Ginger Salsa

Mahimahi is the Hawaiian word for the dolphin fish or dorado. To avoid confusion with the unrelated dolphin, the local name is now being used increasingly nationwide. The firm, moist, and tasty flesh of the mahimahi is deliciously contrasted by the pungently flavored crust. The softly textured chilled salsa provides a cooling counterpoint. I like to serve this dish with the Jasmine Rice (page 152), or Goat Cheese Hash (page 155).

Cucumber-Tomato-Ginger Salsa
(recipe follows)

Garlic-Herb Crust:
¼ cup coarsely chopped garlic
1 teaspoon chopped fresh parsley
1 tablespoon chopped fresh basil

1 teaspoon chopped fresh tarragon
4 anchovy fillets
4 shallots, roughly chopped
(about ½ cup)
1 teaspoon virgin olive oil

. . .

4 mahimahi fillets, about 7 ounces
each
1 teaspoon canola oil

Prepare the salsa and set aside.

Place all the Garlic-Herb Crust ingredients in a food processor or blender, and purée. Coat one side of each mahimahi fillet with this crust and let sit for 10 to 15 minutes. Heat the canola oil in a nonstick sauté pan and sear the crusted mahimahi over high heat for 45 seconds to 1 minute per side for medium doneness.

Place the fish, crust side up, on 4 serving plates and spoon the salsa over and around each serving, letting the juices from the salsa run onto the plates.

Pictured on opposite page

Cucumber-Tomato-Ginger Salsa

1 cup seeded and diced Japanese
cucumber
½ cup seeded and diced red tomato

3 yellow pear tomatoes, cut in half
2 tablespoons finely minced ginger
¼ cup finely minced onion

2 tablespoons soy sauce
2 tablespoons *rayu* (spicy sesame oil)
Salt and freshly ground pepper to taste

Thoroughly combine the ingredients in a mixing bowl and chill.

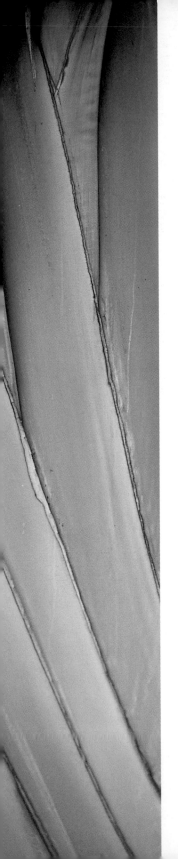

Seared Lemon Grass-Crusted Salmon with Watercress-Ginger Sauce

≫ SERVES 4 ≪

The vibrant, deep green color of the peppery watercress makes a visually arresting sauce. Here, I've deliberately paired a French-style sauce with the Asian flavors of the salmon crust. This recipe can be made equally well with swordfish or another firm-fleshed fish. This recipe goes very well with either Jasmine Rice (page 152) or Japanese White Rice (page 151).

Lemon Grass Crust:
2 tablespoons finely minced lemon grass
1 tablespoon minced garlic
1 tablespoon minced shallot
1 tablespoon minced ginger
1 tablespoon *shichimi*
...

4 salmon steaks, about 7 ounces each
Watercress-Ginger Sauce:
3 tablespoons chopped ginger
1 bunch watercress, leaves only
1 cup *Beurre Blanc* (page 216)
...

¼ cup canola oil
Garnish:
4 sprigs watercress
4 teaspoons red pickled ginger

Combine all the crust ingredients in a mixing bowl. About 5 minutes before you are ready to cook the salmon, thoroughly coat one side of each steak with the crust.

To prepare the sauce, squeeze the ginger in a garlic press and place the extracted juice in a mixing bowl (there should be about 1 tablespoon). Discard the ginger pulp. Bring a saucepan of water to a boil, remove from the heat, and blanch the watercress for about 15 seconds. Drain thoroughly. Mince the watercress leaves and mix them with the ginger juice. Stir the watercress into the *Beurre Blanc*, and keep warm.

Heat a large cast-iron skillet over medium-high heat. Coat the crusted side of the salmon with the canola oil and sear, crusted side first, for about 1½ minutes. Turn over and sear the other side for about 1 minute longer.

To serve, place a salmon steak, crusted side up, in the center of each serving plate and ladle the Watercress-Ginger Sauce around the salmon. Garnish with the watercress sprigs and pickled ginger.

With Neal Aoki and staff at Tropic Fish, Honolulu.

The Honolulu Fish Auction: Where the World Comes to Buy

There are only four major fish auctions held in the United States, and the Honolulu auction is one of the most important. Held by the United Fishing Agency six mornings a week, the Honolulu auction usually begins at 5:30 in the morning. On an average day, fifty buyers representing wholesalers, brokers, fish markets, supermarkets, specialty stores, and restaurants gather to bid on the latest catch. These buyers can visually inspect the fish, which contributes to the Honolulu auction's reputation for high quality.

Brooks Takenaka, manager of the Honolulu Fish Auction.

The largest part of the tonnage in Honolulu is made up of different varieties of tuna (yellowfin, skipjack or aku, albacore, big eye, and bluefin). Swordfish is the next biggest catch. Other types of open-ocean fish sold at the auction are marlin, ono, opah, and mahimahi. Ocean-bottom fish sold in significant quantities include opaka paka, onaga, eshu (all types of snapper), ulua, hapu'upu'u (grouper), and kalikali. Sometimes, fish caught as far away as Fiji, Tonga, Australia, and New Zealand are auctioned in Honolulu.

The auction is a colorful sight. Whole fish are brought into the agency warehouse and laid on slabs for inspection. Tuna are usually the first to be auctioned; wedges of flesh near the tail are removed so the buyers can inspect the coloring, feel the texture, and taste the meat. This is especially important in assessing sashimi-quality tuna (up to

Auctioned snapper, headed for the table.

one-third is destined for the sashimi market). Some of the other fish are cut in half for inspection, but most are left whole. The auctioneer begins by announcing the fish's weight, and then the auction proceeds among the buyers, usually in increments of 10 cents. After the highest bid is made, a tag is attached to the fish to identify the buyer. The fish is then wheeled back out to waiting delivery trucks that are filled with ice. The agency also packs and ships fish in refrigerated airline contain-

ers when successful bidders are representing mainland buyers.

Prices bid for fish vary according to the volume and quality of the supply and the current demand. They can even vary for the same species during the auction, rather like a day at the Stock Exchange. Auction manager Brooks Takenaka colorfully, and accurately, describes the whole auction process as a combination of a circus and a poker game.

The types of fish auctioned and the volume (which can reach as much as 150,000 pounds a day) depends on the season, weather, and which boats have put in. About eighty-five boats based in Honolulu use longlines, and several hundred trawl for bottom fish (no reef fish are auctioned in Honolulu). Most of the fish caught and auctioned here are consumed in Hawaii—local per capita consumption is twice the average for the rest of the United States—although 90 percent of the swordfish are shipped to the mainland.

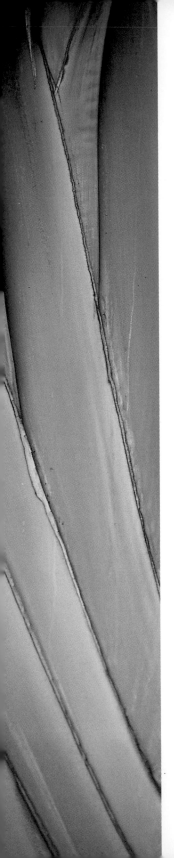

Ono and Pan-Fried Oysters with Lobster-Curry Sauce

Ono, a member of the mackerel family, is better known as "wahoo" in the mainland United States. That name is derived from the early European pronunciation of the Hawaiian island of "Oahu." This is another dish of contrasting flavors and textures. This recipe will also work well with grouper, snapper, or sea bass. Serve with Garlic Spinach (page 157) and Jasmine Rice (page 152), if desired.

Lobster-Curry Sauce:
½ cup Thai Curry Sauce (page 107)
½ cup *Beurre Blanc* (page 216)
2 tablespoons Lobster Paste
   (page 215)
...

4 ono fillets, about 7 ounces each
Salt and freshly ground pepper to taste
2 tablespoons olive oil
2 tablespoons flour
1 egg, beaten
1 cup panko

8 oysters, shucked
1½ cups canola oil

Garnish:
1 each red, green, and yellow bell pepper
1 teaspoon toasted white sesame
   seeds (page 220)

Combine the Thai Curry Sauce, *Beurre Blanc*, and Lobster Paste in a double boiler, and keep warm.

Season the ono with the salt and pepper and coat with the olive oil. Heat a dry cast-iron skillet and sear the ono over medium-high heat for about 1 to 1½ minutes per side for medium-rare. Remove to a platter and keep warm.

Place the flour, egg, and panko in separate shallow bowls. To bread the oysters, dredge them in the flour, then dip in the beaten egg, and finally roll them in the panko. Heat the canola oil in a skillet, and pan-fry the oysters over high heat for about 20 to 30 seconds per side, or until golden brown.

Cut the bell peppers into ½-inch-wide julienne strips; then cut each on the diagonal to form diamond shapes. Blanch the bell pepper pieces in boiling water for 5 seconds and drain. Place the ono fillets on serving plates, and top each fillet with 2 fried oysters. Spoon the Lobster-Curry Sauce around the fish and garnish with bell peppers and sesame seeds.

Pictured on opposite page

Roy's Feasts from Hawaii

Hibachi Tuna with Maui Onion Salad and Ponzu Sauce

My children, Nicole and Roy Jr., love this dish; in fact, it's just about their favorite. If you have any leftover marinade, refrigerate it for another time. Just bring it to a boil after use and keep adding to it. My father had a batch that he kept going for 16 years!

Marinade:

1 cup soy sauce

1 tablespoon chopped garlic

1 tablespoon minced ginger

½ cup sliced scallions

½ cup sugar

...

4 ahi tuna fillets, about 7 ounces each

Maui Onion Salad:

1 large carrot, sliced

1 small Maui onion, julienned

4 ounces Japanese spice sprouts, tops only

½ Japanese cucumber or English hothouse cucumber, seeded and julienned

¼ cup Pink Pickled Ginger (page 219)

1 tablespoon canola oil

4 ounces bean sprouts

...

½ tablespoon toasted white sesame seeds (page 220), for garnish

½ tablespoon black sesame seeds, for garnish

Juice of 1 lemon

Basic Ponzu Sauce (page 217)

Combine the marinade ingredients together in a large mixing bowl and marinate the tuna for about 1 hour. About 30 minutes or so before you're ready to serve, get the hibachi or barbecue grill ready, and prepare the vegetables.

To prepare the salad, combine the carrot, onion, spice sprouts, cucumber, and pickled ginger in a mixing bowl. Heat the canola oil in a sauté pan, and when hot, stir-fry the bean sprouts over high heat for 15 seconds. Transfer to the mixing bowl and toss with the vegetables.

Remove the tuna from the marinade and grill over high heat for 45 seconds to 1 minute per side for medium-rare.

To serve, divide the salad between 4 serving plates. Sprinkle the sesame seeds and lemon juice over the top. Place the tuna on top of the salad and spoon the Basic Ponzu Sauce over the fish.

Evidence of the bounty of Maui's farms.

Seared Lemon Grass-Crusted Swordfish with Thai Curry Sauce

Although the fish in this recipe is prepared in exactly the same manner as the salmon in the recipe on page 102, the curry sauce gives this dish an entirely different taste and appearance.

Thai Curry Sauce:

4 cups unsweetened coconut milk

¼ cup finely minced lemon grass

3 fresh basil leaves

¼ cup palm sugar

½ tablespoon fish sauce

2 tablespoons minced ginger

1½ tablespoons (or more, to taste) red curry paste (preferably Mae Ply brand Matsaman curry paste)

...

Lemon Grass Crust (page 102)

4 swordfish steaks, about 7 ounces each

Salt to taste

¼ cup canola oil

Roy's Mashed Potatoes (page 153)

Garnish:

4 ounces Japanese spice sprouts (optional)

2 tablespoons red pickled ginger (optional)

1 tablespoon minced macadamia nuts (optional)

1 tablespoon black sesame seeds

1 tablespoon toasted white sesame seeds (page 220)

To prepare the curry sauce, combine the coconut milk, lemon grass, basil, palm sugar, fish sauce, and ginger in a heavy-bottomed saucepan and bring to a simmer. Continue to simmer until the sauce reaches the consistency of half-and half, about 15 minutes. Add the curry paste and cook for 5 minutes longer, or until the sauce coats the back of a spoon. Strain and keep warm.

Combine the lemon grass crust ingredients in a mixing bowl. About 5 minutes before you are ready to cook the fish, thoroughly coat one side of each swordfish steak with the crust. Heat a large cast-iron skillet over medium-high heat. Season the swordfish with salt and coat the crusted side of the steak with the canola oil. Sear the swordfish steaks for about 1 to 1½ minutes on the crusted side first, then turn over and sear the other side for about 1 minute longer.

To serve, place a mound of the mashed potatoes in the center of each serving plate and top with a swordfish steak, crust side up. Pour the Thai Curry Sauce around the fish and garnish with the spice sprouts and pickled ginger, if desired. Sprinkle the macadamia nuts, if desired, and sesame seeds all around the swordfish.

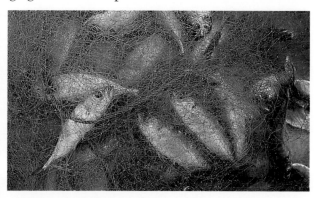

The family catch at Haena Beach, Kauai.

Broiled Hawaiian Swordfish in Miso

⇒ S E R V E S 4 ⇐

In this dish, the marinade serves multiple purposes. It flavors the fish, of course, but it also acts like a ceviche marinade, and "cooks" the fish to a certain degree. Because of this, you should keep the grilling time to a bare minimum, or the fish will dry out. This Japanese style of cooking is called "miso yaki."

Marinade:
⅓ cup white miso (*shiro miso*)
1½ tablespoons sake
2 teaspoons brown sugar
⅔ cup hoisin sauce
1½ tablespoons minced ginger
1½ tablespoons minced garlic
1½ tablespoons fresh orange juice

1 tablespoon chile paste with garlic (preferably Lan Chi brand or a *sambal sekera*)

...

4 swordfish steaks, about 7 ounces each
1 cup red pickled ginger
1 pound Japanese cucumber, seeded, chopped, and peel left on

Garnish:
1 cup canola oil
16 wonton wrappers, julienned
2 ounces Japanese spice sprouts
1 teaspoon black sesame seeds
1 teaspoon toasted white sesame seeds (page 220)
Avocado Salsa (page 164), optional

Combine all of the marinade ingredients in a mixing bowl. Add the swordfish and marinate in the refrigerator for 4 hours.

Prepare the grill. Meanwhile, purée the red pickled ginger in a food processor until it is smooth. Place in a sieve, drain, and set aside. Purée the cucumbers in the food processor until smooth. Place in a clean sieve, drain, and set aside.

To prepare the garnish, heat the oil in a skillet and fry the julienned wonton wrappers for about 30 seconds over medium heat. Drain on paper towels. Lightly toss with the sprouts and sesame seeds.

Grill the swordfish for 45 seconds to 1 minute per side for medium-rare. Spoon out a circle of puréed cucumber on each serving plate, then spoon a smaller circle of pickled ginger in the center of the cucumber. Lay a swordfish steak on the puréed ginger, then top with a mound of the mixed wonton strips. Serve with Avocado Salsa, if desired.

Grilled Miso-Crusted Butterfish with Three Caviars and Avocado

SERVES 6

Butterfish is very rich and flaky, much like salmon, which you may use instead of butterfish in this recipe. The miso marinade draws out some of the moisture of the fish, making the flesh firmer. This dish goes well with Garlic Spinach (page 157).

Miso Marinade:
½ cup white miso (*shiro miso*)
½ cup red miso
1½ tablespoons minced ginger
2 teaspoons minced garlic
½ cup hoisin sauce
⅔ cup sugar

½ cup sake
...
6 butterfish fillets, about 7 ounces each
1½ teaspoons *shichimi*

Garnish:
1½ ounces salmon "pearls" (optional)
1½ ounces *tobiko* caviar (optional)
¾ ounce Sevruga caviar (optional)
1 avocado
1 cup Sweet Ponzu Sauce (page 217)

*I*n a large mixing bowl, combine all the miso marinade ingredients. Sprinkle the butterfish fillets with the *shichimi*, and place in the marinade. Cover and marinate overnight in the refrigerator.

Prepare the grill. Remove the fish from the marinade and grill to desired doneness, about 1½ to 2 minutes per side over medium heat for medium doneness.

Place the grilled butterfish on serving plates. If you are using caviar, spoon the three caviars on the butterfish (you can either combine them, or keep each kind separate, depending on the effect you want). Cut the avocado in half, and remove the pit. Cut each half once lengthwise, and again crosswise. Thinly slice each chunk so the pieces can be fanned out. Garnish each serving of fish with an avocado fan. Serve with the Sweet Ponzu Sauce.

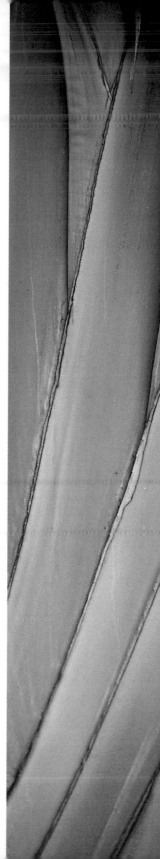

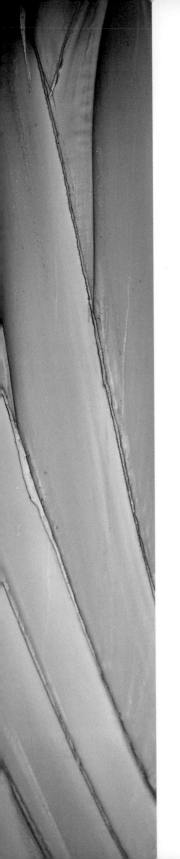

Ulua with Banana-Curry Sauce

Also called jack or jackfish, ulua is a deep-water bottomfish with white meat. It is similar to snapper, grouper, or pompano, which may be used in its place in this recipe. This dish may be served with Tropical Island Salsa.

Banana-Curry Sauce:

1 teaspoon canola oil

1 large banana, peeled and halved lengthwise

¼ cup diced onion

2 tablespoons minced ginger

2 tablespoons diced carrot

2 tablespoons diced celery

1 tablespoon red curry paste (preferably Mae Ploy brand Matsaman curry paste)

3 tablespoons brown sugar

4 cups unsweetened coconut milk

½ cup chopped fresh basil

½ cup chopped fresh cilantro

2 tablespoons finely minced lemon grass

3 kaffir lime leaves

…

1 tablespoon sesame oil

1 teaspoon minced ginger

1 teaspoon minced garlic

1 cup diced shiitake mushrooms

4 cups diced choy sum

1 cup diced napa cabbage

1 teaspoon chile paste with garlic (preferably Lan Chi brand)

4 red bell peppers, roasted, peeled, seeded, and diced (page 220)

3 tablespoons canola oil

2 bananas, peeled and halved lengthwise

2 teaspoons sugar

8 ulua fillets, about 3½ ounces each

Garnish:

Red leaf lettuce or radicchio (optional)

1 tablespoon black sesame seeds

To make the sauce, heat the canola oil on a hot griddle or in a sauté pan, and brown 2 of the banana halves over high heat, about 30 seconds per side. Chop coarsely and transfer to a heavy-bottomed saucepan. Add the remaining sauce ingredients, and bring to a boil. Reduce the heat to medium and reduce the liquid by half, stirring often with a wooden spoon, about 45 minutes. Transfer to a blender or food processor and pulse until semi-smooth. Return to a clean pan and keep warm.

Heat the sesame oil in a heavy skillet, and sauté the ginger, garlic, mushrooms, choy sum, and napa cabbage for about 2 minutes over high heat. Stir in the chile paste and bell peppers, and combine. Transfer to the center of 4 serving plates.

Heat 1 tablespoon of the canola oil on a hot griddle or in a sauté pan, sprinkle the remaining 4 banana halves with the sugar, and sauté the bananas over medium-high heat until lightly browned, about 1 minute per side. Set aside.

Coat the ulua with the remaining 2 tablespoons of the canola oil and heat a large, dry cast-iron skillet. Sear the ulua over high heat for about 1 minute per side for medium doneness. Place 2 fillets over the bed of sautéed vegetables on each plate, and spoon the Banana-Curry Sauce around. Place a browned banana half on top of the ulua. Garnish with any small red leaf lettuce, if desired, and sprinkle the black sesame seeds over the top.

Pictured on opposite page

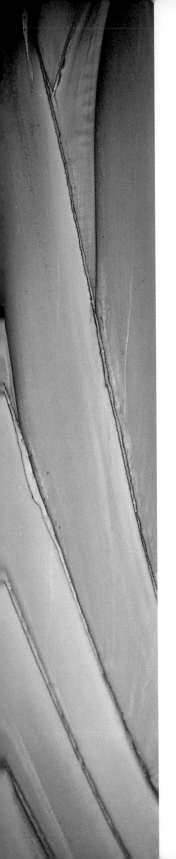

Asian-Style Ono with Spicy Shrimp and Bell Peppers

This is a great-tasting dish that combines the delicate flavors of ono, shrimp, and lobster.

4 jumbo shrimp (about 8 ounces), peeled and deveined, tail left on

2 tablespoons *sriracha* chile sauce

2 tablespoons canola oil

Sauce:

¾ cup *Beurre Blanc* (page 216)

2 tablespoons Lobster Paste (page 215)

1 tablespoon minced ginger

1 tablespoon sesame oil

1 teaspoon soy sauce

Vegetables:

1 teaspoon sesame oil

¼ cup seeded and finely diced red bell pepper

¼ cup seeded and finely diced green bell pepper

¼ cup seeded and finely diced yellow bell pepper

¼ cup finely diced zucchini

...

4 ono fillets, about 7 ounces each

¼ cup canola oil

Salt and freshly ground white pepper to taste

Garnish:

4 teaspoons seeded and finely diced red bell pepper

4 large sprigs fresh Italian parsley

Marinate the shrimp in the chile sauce for 30 minutes. (For an optional presentation, before marinating, butterfly the shrimp, cutting a slit in the upper part of the shrimp and pulling the tail through the slit.) Heat the 2 tablespoons of canola oil in a nonstick pan and sear the shrimp over high heat until just cooked through. Set aside.

To prepare the sauce, combine the *Beurre Blanc* and Lobster Paste in a small saucepan. Squeeze the ginger in a garlic press, adding the juice to the sauce (discard the ginger pulp). Stir in the sesame oil and soy sauce. Keep warm.

To prepare the vegetables, heat the sesame oil in a wok or heavy nonstick pan and stir-fry the bell peppers and zucchini for 30 seconds. Keep warm.

Coat the ono fillets with the ¼ cup of canola oil and season with salt and pepper. Heat a dry cast-iron skillet and sear the ono over medium-high heat for about 1 to 1½ minutes per side for medium-rare.

To serve, place the ono on serving plates and top each fillet with a shrimp. Spoon the sauce around the fish, followed by the stir-fried vegetables. Garnish the ono with the red bell pepper and Italian parsley.

Hane'o'o Fishpond, Maui, and 'A-Lau Island (background).

Roy's Feasts from Hawaii

Seared Ahi with Passion Fruit-Shrimp Salsa

≫ SERVES 4 ≪

With its density and color, ahi is almost like meat. Its deep, rich color fades when exposed to the air, so marinating and cooking it lightly preserves the attractive interior hue. For contrast in taste and texture, I like to serve most ahi dishes with a fruit salsa. Jasmine Rice (page 152) or Thai Potato Croquettes (page 153) make great accompaniments for this dish.

Passion Fruit-Shrimp Salsa
(recipe follows)

4 ahi tuna steaks, about 7 ounces each

3 tablespoons peanut oil
Salt and freshly ground pepper to taste

*P*repare the salsa and set aside.

Coat the ahi steaks with the peanut oil and season with salt and pepper. Heat a dry cast-iron skillet and sear the ahi over high heat for about 15 to 20 seconds each side for rare (about 1 minute each side fro medium-rare). Place the steaks on serving plates and spoon the salsa over the tuna, letting the juices from the salsa run onto the plates.

Passion Fruit-Shrimp Salsa

≫ YIELD: ABOUT 1 CUPS ≪

1 ripe passion fruit

4 or 5 extra-large shrimp (about 4 ounces), peeled, deveined, and diced

2 teaspoons olive oil

¼ cup finely minced Maui onion

½ cup peeled, seeded, and finely diced tomatoes

2 tablespoons finely sliced scallions

1 tablespoon finely minced fresh cilantro

1 teaspoon Tabasco sauce

Salt and freshly ground pepper to taste

*S*coop out the pulp from the passion fruit and press through a fine sieve. Reserve the juice (about 1 tablespoon).

Coat the shrimp in the olive oil and sear in a skillet over high heat until cooked through. Transfer to a stainless steel mixing bowl, add the passion fruit juice and the remaining ingredients, and toss well to combine.

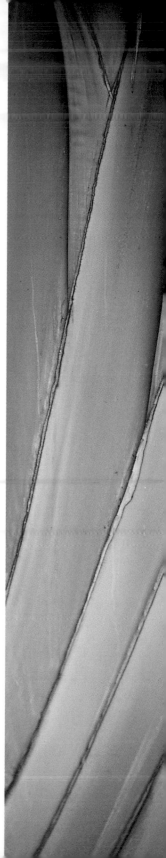

Fish and Shellfish

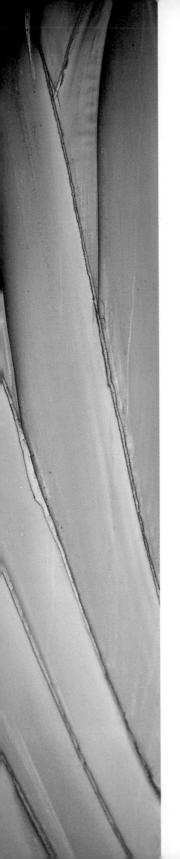

Cassoulet of Shrimp, Opakapaka, Scallops, Oysters, and Clams in Cioppino Broth

Cassoulets are stews from southern France that are usually made with beans and meat. I've given this recipe a twist by using seafood and a cioppino base—a unique flavor from San Francisco. To give this dish a little more of the taste and smell of the sea, we garnish it with ogo, a sea vegetable found in Hawaiian waters. Ask for it at your local fish market or an Asian grocery store; they may be able to get it for you. This dish goes well with Goat Cheese Hash (page 155).

Cioppino Broth:
1 tablespoon olive oil
1 tablespoon chopped garlic
Pinch of saffron threads
1 quart Shrimp Stock (page 214)
1 tablespoon fresh tarragon
1 tablespoon fresh basil
1 tablespoon fresh thyme
2 tablespoons Basic Tomato Sauce
   (page 215)

¼ teaspoon dried red chile flakes
Salt and freshly ground pepper
   to taste

...

16 oysters, in the shell
12 clams, in the shell, scrubbed
½ cup Tuscan-Style White Beans
   (page 156), warmed
¼ cup olive oil

16 to 20 extra-large shrimp (about 1
   pound), peeled and deveined,
   with tails left on (reserve 4 heads
   for garnish, if desired)
12 scallops
1 opakapaka fillet (about 4 ounces),
   cut into 4 pieces

Garnish:
20 fresh chives
Sea vegetables such as ogo

To prepare the broth, heat the tablespoon of olive oil in a stockpot and sauté the garlic over medium-high heat until it is lightly browned, about 30 seconds. Add the saffron, then add the Shrimp Stock, herbs, Basic Tomato Sauce, and chile flakes. Reduce to about 1 quart, simmering over low to medium heat for about 30 minutes. Season with salt and pepper, then strain into a clean saucepan.

Shuck 12 of the oysters, leaving 4 unshucked. Add the unshucked oysters and clams to the broth and poach over high heat until they begin to open. Remove the oysters and clams from the broth and allow them to cool slightly. Meanwhile, spoon the beans into 4 soup bowls. When the oysters and clams are cool enough to handle, pry them open so they can be easily eaten (you can remove the empty half of each shell if you like), and add to the soup bowls.

In a large sauté pan, heat the ¼ cup of olive oil and sear the shucked oysters, shrimp, scallops and opakapaka over high heat to medium-rare, about 30 seconds. Add them to the soup bowls. Bring the cioppino broth to a boil, and pour it over the seafood in the bowls. Garnish with the chives and sea vegetables. If you wish, you can also garnish each bowl with a shrimp head.

Pictured on opposite page (upper right)

Rustic Opakapaka with Tuscan-Style White Beans and Herb-Infused Olive Oil

※ SERVES 4 ※

Opakapaka is one of the most popular fish in Hawaii because of its delicate flesh and versatility—it's great grilled, seared, or steamed. Red snapper or grouper can be used instead of opakapaka.

¾ cup Herb-Infused Olive Oil (recipe follows)

1 tablespoon olive oil

1 red bell pepper, roasted, peeled, seeded, and julienned (page 220)

1 yellow bell pepper, roasted, peeled, seeded, and julienned (page 220)

4 ounces prosciutto, julienned

2 teaspoons chopped garlic

2 tablespoons balsamic vinegar

1 cup Tuscan-Style White Beans (page 156)

4 opakapaka fillets, about 7 ounces each

2 tablespoons canola oil

4 sprigs fresh thyme, for garnish

Prepare the Herb-Infused Olive Oil and set aside. Heat the olive oil in a sauté pan, and sauté the roasted bell peppers, prosciutto, garlic, and balsamic vinegar over high heat for 30 seconds. Stir in the white beans and cook for 1 minute. Remove from the heat and keep warm.

Brush the opakapaka with the canola oil. Heat a dry cast-iron skillet, and when it is hot, sear the fillets for 1 to 1½ minutes per side over high heat for medium doneness.

Place a bed of the bean mixture on each serving plate and top with the opakapaka fillets. Spoon about 3 tablespoons of the herb-infused oil around the edge of the beans on each plate, and garnish with the sprigs of thyme.

Pictured on page 115 (lower left)

Herb-Infused Olive Oil

※ YIELD: 1 CUPS ※

1 cup olive oil

1 tablespoon chopped fresh thyme

1 scallion, sliced

½ teaspoon chopped fresh rosemary

20 fresh basil leaves

1 tablespoon chopped fresh parsley

Warm the olive oil in a sauté pan. Add the thyme, scallion, and rosemary. Turn off the heat and allow to cool. Transfer to a blender, and add the basil and parsley. Purée and strain. Reserve until needed.

Mahimahi with Szechwan-Style Clams and Bell Peppers

SERVES 4

Manila, littleneck or cherrystone clams all work well in this recipe, so use whichever type is available or looks the best. If you buy shucked clams, choose plump ones and make sure the liquid they're sitting in is clear. I like to use sambal sekera to flavor this dish: it's an Indonesian chile paste that has a delicious sweetness as well as heat. Excellent side dishes for this recipe are Crispy Couscous (page 154) or Jasmine Rice (page 152).

1 tablespoon *sambal sekera* (Indonesian chile paste)

½ tablespoon mushroom soy sauce

½ tablespoon olive oil

2½ tablespoons sesame oil

½ green bell pepper, seeded and julienned

½ yellow bell pepper, seeded and julienned

½ red bell pepper, seeded and julienned

1 cup bean sprouts

3 ounces shiitake mushrooms, julienned

½ cup sliced scallions

12 fresh clams, shucked (Manilas, littlenecks, or cherrystones are best)

4 mahimahi steaks, about 7 ounces each

1 tablespoon canola oil

Salt and freshly ground pepper to taste

Garnish:

2 teaspoons black sesame seeds

Olive oil (optional)

Rayu (spicy sesame oil), optional

Soy sauce, optional

Combine the *sambal sekera*, mushroom soy sauce, olive oil, and ½ tablespoon of the sesame oil in a small bowl and set aside. Heat the remaining 2 tablespoons of the sesame oil in a wok or sauté pan and stir-fry the bell peppers and bean sprouts for 30 to 45 seconds over high heat, until lightly browned. Add the shiitake mushrooms and scallions, and sauté for about 30 seconds to 1 minute longer. Add the clams and then slowly add as much of the reserved chile paste mixture as suits your taste. Stir and cook for 15 seconds longer.

Coat the mahimahi steaks with the canola oil, and season with salt and pepper. Heat a dry cast-iron skillet or nonstick pan, and sear the mahimahi over high heat for 45 seconds to 1 minute per side for medium-rare.

Arrange a bed of vegetables and clams on the center of each serving plate, and place the mahimahi on top. Garnish with the black sesame seeds. If desired, drizzle a little olive oil, *rayu*, and soy sauce over the fish.

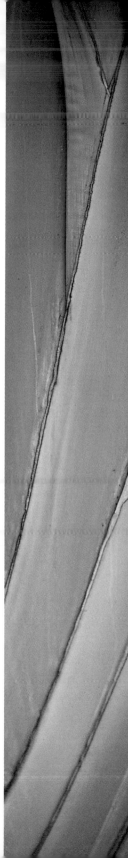

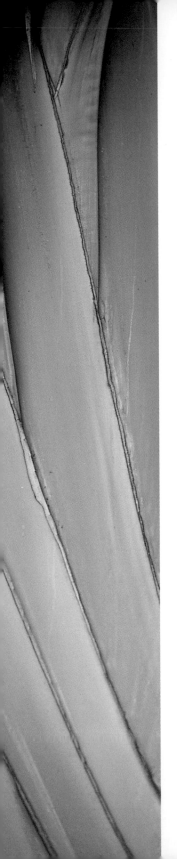

Shrimp Shiu Mai and Hawaiian Prawns with Sesame Butter Sauce

≫ SERVES 4 ≪

Shiu mai was one of my favorite foods while growing up in Japan. I eagerly looked forward to the occasional family outings to the Chinatown district in nearby Yokahama, when I'd eat as many as I could. Shiu mai is still one of my favorites.

Shiu Mai Filling:

8 ounces shrimp, peeled and deveined

¼ cup heavy cream

1 small egg

½ tablespoon grated ginger

½ teaspoon minced fresh basil

½ teaspoon minced fresh thyme

½ teaspoon minced fresh chives

½ teaspoon minced fresh parsley

4 ounces shiitake mushrooms, minced

Salt and freshly ground white pepper to taste

. . .

1 teaspoon cornstarch

2 tablespoons water

12 wonton wrappers

Sesame Butter Sauce:

1 cup *Beurre Blanc* (page 216)

3 tablespoons sesame oil

2 tablespoons unseasoned rice vinegar

. . .

1 tablespoon peanut oil

4 Hawaiian prawns or jumbo shrimp, peeled, head and tail left on

Garnish:

1 tablespoon black sesame seeds

½ tablespoon *shichimi*

4 sprigs fresh basil or 16 stalks fresh chives, each about 2 inches long

To prepare the *Shiu Mai* Filling, purée the shrimp in a food processor. Add the cream, egg, and ginger, and blend well. Transfer to a mixing bowl, and fold in the herbs and mushrooms. Season with salt and pepper, cover, and refrigerate for at least 1 hour.

Line a baking sheet with parchment paper. Combine the cornstarch and water in a small bowl. To make the *shiu mai*, lay out the wrappers on a work surface. Place 1 tablespoon of the filling in the center of each wrapper, and brush the edges with the cornstarch mixture. Gather up the edges of the wrapper, and twist to close. Place on the prepared baking sheet; cover and refrigerate until ready to use (up to 24 hours).

Shortly before serving, prepare the Sesame Butter Sauce by combining the *Beurre Blanc*, sesame oil, and vinegar in a double boiler. Keep warm.

Bring a large saucepan of water to a boil and cook the *shiu mai* until they float to the surface and are cooked through, about 5 minutes. Heat the peanut oil in a sauté pan or skillet, and sear the prawns or shrimp over medium-high heat for 2 minutes per side, or until cooked through.

Ladle ¼ cup of the sauce into the bottom of large soup bowls. Place a prawn or shrimp in the middle, surrounded by 3 *shiu mai*. Sprinkle with the sesame seeds and *shichimi*. Garnish each bowl with a basil sprig or 4 chive stalks.

Pictured on opposite page

Curried Shrimp with Enoki Mushroom-Cucumber Relish

≫ SERVES 4 ≪

One of the food contrasts I enjoy most is spicy curry and a cooling relish or salsa. I especially enjoy shrimp curries. Enoki mushrooms actually look more like sprouts than mushrooms because they are ivory colored with long, thin stems and a tiny round cap. They have a crunchy texture and a pleasant, mild flavor; they can be eaten raw or cooked in soups or stir-fries. Most Asian markets carry them, as do many produce markets (they may also be sold as enokitakes). They are packaged in clumps in plastic bags. To use, cut the mushrooms off the spongy root. Serve this dish with Japanese White Rice (page 151), if desired.

Marinade:

3 tablespoons curry powder

1 tablespoon minced ginger

1 tablespoon minced garlic

½ tablespoon minced lemon grass

⅓ teaspoon minced kaffir lime leaf (optional)

½ cup olive oil

1½ tablespoons light soy sauce (preferably Yamasa brand)

…

1¾ pounds extra-large shrimp (about 30), peeled and deveined

Relish:

1 cup seeded and diced Japanese cucumber

⅓ cup finely diced Maui onion

4 ounces enoki mushrooms, base removed

½ tablespoon grated ginger

2 tablespoons soy sauce

2 tablespoons *rayu* (spicy sesame oil)

2 tablespoons unseasoned rice vinegar

…

1 teaspoon toasted white sesame seeds (page 220), for garnish

Salt and freshly ground pepper to taste (optional)

Combine all the marinade ingredients in a mixing bowl, and marinate the shrimp for 15 minutes. Meanwhile, combine all the relish ingredients in a mixing bowl and toss well.

Heat a heavy dry sauté pan or skillet. Remove the shrimp from the marinade and sear over high heat for 30 seconds per side, or until cooked through.

Garnish with the sesame seeds, add salt and pepper, if desired, and serve with the relish.

Unloading tuna at the Hilo Fish Auction, Big Island.

Roy's Feasts from Hawaii

Kona Crab Cakes in Spicy Butter Sauce

⇛ SERVES 4 ⇚

Crab cakes are a permanent feature on the menu at Roy's. For special occasions, we make them with the rich, meaty Kona crabs that are caught off the leeward (western) coast of the Big Island.

3 tablespoons unsalted butter

½ tablespoon minced garlic

3 tablespoons finely diced onion

3 tablespoons seeded and finely diced red bell pepper

3 tablespoons seeded and finely diced green bell pepper

3 tablespoons finely diced celery

3 tablespoons finely diced carrot

2 tablespoons julienned fresh basil

6 tablespoons heavy cream

Salt and freshly ground white pepper to taste

Spicy Sesame Butter Sauce:

1 cup *Beurre Blanc* (page 216)

¼ cup *rayu* (spicy sesame oil)

1 tablespoon unseasoned rice vinegar

1 teaspoon *shichimi*, or more to taste

…

1¼ pounds crabmeat (Kona crab, if available, or blue crab)

½ cup flour

2 cups panko

2 eggs

1 cup peanut oil

Heat the butter in a sauté pan and sauté the garlic and onion over medium-high heat until lightly browned. Then add the bell peppers, celery, carrot, and basil, and sauté for 1 minute longer. Add the cream and continue cooking until the liquid is reduced by half. Season with salt and pepper. Transfer to a stainless steel bowl and chill for about 1 hour.

Combine all the sauce ingredients in a double boiler, stirring thoroughly to incorporate. Keep warm.

Add the crabmeat to the chilled vegetable mixture and mix thoroughly. Form into 8 balls and squeeze them gently to remove any excess liquid (they should be moist and creamy, but not oozing liquid). Flatten into patties. Place the flour and panko on separate plates and beat the eggs in a shallow bowl. Lightly coat the crab cakes in the flour, then in the egg, and finally dredge evenly in the panko. Heat the peanut oil in a sauté pan. When hot, cook the crab cakes over medium heat and brown evenly, about 1½ minutes per side.

Ladle a little sauce onto each serving plate and serve 2 crab cakes per person.

Seacliffs and Kalaupapa Peninsula, Molokai.

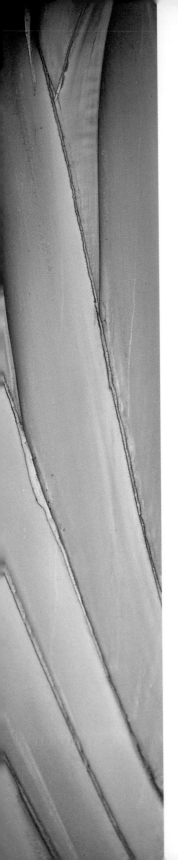

Grilled Spiny Lobster with Bean Thread Noodles and Macadamia Nuts

I prefer the firmer textured spiny lobsters (also called rock lobsters) to Maine lobsters, but you may use either in this recipe. The small, colorful warm-water spiny lobsters have a sweeter taste than the cold-water lobsters. They also yield almost all tail meat and no claw meat, so they're easier to eat. Bean thread noodles are sold in Asian markets and are called different names; they may be labeled cellophane noodles, saifun, or vermicelli.

2 spiny lobster tails, about 7 or 8 ounces each

2 tablespoons peanut oil

6 to 8 ounces bean thread noodles

Sauce:

1 teaspoon sesame oil

½ cup finely angle-cut scallions

5 tablespoons soy sauce

1½ tablespoons sugar

1½ teaspoons grated ginger

1 teaspoon minced garlic

Garnish:

1 teaspoon vegetable oil

2 tablespoons seeded and julienned red bell pepper

2 tablespoons seeded and julienned green bell pepper

2 tablespoons seeded and julienned yellow bell pepper

1 teaspoon black sesame seeds

1 teaspoon toasted white sesame seeds (page 220)

2 tablespoons crushed toasted macadamia nuts (page 222)

2 teaspoons *furikake* (optional)

4 sprigs fresh cilantro

Prepare the grill. Brush the lobster with the peanut oil and grill for about 5 minutes, or until done. Remove the meat, dice it, and set aside.

Bring a saucepan of water to a boil, and cook the bean thread noodles for about 5 minutes, or until tender. Rinse under cold water, drain, and reserve.

To prepare the sauce, heat the sesame oil in a sauté pan and sauté the scallions for 10 to 15 seconds over high heat. Quickly add the soy sauce, sugar, ginger, and garlic, stir together, and immediately remove from the heat. Set aside.

Heat the vegetable oil in a sauté pan and sauté the bell peppers for 15 seconds over high heat, or until soft, and set aside.

Heat the cooked bean thread noodles gently in the sauce. When the sauce has been completely absorbed by the noodles, add the diced lobster and remove from the heat. Transfer to serving bowls and garnish with the bell peppers, sesame seeds, and macadamia nuts. Sprinkle the *furikake* around the edge of each plate, if desired; top with the cilantro sprigs.

Pictured on opposite page

Meat and Poultry

*W*hen you think of Hawaiian food, the luau, featuring a pit-roasted pig, is probably the first thing that springs to mind. The Hawaiian luau is a festive event dating from early tribal days, and is still a popular celebration that is held on the islands to mark weddings, birthdays, anniversaries, family gatherings, and other significant occasions. Originally, luaus were convivial ritual feasts that aspired to invoke the spirits of the gods. Pig and moa (fowl) were the favored offerings. Modern-day Hawaiian luaus typically feature these as well as fish dishes, ribs and tropical fruit accompaniments.

For centuries, pigs were used in Hawaii as barter and as payment to tribal chiefs. The commander of Captain Cook's expedition visiting Kauai wrote in 1779, "The natives bring aboard so many hogs we know not what to do with them, so are oblig'd to give up that trade for the present." Chicken and game birds such as goose (nene), duck, and plover, usually pit-cooked in underground imu ovens, were regarded as less flavorful than pig and were less popular. (Domesticated dog, one traditional source of meat in ancient Hawaii —as in pre-Columbian Mexico—was also cooked in the imu.)

Beef was introduced to Hawaii in the late eighteenth century (see page 133). Today, visitors are amazed to discover that the Parker Ranch on the Big Island is the second-largest cattle ranch in the United States. Texans are particularly disbelieving!

Lanai Venison in Red Currant-Cabernet Sauce with Pesto Potatoes

Lanai used to be known as the Pineapple Island because most of it was a pineapple plantation owned by the Dole Company. In recent years, most of Hawaii's pineapple industry has moved to Southeast Asia because of the lower growing costs, and Lanai's economy has been dramatically transformed. These days, it mostly revolves around resorts and a large game reserve where venison is raised. The red currants give the rich sauce a fruity dimension that complements the complex flavors of the meat. If fresh red currants are unavailable, use defrosted frozen fruit.

Marinade:

¼ cup olive oil

1 tablespoon minced garlic

1 tablespoon minced fresh basil

1 tablespoon grated ginger

Salt and freshly ground pepper
   to taste

…

4 venison loin steaks, about 6
   ounces each, trimmed of fat

Red Currant-Cabernet Sauce:

¼ cup cabernet sauvignon

1 tablespoon sugar

¼ cup fresh red currants

1 cup Cabernet Sauce (page 216)

4 tablespoons chilled unsalted
   butter, chopped (optional)

…

½ cup Pesto (page 214)

3 cups Roy's Mashed Potatoes
   (page 153)

½ cup *Beurre Blanc* (page 216)

1 cup fresh red currants, for garnish

4 sprigs fresh rosemary, for garnish

Combine the marinade ingredients in a shallow dish. Make sure the venison steaks are of a consistent thickness: pound out thicker portions with a mallet, if necessary. Place the steaks in the marinade, coating thoroughly, cover, and marinate overnight in the refrigerator.

To prepare the sauce, combine the wine, sugar, and red currants in a large saucepan. Reduce over medium-high heat, stirring constantly until the sauce is thick enough to coat the back of a spoon, about 2 to 3 minutes. Stir in the Cabernet Sauce. If desired, whisk in the butter a little at a time, and incorporate thoroughly. Keep the sauce warm in a double boiler.

Prepare the grill. Gently fold ¼ cup of the Pesto into the prepared mashed potatoes so that they are not uniformly green but a mixture of green and white. Warm the *Beurre Blanc* in a double boiler. Remove the venison from the marinade and grill to the desired doneness, about 2 to 3 minutes per side for medium-rare.

Place the potatoes in a neat circle in the center of each serving plate. Slice the venison steaks and arrange on top of the potatoes. Pour the Red Currant-Cabernet Sauce around, and overlay with the *Beurre Blanc*. Drizzle the remaining ¼ cup of Pesto over the sauces and top the sauces with the red currants. Garnish the venison with a sprig of rosemary.

Pictured on page 128 (lower right)

Grilled Pork Medallions with Watercress Salad and Shoestring Potatoes

Ideally, the pork for this recipe should be marinated overnight, so the meat will have time to take on the flavors of the marinade. However, if you want to cook it the same day, you can cut the time to 3 or 4 hours, and it will be almost as good. To get really crisp shoestring potatoes, soak them in water for an hour to remove the excess starch, then drain and pat dry thoroughly before frying.

Marinade:

1 quart warm water

1 green bell pepper, seeded and chopped

½ onion, chopped

2 bay leaves

10 black peppercorns

½ cup sugar

. . .

1 boneless pork loin, about 1¾ pounds, trimmed of fat

1 large baking potato, unpeeled

Mushroom-Watercress Bed:

2 tablespoons sesame oil

½ teaspoon minced ginger

½ teaspoon minced garlic

4 ounces shiitake mushrooms, sliced

½ cup watercress stems

1 cup seeded and finely julienned red bell pepper

2 cups bean sprouts

½ tablespoon oyster sauce

1 teaspoon toasted white sesame seeds (page 220)

. . .

1 quart canola oil, for deep frying

Watercress Salad:

3 tablespoons olive oil

⅛ teaspoon minced ginger

⅛ teaspoon minced garlic

½ teaspoon chile paste with garlic (preferably Lan Chi brand or a *sambal sekera*)

3 tablespoons unseasoned rice vinegar

½ cup seeded and julienned red bell pepper

½ cup seeded and julienned yellow bell pepper

8 ounces watercress leaves

3 tablespoons crushed toasted macadamia nuts (page 220)

Combine the marinade ingredients in a large bowl and marinate the pork overnight in the refrigerator.

Cut the potato into ½-inch julienne (a mandoline works best for this). Soak in a bowl of water for up to 1 hour.

Shortly before you're ready to cook the pork, prepare the grill and prepare the Mushroom-Watercress Bed. Heat the sesame oil in a wok or sauté pan and stir-fry the ginger, garlic, mushrooms, watercress stems, and bell pepper over medium heat for about 1 minute. Add the bean sprouts and oyster sauce, sauté for 30 seconds longer, and add the sesame seeds. Remove from the heat and reserve.

Remove the pork from the marinade and grill to the desired doneness, about 7 or 8 minutes per side over high heat for medium doneness. Remove and cut into 12 slices.

While the meat is on the grill, drain the shoestring potatoes, and dry thoroughly with paper towels. Heat the canola oil in a deep-fryer or large saucepan, and fry the shoestring potatoes over high heat for 2 to 3 minutes, or until browned and crisp. Drain on paper towels.

Pictured on opposite page (upper left)

To prepare the watercress salad, heat the olive oil in a large sauté pan, and lightly brown the ginger and garlic over medium-high heat. Stir in the chile paste, vinegar, and bell peppers, remove from the heat, and transfer to a large salad bowl. Add the watercress leaves and macadamia nuts, and toss with one-quarter of the shoestring potatoes.

Arrange a mushroom-watercress bed in the center of each serving plate, and top with 3 slices of the grilled pork. Place the watercress salad on top of the pork and the remaining shoestring potatoes on top of the watercress salad.

Grilling up a storm at Roy's, Honolulu; that's the imu oven in the background.

THESE PANIOLOS AT ULUPALAKUA RANCH on Maui work the 5,000 head of cattle and 1,000 sheep that graze over 25,000 acres on the slopes of Mount Haleakala. The ranch was once a sugar plantation—the old mill that was once the largest on Maui can still be seen here—but it was turned over to livestock in the 1890s. Today, Ulupalakua Ranch is one of the state's main suppliers of locally raised Hawaiian beef.

The original *paniolos*—three Mexican cowboys—were brought to Hawaii by King Kamehameha III in the early 1840s to round up wild cattle and to supervise the development of a beef herd. (*Paniolo* is the local abbreviation for *españolos*, or "Spanish.") These three *amigos* taught local Hawaiians their cowboy skills, and some of their descendants four and five generations on, still ride the Hawaiian range today.

Roy's Feasts from Hawaii

Rack of Lamb with Bangkok Curry Sauce

Most of our lamb is imported, but from time to time we are able to obtain excellent locally raised lamb from Niihau, an isolated, privately owned island off Kauai.

⫸ SERVES 4 ⫷

Bangkok Curry Sauce:

1 red bell pepper, roasted, peeled, seeded, and puréed (page 220)

2 tablespoons minced ginger

2 tablespoons minced garlic

2 tablespoons finely minced lemon grass

1 cup chopped onion

1 tablespoon chopped shallot

4 kaffir lime leaves

¼ cup green curry paste (or regular curry paste)

3 tablespoons creamy peanut butter

2 cups unsweetened coconut milk

½ cup heavy cream

2 tablespoons soy sauce

1 tablespoon fish sauce

2 tablespoons unseasoned rice vinegar

½ bunch fresh cilantro, chopped

4 fresh basil leaves, chopped

2 tablespoons cornstarch

¼ cup water

. . .

4 racks of lamb, each with 4 ribs

Salt and freshly ground pepper to taste

1 to 2 tablespoons vegetable oil

Vegetables:

2 tablespoons canola oil

½ cup julienned red bell pepper

½ cup julienned yellow bell pepper

½ cup julienned green bell pepper

½ cup julienned eggplant

½ cup bean sprouts

½ teaspoon minced garlic

1 teaspoon minced ginger

Garnish:

1 teaspoon toasted white sesame seeds (page 220)

1 teaspoon black sesame seeds

Place all the sauce ingredients, except for the cornstarch and water, in a heavy saucepan. Bring to a boil, stirring frequently. Lower the heat to low and simmer for about 45 minutes to reduce the liquid. In a small bowl, add the water to the cornstarch and stir until smooth. Add to the sauce, stir until the sauce thickens, then remove from the heat.

Prepare the grill. Season the lamb with salt and pepper, and lightly brush with the vegetable oil. Grill to the desired doneness, about 5 minutes per side for medium-rare.

To prepare the vegetables, heat the canola oil in a large sauté pan or wok, and when hot, stir-fry all the vegetable ingredients over high heat for 1 minute.

Arrange a bed of the vegetables in the center of each serving plate. Cut the grilled racks of lamb into chops and arrange 4 chops per serving around the vegetables (lean the chops inwards so the ribs intertwine over the vegetables). Spoon the Bangkok Curry Sauce around the vegetables and lamb, and garnish by sprinkling the sesame seeds over all.

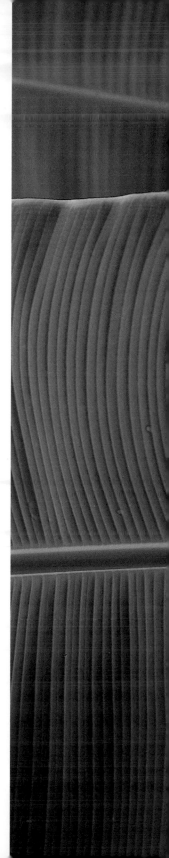

Parker Ranch Filet Mignon with Pan-Crisped Onions and Honey-Mustard Sauce

The Parker Ranch, headquartered in Waimea on the Big Island, is so large that it's contained by eight hundred miles of fence. Most of the ranch's livestock is exported, but a limited amount of Parker Ranch beef is sold locally, especially in Hilo. When buying filet mignon (the small end of the tenderloin), look for a thickness of 1½ to 2 inches.

Honey-Mustard Sauce:

¼ cup peanut oil

2 Maui onions, chopped (about 1 cup)

8 cloves garlic, minced

¾ cup chopped carrots

¾ cup chopped celery

4 bay leaves

5 black peppercorns

1 cup port or cabernet sauvignon

1 quart Veal Stock (page 213)

1 cup whole-grain mustard

⅓ cup honey

10 tablespoons chilled, unsalted butter, chopped

Onions:

1 cup peanut oil

1½ cups flour

4 large Maui onions, very finely julienned

Garnish (optional):

½ zucchini

½ yellow squash

½ carrot

…

4 filets mignon, about 8 ounces each

Salt and fresh ground pepper to taste

To prepare the sauce, heat the peanut oil in a heavy saucepan and sauté the onions, garlic, carrots, celery, bay leaves, and peppercorns over medium-high heat for 3 to 5 minutes, stirring occasionally until golden brown. Deglaze the pan with the port or cabernet, and add the stock, mustard, and honey. Reduce the liquid to about 2½ cups, stirring constantly until the sauce is thick enough to coat the back of a spoon. Strain through a fine sieve into a clean pan (discard the solids) and return to the heat. Whisk in the butter, a little at a time, and incorporate thoroughly. Keep the sauce warm in a double boiler.

To prepare the onions, heat the peanut oil in a heavy saucepan (there should be enough to come at least 1½ inches up the sides of the pan). Place the flour on a plate and lightly dredge the onions in the flour. When the oil is hot, fry the onions for about 5 to 7 minutes over medium-high heat, turning constantly but gently, until golden brown. Drain on paper towels, and keep warm.

To prepare the optional vegetable garnish, cut the zucchini, squash, and carrot into neat ovals about the size of a clove of garlic. Steam for a minute or two, drain, and set aside.

Prepare the grill. Season the filets with salt and pepper. Grill for about 3 to 4 minutes per side for medium-rare.

Place a filet in the center of each serving plate and spoon the sauce around the meat. Place a handful of the onions on top of the filet. If desired, arrange the vegetables around the filet with a sunburst effect.

Parker Ranch: In the Shadow of the Volcano

There are several hundred cattle ranches on the Hawaiian islands, but the Parker Ranch is by far the largest. It lies in the northwest part of the Big Island, on the rolling lower slopes of dormant Mauna Kea. At more than 210,000 acres, the ranch is the second largest in the United States (exceeded in size by only the Deseret Ranch in Florida). It is surely the most spectacular, with the (sometimes snowcapped) volcano as its backdrop, lush green grass refreshed by rapidly moving showers brought by the trade winds, and groves of stately old trees dotting the landscape.

The ranch currently owns up to 50,000 head of cattle, although some of these are dispersed in Canada and states such as New Mexico, Texas, Oklahoma, Kansas, and California for grazing before being sold on the mainland. More than 21,000 of the herd are breeding cows; over 1,000 are bulls. Three main breeds are raised on the ranch: Herefords, Angus, and Brangus (a Brahma/Angus crossbreed).

The origins of the ranch can be traced back to Hawaii's first cattle, which were presented as a gift to King Kamehameha III in 1793 by British naval captain George Vancouver. Before long, however, the cattle were running wild and destroying farmland and forests alike. King Kamehameha III commissioned John Palmer Parker, a former New Englander and court fa-

Paniolos in the cattle corral at Parker Ranch.

Paniolo Yutaka Kimura.

vorite, as his agent to bring the animals under control, which he succeeded in doing. The hides and meat proved highly profitable for both Parker and the king, and Parker often took payment in the form of cattle. In 1847, Parker received a small land grant from the king, and together with extensive lands granted to his wife, a royal princess, the foundation of the Parker Ranch was created. In due course, John Parker purchased considerably more contiguous acreage and leased other grazing lands.

While the fortunes of the ranch fluctuated during the lifetimes of subsequent generations, steady profitability has prevailed during the most recent decades. In 1992, Richard Smart, owner of the ranch and great-great-great-grandson of John Palmer Parker, died. His will arranged for the ranch to be run as a working business by a foundation trust.

Veal Chops with Mediterranean Vegetables and Madeira Tomato Sauce

As this recipe proves, Madeira wine works very well in sauces and cooked dishes, adding both richness and flavor. You can substitute a beef steak for the veal, if you prefer.

Madeira Tomato Sauce:
¼ cup canola oil
8 cloves garlic, minced
1 onion, chopped
1 carrot, chopped
1 stalk celery, chopped
4 bay leaves
5 black peppercorns
2 tablespoons sugar
4 tomatoes, peeled, seeded, and diced
1 cup red wine

3 cups Madeira wine
1 quart Veal Stock (page 213)
Mediterranean Vegetables:
¾ cup olive oil
2 teaspoons minced garlic
8 ounces eggplant, cut into ½-inch slices
8 ounces yellow squash, cut into ½-inch slices
8 ounces zucchini, cut into ½-inch slices
2 teaspoons minced fresh rosemary
2 teaspoons minced fresh thyme

2 teaspoons minced fresh basil
4 Roma tomatoes, cut in half
2 tablespoons Pesto (page 214)
. . .
4 veal chops, about 6 to 7 ounces each
Salt and freshly ground pepper to taste
1 tablespoon finely sliced fresh chives, for garnish
12 whole fresh chives, for garnish (optional)

To prepare the sauce, heat the canola oil in a saucepan and sauté the garlic, onion, carrot, celery, bay leaves, and peppercorns over medium heat for about 5 minutes, or until the vegetables are golden brown. Add the sugar and caramelize for about 2 minutes, stirring continuously. Stir in the tomatoes, and deglaze with the red wine and Madeira. Reduce the liquid by two-thirds. Add the Veal Stock and once again reduce the liquid by two-thirds. Strain the sauce into a clean pan (discard the solids) and continue reducing the sauce until it coats the back of a spoon (there should be about 1 cup of sauce). Keep warm in a double boiler.

To prepare the vegetables, place ½ cup of the olive oil and the garlic on a large platter. Place the eggplant, squash, and zucchini slices on the platter, sprinkle with the minced herbs, and coat thoroughly. Over a hot grill, or in a large skillet over high heat, sear the vegetables until tender, about 2 minutes per side. Cool, dice, and set aside. Coat the cut side of the tomato halves with 1 tablespoon of the Pesto and sear the cut side on the hot grill or in a skillet for about 15 seconds. Cool, cut into chunks, and set aside.

Flatten the veal with a mallet to an even thickness of about 1¼ inches. Coat the veal with the remaining 1 tablespoon Pesto, and season lightly with salt and pepper. Heat the remaining ¼ cup of olive oil in a skillet and sear the veal over medium-high heat until browned on both sides, about 3 minutes per side for medium-rare.

Place the prepared vegetables in a saucepan, add ½ cup of the Madeira Tomato Sauce, and bring to a simmer. Transfer the vegetables to serving plates and top with the veal. Drizzle the remaining sauce around the veal and sprinkle with the sliced chives. If desired, place the whole chives upright in the vegetables.

Pictured on opposite page

Venison with Grilled Vegetable Gratin and Cognac Peppercorn Sauce

We serve top-quality, local venison at Roy's whenever we can. Guests sometimes express apprehension that venison might taste too gamey for their liking, but with modern processing techniques, this is not a problem. Venison is one of the most healthful and flavorful red meats available, and it's at its best when matched with a complex, wine-based sauce like the one presented here.

Cognac Peppercorn Sauce:
2 tablespoons unsalted butter
¾ teaspoon minced shallot
1 teaspoon crushed black
   peppercorns
½ cup cognac or brandy

¾ cup heavy cream
¼ cup Cabernet Sauce (page 216)
...
¼ cup olive oil
1 teaspoon minced garlic
1 teaspoon minced lemon grass
   (optional)

1 teaspoon crushed black
   peppercorns
Salt to taste
1¾ pounds venison loin, trimmed
   of fat and cut into 4 portions
Grilled Vegetable Gratin (recipe follows)

To prepare the sauce, heat the butter in a saucepan and sauté the shallot and peppercorns over medium heat for about 1 minute. Add the cognac or brandy, and carefully flame to burn off the alcohol. Reduce the liquid for about 2 minutes, or until 1 teaspoon is left. Add the cream and reduce by one-third, about 2 minutes. Stir in the Cabernet Sauce and reduce until the sauce is thick enough to coat the back of a spoon. Keep warm in a double boiler.

Prepare the grill. Combine the olive oil, garlic, lemon grass, peppercorns, and salt in a shallow bowl, and thoroughly coat the venison. Grill the venison to the desired doneness, about 2 to 3 minutes for medium-rare. Cut each loin portion into 6 or 7 slices.

Arrange the Grilled Vegetable Gratin on one half of each serving plate, broil or bake to melt the cheese, then arrange the sliced venison on the other half of the plates. Ladle the sauce beside the venison.

Grilled Vegetable Gratin

1 Japanese eggplant, sliced
1 yellow squash, sliced
1 zucchini, sliced

1 or 2 tomatoes, sliced
1 or 2 Maui onions, sliced
½ tablespoon minced garlic

½ cup olive oil
4 ounces shredded mozzarella cheese

Prepare the grill. Place the olive oil in a mixing bowl, add all of the vegetables, and marinate for 1 to 2 minutes. Remove and grill until tender. When ready to serve, sprinkle the grilled vegetables with the mozzarella and broil (or bake) until the cheese melts.

Note: Feel free to vary the vegetables, depending on your personal preference and the availability of produce. This also makes a good vegetable side dish for fish, pork, and lamb.

Braised Pork with Island-Style Applesauce

4 to 5 pounds boneless pork shoulder or
    pork butt, trimmed of fat

¼ cup canola oil

1 cup diced onion

¾ cup diced carrots

¾ cup diced celery

3 bay leaves

3 star anise

1 tablespoon black peppercorns

1 stalk lemon grass, cut in half

½ vanilla bean, split in half
    lengthwise

2-inch length of ginger

2 cups red wine

2 quarts Chicken Stock (page 213)

1 bunch fresh cilantro, tied

1 bunch fresh mint, tied

½ cup chilled unsalted butter, chopped

Saffron Sauce (optional):

10 saffron threads

¼ cup water

½ cup *Beurre Blanc* (page 216)

…

Island-Style Applesauce (recipe follows)

3 cups Chicken Stock (page 213)

Roy's Mashed Potatoes (page 153)

Garlic Spinach (page 157)

4 sprigs fresh thyme, for garnish

2 apples, cored, quartered, and
    sliced, for garnish (optional)

$\mathcal{C}$ut the pork into 4 pieces and roll up, tying each piece with butcher's twine to secure. Heat the canola oil in a stockpot and sear the pork on all sides over high heat, until golden brown. Add the onion, carrots, and celery to the stockpot, together with the bay leaves, star anise, peppercorns, lemon grass, vanilla bean, and ginger. Sauté for 2 minutes and then add the wine, stock, cilantro, and mint. Bring to a boil, reduce the heat, and simmer for 1½ hours, or until the meat is tender.

Remove the pork and set aside. Skim off any impurities and reduce the liquid over medium-high heat to about 2 cups, or until it coats the back of a spoon. Strain through a fine sieve into a clean saucepan. Over low heat, whisk in the butter, a little at a time to form a brown sauce. Keep warm in a double boiler. To prepare the Saffron Sauce, place the saffron and water in a small saucepan and reduce over low heat to 1 teaspoon. Warm the *Beurre Blanc* in a double boiler, and stir in the saffron mixture.

Prepare the applesauce.

In a saucepan, reheat the pork in the 3 cups of Chicken Stock. When warmed through, remove and untie the pork. Spoon the mashed potatoes on one side of each serving plate and the spinach next to the potatoes. Place the pork in the center of the plate and top it with the applesauce. Ladle the brown sauce around and, if used, spoon the Saffron Sauce over the brown sauce. Garnish the apple-sauce with a sprig of thyme, and, if desired, decorate each plate with the sliced apple arranged in a fan.

Island-Style Applesauce

6 Granny Smith apples, peeled,
    cored, and sliced

2 tablespoons strained fresh passion
    fruit juice or passion fruit nectar

½ cup mirin

2 tablespoons unseasoned rice vinegar

2 tablespoons honey

½ vanilla bean, split in half
    lengthwise

1 star anise

2-inch length of ginger

$\mathcal{P}$lace all of the ingredients in a large saucepan and cook over medium heat for 30 minutes, or until the apples are soft and falling apart. Remove the vanilla bean, star anise, and ginger, and discard. Transfer the apples and liquid to a food processor or blender and purée. Serve hot or cold.

Mongolian-Style Grilled Short Ribs with Leeks au Gratin and Mashed Potatoes

❧ SERVES 4 ❧

These spicy ribs are perfect for a summer barbecue. The leeks go well with most entrées, including fish.

¼ cup canola oil
4 pounds beef short ribs
1 onion, diced
1 carrot, diced
1 stalk celery, diced
1 tomato, diced
1 bay leaf

5 black peppercorns
1 cup red wine
2 quarts water

Mongolian Marinade:
1 cup hoisin sauce
1 teaspoon minced garlic
1 teaspoon minced ginger

2 tablespoons honey
2 tablespoons chile paste with garlic
(preferably Lan Chi brand or a *sambal sekera*)

...

Roy's Mashed Potatoes (page 153)
Leeks au Gratin (recipe follows)

Heat 2 tablespoons of the canola oil in a large saucepan and brown the ribs on all sides over high heat. Remove the ribs and reserve. Lower the heat to medium-high, add the remaining canola oil to the pan, and sauté the onion, carrot, celery, tomato, bay leaf, and peppercorns for about 5 minutes, or until golden brown. Return the ribs to the pan and add the wine and water. Simmer over low heat for 1½ hours, or until the meat is tender. Strain through a sieve and discard the vegetables.

While the ribs are simmering, combine the marinade ingredients in a bowl and set aside. Prepare the Potatoes and the Leeks au Gratin. Prepare the grill.

Carefully remove the rib meat from the bones, brush the meat well with the marinade, and finish on a hot grill. Serve with the potatoes and leeks.

Leeks au Gratin

16 leeks, about ½-inch in diameter
½ cup Chicken Stock (page 213)

¼ cup grated Swiss cheese
1 cup heavy cream

Salt and freshly ground pepper
to taste

Preheat the oven to 375 degrees. Cut the roots off the leeks and trim away the upper part, leaving all the white part and about 3½ inches of the green. Wash thoroughly and place in a large earthenware dish, leaving about 1 inch between the leeks and the side of the dish so the leeks don't burn. Add the Chicken Stock and cover with foil. Bake for about 30 minutes, or until tender and the liquid has evaporated. Turn the oven up to 400 degrees. Remove the foil, combine the cheese and cream, pour it over the leeks, and season with salt and pepper. Bake, uncovered, for about 20 minutes, or until the cheese sauce has thickened and turned golden brown.

Roy's Feasts from Hawaii

Chicken Katsu with Crispy Eggplant Chips and Maui Onion Salad

In Japanese, katsu means food that has been breaded and fried, usually a pork cutlet or chicken breast. When I was a kid, my mother used to make chicken katsu sandwiches for my school lunches. The chicken katsu in this recipe is pretty much like my mother's—I've just embellished it a little.

2 eggs
1 teaspoon *shichimi*
1 cup flour
2 cups panko
4 boneless half chicken breasts,
    skin removed

Eggplant Chips:
Cottonseed or canola oil,
    for deep-frying
2 Japanese eggplant, cut on the
    diagonal into ⅛-inch-thick slices
Kosher salt to taste
…

Maui Onion Salad (page 60)
Basic Ponzu Sauce (page 217)
Garnish:
1 tablespoon sliced red pickled ginger
¼ cup Japanese spice sprouts (optional)
1 teaspoon *furikake* (optional)

In a bowl, beat the eggs with the *shichimi* until foamy. Place the flour and panko on separate large plates. Dredge the chicken in the flour, dip in the egg mixture, and then in the panko, coating thoroughly. Cover and refrigerate until ready to cook.

To prepare the chips, heat the oil in a deep-fryer or large saucepan. When hot, fry the sliced eggplant for 2 to 3 minutes over medium-high heat, until flesh is golden brown and crisp. Remove with a slotted spoon and drain on paper towels. Sprinkle with the kosher salt and keep warm.

Strain the frying oil through a fine sieve into a clean sauté pan or skillet (about ½ inch of oil will do). Reheat the oil and pan-fry the breaded chicken breasts over medium-high heat for about 4 minutes on each side, or until crispy and golden brown.

Place a mound of the Maui Onion Salad in the center of each serving plate. Slice the chicken breasts and place on top of the salad. Ladle the ponzu sauce over the chicken and top with the eggplant chips. Garnish with the red ginger and, if desired, with the spice sprouts and *furikake*.

Crispy Lemon Grass Chicken with Red Wine Curry Sauce

The batter used for coating the chicken gives this dish an attractive tangy taste and a crunchy texture. The flavorful curry sauce is another Euro-Asian favorite of mine.

Lemon Grass Batter:

½ cup rice flour

1½ tablespoons finely minced lemon grass

3 tablespoons soy sauce

½ teaspoon minced ginger

½ teaspoon minced garlic

1 tablespoon water

2 or 3 ice cubes

Vegetables:

¼ cup julienned carrot

¼ cup Japanese spice sprouts

½ Maui onion, very finely julienned

1 teaspoon black sesame seeds

1 tablespoon sliced red pickled ginger

1 tablespoon Pink Pickled Ginger (page 219)

1 tablespoon *furikake*

2 tablespoons light soy sauce (preferably Yamasa brand)

1 tablespoon unseasoned rice vinegar

Red Wine Curry Sauce:

1 teaspoon peanut oil

½ banana, peeled and sliced

1 cup chopped onions

4 kaffir lime leaves

1 tablespoon chopped shallot

2 tablespoons chopped ginger

2 tablespoons chopped garlic

2 tablespoons finely minced lemon grass

¼ cup red curry paste (preferably Mae Ploy brand or Matsaman curry paste)

2 cups unsweetened coconut milk

½ cup heavy cream

½ bunch fresh cilantro, chopped

4 fresh basil leaves, chopped

1 tablespoon fish sauce

2 tablespoons unseasoned rice vinegar

¼ cup water

2 tablespoons cornstarch

…

½ cup Cabernet Sauce (page 216)

…

4 boneless half chicken breasts, skin removed

To prepare the batter, combine the rice flour, lemon grass, soy sauce, ginger, garlic, and water in a mixing bowl. Mix well and then add the ice cubes. Set aside in the refrigerator.

To prepare the vegetables, put all the ingredients in a large stainless steel bowl and toss lightly. Keep refrigerated.

To prepare the sauce, heat the peanut oil in a skillet and sear the banana over high heat until caramelized. Chop the banana and transfer to a heavy-bottomed saucepan. Add the remaining sauce ingredients, except for the water and cornstarch, and bring to a boil. Turn down the heat to low and reduce the mixture for about 40 to 45 minutes, stirring frequently, until it is slightly syrupy. In a small bowl, add the water to the cornstarch and stir until smooth. Add to the sauce and stir until the sauce thickens. Whisk into the Cabernet Sauce until incorporated and the color is even. Strain through a fine mesh strainer into a double boiler and keep warm while cooking the chicken.

Dredge the chicken breasts in the reserved batter to coat thoroughly. Heat a heavy, dry, nonstick sauté pan (or heat 2 tablespoons canola oil in a regular skillet) and sauté the chicken breasts over medium-high heat for 4 to 5 minutes on each side, until crispy and golden brown.

Slice the chicken breasts, and arrange on warm serving plates. Place the vegetables on top of the chicken and pour the Red Wine Curry Sauce around.

Grilled Chicken with Black Bean Mango Salsa and Crispy Taro

Taro is a highly versatile root vegetable—it can be roasted, boiled, steamed, ground into flour, or pounded to make poi. Here, I slice it into shoestrings and fry it. Commercial taro chips, with their nutty flavor, are a popular alternative to potato chips in Hawaii.

Black Bean Mango Salsa
  (recipe follows)
1 pound large taro, peeled and cut
  into ⅛-inch julienne

1 quart canola or vegetable oil
4 boneless half chicken breasts,
  with skin on
Salt and freshly ground pepper to taste

2 tablespoons olive oil
1 small bunch fresh chives,
  for garnish

Prepare the Black Bean Mango Salsa and set aside. Soak the taro in a bowl of cold water for 30 minutes. Rinse well under running water, drain, and pat dry. Heat the oil in a deep-fryer or large saucepan. When the oil is hot, deep-fry the taro over high heat for about 2 to 3 minutes, until crispy and golden brown. Remove and drain on paper towels.

Prepare the grill. Season the chicken with salt and pepper, and coat with the olive oil. Grill for about 5 minutes per side for medium doneness.

To serve, place about ¾ cup of the Black Bean Mango Salsa in the center of each serving plate. Slice the chicken and stack the slices on top of the salsa. Top with the taro fries and garnish with the chives.

Pictured on opposite page

Black Bean Mango Salsa

½ cup dried black beans, rinsed
2 tablespoons olive oil
½ cup diced onion
½ cup seeded and diced red bell pepper
¼ cup diced celery

⅛ teaspoon ground cumin
⅛ teaspoon pure red chile powder
⅛ teaspoon cayenne powder
Salt and freshly ground pepper to taste

2 tablespoons red wine vinegar
½ cup diced mango (or papaya,
  if you prefer)
½ cup diced watermelon

Put the beans in a saucepan with enough water to cover by 1 or 2 inches. Bring to a boil, reduce the heat, and simmer, covered, until tender, about 45 minutes to 1 hour. Stir the beans occasionally and add more water if necessary. Strain and reserve.

Heat the olive oil in sauté pan and lightly brown the onion over medium-high heat. Stir in the bell pepper, celery, cumin, chile powder, and cayenne, and sauté for 1 minute. Transfer to a stainless steel bowl and season with salt and pepper. Add the cooked beans and the remaining ingredients; toss well to combine. Chill. If you are preparing the salsa ahead of time, add the mango and watermelon just before serving.

Roy's Chinatown Duck with Plum-Peach Sauce

❖ SERVES 4 ❖

Almost all Chinatowns have special delicatessens where you can buy delicious, freshly prepared roast duck any day of the week. This recipe is for those people who don't have access to ready-made Chinatown duck—and for those who want to try duplicating the duck we serve in our restaurants. Part of the secret to our duck lies in the special curing process we use to flavor it and to make the skin crispy. You need to allow at least two days for this; three would be even better. The accompanying Plum-Peach Sauce is my version of the traditional Chinese plum sauce that is always served with roast duck.

2 Long Island ducklings, 5 to 6 pounds each, neck and wings removed

2 tablespoons salt

2 tablespoons freshly ground pepper

20 scallions, roots trimmed

Marinade:

4 quarts water

1½ cups honey

½ cup hoisin sauce

¼ cup soy sauce

6 tablespoons sesame oil

¼ cup unseasoned rice vinegar

2 tablespoons chile paste with garlic (preferably Lan Chi brand)

¼ cup minced ginger

1½ tablespoons minced garlic

2 tablespoons chopped fresh cilantro leaves

Plum-Peach Sauce:

6 tablespoons sugar

¼ cup red wine vinegar

1½ cups Japanese plum wine

2 or 3 fresh plums, pitted and quartered

½ cup canned peaches, with syrup

¼ cup finely minced ginger

1 quart Duck Stock or Chicken Stock (page 213)

Vegetables:

2 tablespoons sesame oil

2 teaspoons minced garlic

2 teaspoons minced ginger

2 whole baby bok choy (Chinese white cabbage)

16 water chestnuts, peeled and sliced

4 ounces shiitake mushrooms, quartered

½ cup rehydrated and julienned dried black mushrooms

½ cup scallions, cut into thin 1-inch-long strips

1 teaspoon oyster sauce

1 teaspoon or more chile paste with garlic (preferably Lan Chi brand or *sambal sekera*)

Salt and freshly ground pepper to taste

...

2 fresh peaches, pitted and sliced, for garnish

*S*eason the cavity of the ducks with the salt and pepper, and place 10 scallions inside each. Refrigerate overnight, but no longer than 12 hours, allowing as much of the surface of the duck to be exposed to air as possible—do not wrap in plastic. The ducks could also be hung to dry in a cool, airy place.

At the end of this period, combine all the marinade ingredients in a large nonreactive saucepan or stockpot and bring to a boil. Remove from the heat and submerge the ducks in the marinade for about 30 minutes. Remove the ducks and stand them in the refrigerator (or hang them) overnight. Refrigerate the marinade, too. The next day, reheat the marinade, and marinate the ducks again for 30 minutes. Return to the refrigerator overnight.

To roast the ducks, preheat the oven to 500 degrees. Set the ducks in a large roasting pan and roast for 10 to 15 minutes, or until the skin becomes crispy. Reduce the heat to 300 degrees and roast for 30 minutes longer, or until the juices run clear when a skewer is inserted in the thigh. Let rest briefly before serving.

To prepare the sauce, heat the sugar in a heavy-bottomed saucepan and caramelize over low heat. Add the vinegar, stir well, and reduce over medium heat until syrupy. Deglaze the pan with the plum wine, and add the plums, peaches, and ginger. Reduce the liquid by half and then add the stock. Reduce further to a saucelike consistency, about 5 to 10 minutes. Strain, and keep warm in a double boiler.

To prepare the vegetables, heat the sesame oil in a wok or large skillet. When very hot, add the garlic and ginger, and stir-fry over medium-high heat for 10 seconds. Add the bok choy, water chestnuts, shiitake mushrooms, black mushrooms, and scallions, and stir-fry briefly. Add the oyster sauce, chile paste, salt, and pepper, and stir-fry until the bok choy is slightly wilted.

To serve, carve the legs off the ducks, leaving them in one piece, and trim away any excess fat. Carefully cut the duck breast away from the carcass, along with the skin. Again, trim off any excess fat, then slice each half breast into 3 or 4 pieces. Place a mound of the stir-fried vegetables on each serving plate and top with the sliced duck breast and a leg. Ladle the sauce around the vegetables and garnish with the peaches.

Cattle grazing on Palawai grasslands, formerly pineapple fields, Lanai.

Gratin of Corn-Fed Turkey with Johnny Apple Stuffing and Creamed Spinach

This recipe is a loose interpretation of the roast turkey dish I prepared one Thanksgiving in my high school home economics course. We were all allowed to bring one guest, and I invited my career counselor. The dish must have come out pretty well because after the dinner, he suggested that I train as a professional chef. In a way, my whole career evolved out of that meal I prepared so many years ago.

1 teaspoon minced garlic
1 tablespoon minced fresh basil
1 tablespoon minced lemon grass
1½ pounds boneless turkey breast, with skin on (preferably corn-fed turkey)
Salt and freshly ground white pepper to taste
2 ounces pork caul fat or bacon

Stuffing:

1 tablespoon olive oil
¼ cup diced onion
¼ cup diced bacon
¼ cup diced celery
½ teaspoon minced fresh sage

1 teaspoon minced fresh thyme
½ teaspoon crushed dried bay leaves
½ teaspoon poultry seasoning
2 cups Chicken Stock (page 213), reduced to 1 cup
4 cups diced French or Italian bread, toasted
1 cup chopped shiitake mushrooms
½ cup peeled, cored, and diced apples

Gratin:

3 egg yolks
2 tablespoons water
1 tablespoon fresh lemon juice
⅔ cup softened unsalted butter
1 tablespoon minced shallots

1 teaspoon crushed black peppercorns
1 cup red wine vinegar
1 tablespoon minced fresh tarragon
½ tablespoon tomato paste
¼ cup whipped cream
2 tablespoons Cabernet Sauce, optional (page 216)

Creamed Spinach:

2 tablespoons unsalted butter
1 pound spinach, stems removed
1 teaspoon minced garlic
½ cup heavy cream
Salt and freshly ground pepper to taste

Preheat the oven to 350 degrees. Combine the garlic, basil, and lemon grass in a small mixing bowl. Pound the turkey breast flat so that it will cook more uniformly, and coat it with the garlic and herb mixture. Season with salt and pepper, and wrap with the caul fat or lay the bacon over the turkey breast. Place in a roasting pan and roast in the oven for 20 minutes, or until cooked to medium doneness. Remove from the oven, and, when cool enough, take off the skin. Allow to rest for about 30 minutes before slicing.

Meanwhile, prepare the stuffing. Heat the olive oil in a large saucepan, and sauté the onion and bacon over medium heat until the onion is golden brown, about 1½ to 2 minutes. Add the celery, sage, thyme, bay leaves, and poultry seasoning and continue to cook for about 1 minute. Add the chicken stock and bring to a boil. Add the bread, mushrooms, and apples. Mix thoroughly. Transfer the mixture to a baking pan, and bake, uncovered, in the oven for 10 minutes at 400 degrees.

To prepare the gratin, first make a hollandaise sauce. Vigorously whisk together the egg yolks, water, and lemon juice in a double boiler, until the mixture begins to thicken and turn pale yellow. Slowly whisk in the softened butter, a little at a time, until thoroughly incorporated. Add a little more water if the sauce is too thick. Combine the shallots, peppercorns, vinegar, and tarragon in another saucepan and reduce over low heat until the mixture is almost dry. Transfer to a stainless steel bowl set over a pan of warm water, add ¾ cup of the hollandaise sauce, and combine. Add the tomato paste, whipped cream, and Cabernet Sauce, if using. Combine thoroughly, and keep warm in a double boiler.

To prepare the spinach, heat the butter in a large sauté pan and sauté the spinach with the garlic over high heat for about 30 seconds, while stirring. Add the cream and cook for about 2 minutes, or until the cream thickens. Season with salt and pepper, and keep warm.

Preheat the broiler. Place 4 mounds of the baked stuffing on a baking sheet. Thinly slice the turkey, and arrange 7 or 8 slices on top of each mound of stuffing. Cover the turkey with a thin layer (⅛ to ¼ inch) of gratin. Broil for about 1 minute, or until golden brown.

Arrange a bed of the creamed spinach on serving plates. Carefully transfer the turkey, gratin, and stuffing from the baking sheet and place on top of the spinach.

Side Dishes and Salsas

*T*he recipes in this chapter are versatile accompaniments that I often use at Roy's. As the preceding fish and meat recipes demonstrate, the sides can be used with a variety of dishes, as well as in different combinations. They fall into two main categories: starches (potatoes and grains) and vegetables. Most are good examples of the disparate culinary styles that I like to combine in the food that I prepare—from Thailand to Japan, North Africa, Italy, France, and back again to the United States. Feel free to mix and match as you see fit.

The first time I ever tasted a salsa I was in my early twenties and living in California. I've since made up for lost time; I started making them at 385 North, and now I love to add a freshly made salsa to fish and meat, especially when its color, flavor, or texture will provide an additional dimension or an interesting contrast to the dish. There's nothing like the refreshing simplicity of a plain salsa made with tomatoes, avocado, onion, or jalapeños.

Salsas may be Latin American in origin, but I enjoy adapting their essential nature to ingredients drawn from around the Pacific Rim. The main consideration, as usual, is that they are made with fresh local produce. This is particularly important for salsas, which are mostly uncooked and consequently reflect the quality of the raw ingredients.

Japanese White Rice

We serve a small plate of Japanese rice with almost every fish entrée at Roy's—it's an Asian tradition that our regular customers love. Japanese rice is a short-grain rice; it's starchier than the long-grain rice that the Chinese favor and when cooked is somewhat stickier and chewier. Short-grain rice is available in most supermarkets under various brand names. It may be labeled medium grain; Calrose is a common variety. Don't buy sweet (glutinous) rice.

Rice can be cooked in a pan on the stovetop, but an automatic electric rice cooker makes the job much simpler and eliminates virtually all the guesswork. For either method, rinse 2 cups of short-grain rice in repeated changes of cold water until the water no longer looks milky (you could also put the rice in a strainer and run it under cold water). Soak the rice in fresh water for 1 hour and drain. Then, if you're using a rice cooker, put the rice in the cooker, add water to the 2-cup mark, cover, and turn the cooker on.

To cook on the stovetop, put the rice and 2 cups of water in a heavy-bottomed saucepan with a tight-fitting lid. Bring to a boil, lower the heat, cover, and cook until the rice is soft and sticky and the water has evaporated, about 15 minutes.

Note: Two cups of uncooked rice will yield about 6 cups of cooked rice, enough for 4 to 6 servings. If you are starting with more or less than 2 cups of rice, you may have to adjust the water somewhat (e.g., 3 cups of rice will probably take slightly less than 3 cups water, 1 cup of rice slightly more than 1 cup of water).

Waterfall and rainforest on the windward Hamakua Coast, Big Island.

Jasmine Rice

⇒ SERVES 4 ⇐

The highly aromatic Thai jasmine rice is a long-grain variety. You can serve it plain, or add diced vegetables and/or fruit to it, as I have done here. It's especially good with fish or chicken. Many regular markets carry jasmine rice; if yours doesn't, look for it at an Asian grocery store.

2 cups jasmine rice

2½ cups water

2 tablespoons olive oil

¼ cup finely diced onion

¼ cup peeled, cored, and finely diced apple

2 tablespoons seeded and finely diced red bell pepper

2 tablespoons finely diced orange segments

3 tablespoons minced fresh basil

Salt and freshly ground pepper to taste

Thoroughly rinse the rice in cold water until the water is clear, and drain. Put the rice in a saucepan with the 2½ cups fresh water and bring to a boil. Reduce the heat and simmer, covered, for 5 minutes, until the water has evaporated and the rice is just cooked but firm to the bite and not soft (the rice should have a risotto-like texture). You can also cook the rice in a rice cooker, but it may take a little longer.

Heat the olive oil in a sauté pan or skillet, and sauté the onion, apple, bell pepper, and orange over medium-high heat for 30 seconds. Remove from the heat, add the cooked rice and the basil, mix thoroughly, and season with salt and pepper.

Harvesting sweet potatoes on George Mokuau's farm, Molokai.

Roy's Feasts from Hawaii

Roy's Mashed Potatoes

※ SERVES 4 TO 6 (ABOUT 4 CUPS) ※

Sometimes, there's nothing quite like good old fashioned mashed potatoes. It's a classic comfort food that goes well with almost everything. I like to add a little garlic to the potatoes; if you like garlic, you can increase the amount, and if you don't, you can leave it out completely.

2 pounds potatoes, peeled and cut into large dice

½ tablespoon salt

1 teaspoon plus 2 tablespoons unsalted butter

½ teaspoon minced garlic, or to taste

1 cup milk

Salt and freshly ground white pepper to taste

Preheat the oven to 300 degrees. Bring a saucepan of water to a boil, add the potatoes and salt, and cook over medium heat until tender, about 15 to 20 minutes. Drain the potatoes and put them in an ovenproof bowl. Whip with an electric mixer until smooth and fluffy. Place in the oven for 2 or 3 minutes so the excess moisture evaporates.

Melt 1 teaspoon of the butter in a small saucepan, and sauté the garlic over low heat for 15 seconds. Stir the garlic into the potatoes. Place the remaining 2 tablespoons butter and the milk in the saucepan, bring to a boil, and stir into the potatoes. Whisk until thoroughly combined and smooth (about 2 minutes if using an electric mixer at medium speed), and season with salt and pepper.

Thai Potato Croquettes

※ SERVES 4 TO 5 ※

This recipe makes for a delicious, if unusual, side dish. It's especially good with chicken and red meat. For a stronger flavor, add more Thai Peanut Dip.

¼ cup Thai Peanut Dip (page 20)

4 cups Roy's Mashed Potatoes (see preceding recipe)

2 eggs

1 cup milk

½ cup flour

2 cups panko

1 cup canola or peanut oil

In a mixing bowl, thoroughly combine the peanut dip and mashed potatoes. Whisk the egg and milk together in a separate bowl to make an egg wash. Place the flour and panko on separate plates. Form the potatoes into 2-inch patties about ½ inch thick. Dredge in the flour, then in the egg wash, and finally in the panko, making sure the potatoes are well coated.

Heat the canola oil in a large sauté pan, and pan-fry the croquettes over medium heat until both sides are crispy and browned. Remove and drain on paper towels.

Crispy Couscous

≫ SERVES 6 TO 8 ≪

Couscous is the staple starch of North Africa, where, much like rice, it is served with stews of all kinds—vegetable, meat, poultry, fish. It looks like a fine-grained rice, but is actually made from semolina flour. The couscous that you buy in the market has been presteamed, so preparing it is just a matter of adding boiling water to it. You can serve it plain, or dress it up, as I have done here.

1 cup couscous

¾ cup boiling water

1 large potato, peeled and cut into large dice

1 tablespoon sesame oil

1 tablespoon minced ginger

2½ teaspoons minced garlic

¼ cup finely diced carrot

¼ cup seeded and diced red bell pepper

¼ cup finely diced sugar snap peas

½ cup coarsely chopped fresh basil

½ cup chopped fresh cilantro

1 cup heavy cream

1 tablespoon oyster sauce

½ cup semolina flour

2 tablespoons peanut oil

Salt and freshly ground white pepper to taste

Place the couscous in a large mixing bowl, add the ¾ cup (or slightly more) boiling water, cover, and let sit for 10 minutes. Meanwhile, boil the potato in lightly salted water until very soft, about 20 minutes. Drain and set aside.

Heat the sesame oil in a heavy skillet and sauté the ginger, 2 teaspoons of the garlic, the carrot, bell pepper, and sugar snap peas over high heat for 15 seconds. Mix into the couscous. When cool, stir in the basil and cilantro.

Heat the cream in a saucepan and reduce to ¼ cup. Place the cooked potatoes in a mixing bowl, and add the reduced cream and the remaining ½ teaspoon garlic. Add the oyster sauce, and beat with a whisk until smooth. Add to the couscous mixture and thoroughly incorporate. Form into 6 to 8 patties, about 2½ inches in diameter and ½ inch thick. Place the semolina flour on a plate and dredge the patties in the flour to lightly coat. Heat the peanut oil in a sauté pan or skillet, and when hot, pan-fry the couscous cakes over medium-high heat until browned on both sides. Remove and drain on paper towels. Season with salt and pepper.

Goat Cheese Hash

⫸ SERVES 4 ⫷

I first cooked this hash at a wine dinner we held at Roy's with Jim Clendenen, the owner and winemaker for Au Bon Climat. It's another side dish containing intense flavors, including my favorite goat cheese produced by the Sayres on their Big Island farm (see page 15). This recipe makes a great side for chicken, pork, and most fish (at the wine dinner, it was served with swordfish).

2 ounces sun-dried tomatoes
  (not oil-packed)
2 tablespoons plus ¼ cup olive oil
2 teaspoons minced garlic

4 ounces shiitake mushrooms, sliced
4 ounces spinach leaves, chopped
8 ounces fresh goat cheese
1½ cups Roy's Mashed Potatoes
  (page 153)

3 tablespoons chopped fresh basil
Salt and freshly ground white pepper
  to taste

*S*oak the sun-dried tomatoes in warm water for 30 minutes or so, until they are soft and fully rehydrated, and then chop them. Heat 2 tablespoons of the olive oil in a large sauté pan. Sauté the garlic and mushrooms over medium heat for 30 seconds. Add the spinach and sun-dried tomatoes, and sauté for 30 seconds longer. Transfer to a mixing bowl and add the goat cheese, mashed potatoes, basil, salt, and pepper. Combine thoroughly and divide into 4 portions. Shape into patties about ½ inch thick. Heat the ¼ cup of olive oil in a heavy skillet, and when hot, pan-fry the hash for about 1½ minutes per side, or until nicely browned.

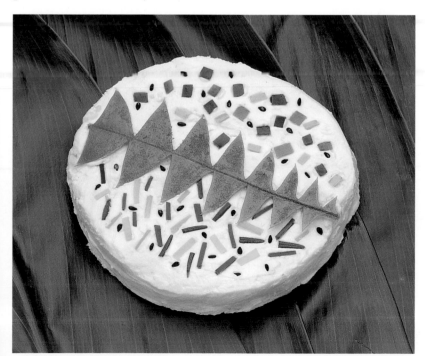

Fresh goat cheese resting on a ti leaf.
Photo by Lois Ellen Frank.

Tuscan-Style White Beans

This is a satisfying and flavorful Mediterranean-style side dish. For a more pronounced tomato flavor, you can add a cup of Napoletana Sauce (page 218). Serve with fish or meat (it is especially good with lamb).

2 tablespoons olive oil
1 tablespoon minced garlic
¼ cup finely diced onion
¼ cup finely diced pancetta
2 tablespoons finely diced celery

2 tablespoons seeded and finely diced red bell pepper
2 tablespoons finely diced carrot
1 tomato, peeled, seeded, and diced
1 teaspoon finely minced fresh thyme

1 teaspoon finely minced fresh rosemary
1 cup dried white navy beans
5 cups Chicken Stock (page 213)
Salt and freshly ground pepper to taste

Heat the oil in a large saucepan, and sauté the garlic, onion, pancetta, celery, bell pepper, and carrot over medium heat for about 2 minutes, until the pancetta renders its fat and becomes a little crispy. Add the tomato, thyme, and rosemary, and stir for 15 seconds. Add the beans and stock, and simmer over medium-low heat for 30 to 45 minutes, or until the beans are just soft but still firm in texture. Season with salt and pepper.

Variation: For **Black Beans**, follow the directions above, substituting 1 cup dried black beans for the white beans, omitting the rosemary, and adding ½ teaspoon achiote powder, if desired.

MOM-AND-POP BUSINESSES are a way of life for many Hawaiians, and a big part of the essential island *ohana*, or spirit. One of the landmarks on the North Shore of Oahu, the Matsumoto Grocery, is one such family operation, and my grandparents' general store, the Yamaguchi Market on Maui, was another. Two of the most popular independent markets on the islands today, Tropic Fish (see page 48) and Tamashiro Market (see page 35), started out as mom-and-pop stores.

Mom-and-pop stores first sprang up as the big sugar and pineapple plantations became established. Their purpose was to service the plantation workers, and they have always sold a wide range of goods, from food to flowers, hardware, and clothing. There are still several examples of these neighborhood stores in Honolulu, although the most successful are having to change with the times as the big stores and chains increasingly dominate the retail trade.

Garlic Spinach

This is a very simple method of cooking spinach lightly with a little additional flavor
Serve as a side with just about anything.

2 tablespoons olive oil
1 teaspoon minced garlic

1 pound spinach leaves
2 tablespoons unsalted butter

Salt and freshly ground pepper
to taste

Heat the oil in a large sauté pan and when very hot, sauté the garlic for 5 seconds. Add the spinach and stir for 1 minute over medium-high heat, until it is wilted and just barely cooked. Swirl in the butter and season with salt and pepper. Remove from the heat and drain off the excess liquid.

Thai-Style Curried Vegetables

Add or substitute vegetables of your choice, and adjust the heat to taste by adding more or less curry powder. I like to serve this side dish with meat and poultry.

2 tablespoons canola oil
2 kaffir lime leaves, minced
2 garlic cloves, minced
1 teaspoon finely minced lemon grass
1 large Japanese eggplant, sliced

1 cup sliced string beans
1 cup seeded and julienned
red bell pepper
1 to 2 ounces miniature corn or
regular fresh corn kernels

1 or 2 ounces water chestnuts,
chopped
1 cup whole shiitake mushrooms
1 teaspoon curry powder, or to taste
¼ cup Thai Peanut Dip (page 20)

Heat the oil in a wok, and when very hot, stir-fry the lime leaves, garlic, and lemon grass over high heat for about 10 seconds. Stir in the eggplant, beans, bell pepper, corn, water chestnuts, and mushrooms, and stir-fry for 1 minute longer. Add the curry powder; after 15 seconds, add the Thai Peanut Dip and stir-fry for another 30 seconds. Remove from the heat and serve.

Asian Ratatouille

Ratatouille is a versatile vegetable dish from the Provençal region of France. Typically, it contains eggplant, tomatoes, zucchini, and bell peppers that are stewed with various herbs. In this recipe, I've given it a distinctly Asian accent by adding the assertive flavors of ginger, lemon grass, lime leaves, oyster sauce, and chile sauce. Serve with fish or lamb.

2 tablespoons sesame oil

2 tablespoons extra virgin olive oil

2 teaspoons minced ginger

1 tablespoon finely minced lemon grass

2 kaffir lime leaves, very finely julienned

1 tablespoon minced garlic

¼ cup seeded and diced red bell pepper

¼ cup seeded and diced yellow bell pepper

½ cup diced onion

½ cup broccoli florets

½ cup diced Japanese eggplant or regular eggplant

¼ cup diced yellow zucchini

¼ cup diced green zucchini

½ tablespoon oyster sauce

1 teaspoon sweet chile sauce (preferably Lingham's brand), or more to taste

¼ cup Chicken Stock (page 213)

¾ teaspoon black sesame seeds

¾ teaspoon toasted white sesame seeds (page 220)

½ cup chopped fresh cilantro

⅓ cup peeled, seeded, and diced tomato

2 tablespoons toasted sliced almonds (page 220), for garnish

$\mathcal{H}$eat the sesame oil and olive oil in a large heavy saucepan, and stir-fry the ginger, lemon grass, lime leaves, and garlic over medium-high heat for 15 to 30 seconds, or until just browned. Add the bell peppers, onion, and broccoli, and stir-fry another 2 minutes, or until golden brown. Add the eggplant and zucchini, and stir-fry 2 to 3 minutes longer. Add the oyster sauce, chile sauce, and Chicken Stock, and cook for 5 minutes to reduce the liquid. Add the sesame seeds, cilantro, and tomato, and simmer for 10 minutes more. Transfer to a bowl and chill. Serve garnished with almonds.

Tomato harvesting at Jefts Farms, Molokai.

Roy's Feasts from Hawaii

The Kula Agricultural Co-operative: Premium Quality from Maui's Small Farms

Kula, lying at an elevation of between 1,500 and 4,000 feet on the lower slopes of Maui's Mount Haleakala, is the agricultural center of Maui. A wide variety of vegetables grow here, including cabbage, bok choy, cauliflower, broccoli, daikon, sweet corn, tomatoes, lettuce, cucumbers, and squash, all flourishing in the rich volcanic soil with the best views

Kula growers Earl and Linda Fujitani with their daughters, Sandy (left) and Tracy.

any vegetable has the right to enjoy. In addition, the region is a center for flower and plant nurseries; proteas, carnations, and chrysanthemums all grow in dazzling abundance.

The Kula Co-operative, which is one of the most active and successful agriculture co-ops in Hawaii, was formed in 1934. It is made up of small-scale farmers who hold, on average, 20 acres of land. About half of all the vegetable growers in the Kula district are members. Many of the growers here are descendants of Japanese sugar and pineapple workers who bought land after their plantation contracts expired. Much of the co-operative's produce is marketed locally, but

Kula sweet onion fields, Maui.

the co-op also ships to the mainland, through California.

Henry Koja, the co-operative's field manager, and Harry Hashimoto, the co-operative's president, took me on a tour of some of the farms in Kula. Henry explained that the co-operative used to be based on tomatoes until a few years ago, but diversification has changed all that. The farmers in the district are nothing if not versatile, and the co-operative helps them identify supply needs and market niches.

At Howard Hashimoto's farm, the primary crop is cabbage, but he rotates part of his land with onion and daikon, and on the particular day I visited he was busy harvesting three acres of sweet Maui onions. Some of his crop was drying under a huge tent while he packed the finished onions into 50-pound bags destined for the mainland market. Howard's three acres might yield up to 35,000 pounds of onions, and that'll make plenty of Maui onion and tomato salads!

Maui onions, hybrids of the Vidalia onion, were developed as a specialized Hawaiian crop in the 1950s, although

regular onions had been grown in Kula for decades before that. Sweet onions take six months to reach maturity, peak size, and sweetness. On the mainland, sweet onions are generally grown in the winter months as they prefer less daylight, but because there's not much difference between the length of days in winter and summer in Hawaii, and because the winter here tends to be too wet, Howard and most other farmers grow onions in summer, harvesting them in the fall. In 1993, 400,000 pounds of Maui onions were exported, 140,000 more than in 1992.

Another major crop in Kula is green cabbage; Henry Koja estimates that 90 percent of all green cabbage sold in the state is grown on Maui, and Hawaiians consume about 300,000 pounds of cabbage every week. Although none is left to export, about one million pounds of bok choy is shipped to California each year between February and April, when the local supply there is out of season. When we visited Earl and Linda Fujitani in their cabbage fields, they told me that they've grown broccoli and bok choy at various times in the eight years they have been farming here. At the time we visited, they were growing seven acres of vibrant green and red cabbage. Earl explained that his decisions regarding what to grow are based on demand, season, rotation, and what grows best in his soil—considerations that summarize the position of most of the Kula farmers.

Creamed Corn

This is a good all-purpose side dish to make when sweet fresh corn hits the market.

2 ears corn, with husks intact
2 tablespoons unsalted butter
⅛ teaspoon minced garlic

1 shallot, minced
⅛ teaspoon minced fresh thyme
1 tablespoon seeded and minced red bell pepper

½ cup heavy cream
Salt and freshly ground white pepper to taste

Grill the ears of corn in their husks for about 10 minutes, turning after 5 minutes to cook evenly. When cool enough to handle, remove the husks and, holding the ears upright on a work surface, cut downwards with a knife to remove the kernels. Heat the butter in a sauté pan and sauté the corn kernels, garlic, shallot, and thyme over medium heat for 1 minute. Add the bell pepper and cream, and cook, stirring, for 1½ minutes longer, or until somewhat thickened. Season with salt and pepper.

Red Bell Pepper Mousse

SERVES 4

With this recipe, you can add more or less cream, to taste. The more you add, the smoother the mousse, but you will decrease the pronounced bell pepper flavor. Wonderful with fish and lobster.

2 large red bell peppers
1 tablespoon olive oil, or more as needed

½ cup to 1 cup heavy cream, whipped until stiff

Salt and freshly ground white pepper to taste

Preheat the oven to 500 degrees. Coat the bell peppers with the olive oil, and place in a roasting pan or baking dish. Cover and roast in the oven for 10 to 15 minutes. Plunge the bell peppers into ice water. Drain and peel; remove the seeds, and pat dry with paper towels. Coarsely chop the peppers, transfer to a food processor, and purée until smooth.

Transfer the purée to a saucepan and cook over low heat for about 5 minutes, stirring, or until most of the moisture evaporates and the purée is very thick. Transfer to a mixing bowl and refrigerate for 1 hour. Using a rubber spatula, fold the whipped cream into the bell pepper purée and blend together thoroughly. Season with salt and pepper, and refrigerate until ready to serve.

160   *Roy's Feasts from Hawaii*

Island Mint Chutney

Chutneys are usually made with fresh or dried fruits that are stewed with vinegar, sugar, and various spices. They are the classic accompaniment for curries, but don't limit yourself. This tropical version, for instance, is also good with grilled or roasted pork, lamb, or game.

½ cup raspberry vinegar

¼ cup red wine vinegar

½ cup peeled, cored, and diced fresh pineapple

½ cup peeled, seeded, and diced papaya

½ cup peeled, pitted, and diced mango

½ cup peeled, cored, and diced apple

½ cup diced orange segments

3 tablespoons honey

1 cup white wine

1 tablespoon seeded and julienned red bell pepper

1 tablespoon seeded and julienned green bell pepper

1 tablespoon seeded and julienned yellow bell pepper

1 bay leaf

4 black peppercorns

2 tablespoons chopped fresh mint leaves

Place the vinegars in a large nonreactive saucepan and reduce over high heat to ¼ cup. Lower the heat to medium, add the pineapple, papaya, mango, apple, and orange, and stir together. Then add the honey, wine, and bell peppers. Tie up the bay leaf and peppercorns in a small square of cheesecloth and add it to the pan. Continue cooking until the liquid has reduced by half; discard the cheesecloth bag and strain the mixture into a clean pan, reserving the fruit. Reduce the liquid until it becomes syrupy, and add back the reserved fruit. Continue to cook another 15 minutes. Remove from the heat, let cool, and stir in the mint. Store in the refrigerator.

Papaya trees, Big Island.

Asian Salsa

This robust salsa stands up well to the complex flavors of red meat. It can also be used with pork or tuna.

1 ripe tomato, peeled, seeded, and diced

½ cup peeled, pitted, and diced ripe avocado

2 tablespoons finely diced onion

1 tablespoon red pickled ginger, minced

1 cup seeded and diced Japanese cucumber, unpeeled

2 tablespoons Thai Peanut Dip (page 20), slightly warmed

½ teaspoon *sriracha* chile sauce

Juice of 2 limes

Juice of 1 orange

¼ cup julienned fresh opal basil

1 tablespoon very finely minced lemon grass

½ cup chopped fresh cilantro

1 kaffir lime leaf, very finely minced

1 teaspoon *shichimi*

Place all the ingredients in a mixing bowl and toss well to combine. Chill before serving.

Shiitake Mushroom and Corn Salsa

Shiso is a hardy Japanese herb with a somewhat minty, lemony taste. The heart-shaped green leaves are chopped up and used to flavor a wide assortment of dishes—vegetables, rice, soups, sushi, and, in this case, a salsa. Fresh shiso *leaves can usually be found in Asian markets. If unavailable, use mint, preferably lemon mint, if you can find it. This salsa is good with fish or poultry.*

10 large shiitake mushroom caps

2 tablespoons olive oil

2 tablespoons sesame oil

⅔ cup fresh corn kernels (from 1 large ear)

½ cup diced Maui onion

1 tablespoon minced ginger

1 tablespoon minced garlic

Salt and freshly ground pepper to taste

1 ripe tomato, diced

¼ cup finely chopped scallions

¼ cup chopped fresh cilantro

Juice of 1 lemon

3 *shiso* leaves (or 10 mint leaves), finely julienned

1 tablespoon light soy sauce (preferably Yamasa brand)

1 teaspoon unseasoned rice vinegar

¼ cup Japanese spice sprouts, top half only

Prepare the grill. Brush the shiitakes with 1 tablespoon of the olive oil and grill until tender. Dice and transfer to a mixing bowl. Heat the remaining 1 tablespoon of olive oil and the sesame oil in a large heavy skillet and sauté the corn kernels, onion, ginger, and garlic over medium-high heat until lightly browned. Remove from the heat, season with salt and pepper, and spread on a cookie sheet to cool. When cool, add to the mushrooms in the bowl, along with all the remaining ingredients. Toss gently but thoroughly, and chill.

Cucumber Caper Relish

Serve with chicken or meaty fish.

1 tablespoon olive oil

½ teaspoon *rayu* (spicy sesame oil)

1 tablespoon grated ginger

¼ teaspoon minced garlic

4 ounces cucumber, peeled, seeded, and diced

¼ cup diced tomato

¼ teaspoon soy sauce

1 tablespoon capers

⅛ teaspoon salt

Freshly ground pepper to taste

Heat the oils in a skillet and sauté the ginger and garlic over high heat for 5 seconds. Add the cucumber and tomatoes and remove from the heat immediately. Add the soy sauce, capers, salt, and pepper and thoroughly combine. Store in the refrigerator.

Black Bean Papaya Relish

This relish is similar to the Black Bean Mango Salsa on page 142, except that is more highly seasoned and the flavors are more complex. Like that salsa, it goes well with fish, poultry, and meat.

Beans:

1½ tablespoons olive oil

¼ cup diced onion

¼ cup diced bacon

4 cups Chicken Stock (page 213)

½ cup dried black beans, rinsed

½ dried ancho chile, seeded

½ bunch fresh cilantro, chopped

½ tablespoon cumin seeds

½ tablespoon pure red chile powder

…

1 cup peeled, seeded, and diced ripe, firm papaya

2 tablespoons seeded and finely diced red bell pepper

2 tablespoons seeded and finely diced yellow bell pepper

2 tablespoons peeled and finely diced jicama

½ jalapeño chile, roasted, seeded, and minced (page 220)

½ tablespoon tamarind paste

Zest and juice of 1 or 2 limes

¼ cup coarsely chopped fresh cilantro

½ tablespoon chopped fresh mint

Heat the oil in a large heavy saucepan and sauté the onion and bacon over medium-high heat until brown. Add the stock, beans, ancho chile, cilantro, cumin, and chile powder, and simmer, covered, for about 2 hours, or until the beans are tender. Stir occasionally and add more stock or water if necessary. When the beans are done, strain and transfer to a mixing bowl. Add the remaining ingredients and toss gently to combine. Chill before serving.

Avocado Salsa

I prefer to use the dark, bumpy-skinned Hass avocado for this salsa because I like its smooth, buttery texture and rich, nutty flavor. You can buy small bottles of chile pepper water in specialty or gourmet stores if you don't have time to make your own. Serve this salsa with chicken, pork, or fish (it's especially good with tuna, ono, opah, or swordfish), or serve it with tortilla chips as an appetizer.

1 to 2 ½-inch-thick slices peeled and cored fresh pineapple

1 firm ripe avocado, peeled, pitted, and diced (reserve the pit)

¼ cup diced ripe tomato

2 tablespoons finely diced red onion

½ cup minced scallions

½ jalapeño chile, seeded and minced

¼ Granny Smith apple, peeled, cored, and diced

Juice of 2 to 3 limes

½ tablespoon chile pepper water, or more to taste (see Roasted Tomato Salsa headnote, page 166)

¼ cup chopped fresh cilantro

Salt and freshly ground pepper to taste

Grill the pineapple slices until browned and caramelized, or sauté in a dry pan or skillet. Dice the pineapple, and place with all the other ingredients in a mixing bowl. Toss gently to thoroughly mix. Place the reserved avocado pit in the salsa to help prevent the salsa from browning (remove before serving). Store in the refrigerator in a covered plastic container.

Kauai Sunrise papayas.

Sun-Dried Tomato Relish

I wish I could say that all of my recipes were invented in a flash of creative inspiration, but this is not always the case. For example, this recipe came about after I realized I had ordered too many sun-dried tomatoes for the restaurant! The salsa also contains green (unripened) papaya, which adds a little crunch. This is an all-purpose accompaniment that's particularly suited to pork, chicken, and most fish.

½ cup sun-dried tomatoes
  (not oil-packed)

¼ cup white wine (optional)

2 fresh basil leaves

1 clove roasted garlic (page 220),
  minced

1 teaspoon peanut oil

½ tablespoon capers

2 tablespoons finely diced fennel root

2 tablespoons seeded and diced
  roasted red bell pepper (page 220)

2 tablespoons grated green papaya

1½ tablespoons finely julienned
  fresh basil

Juice of ¼ large lemon

Zest of ¼ large lemon

3 tablespoons extra virgin olive oil

Place the sun-dried tomatoes in a bowl with the wine (if using), basil leaves, and garlic. Add warm water to cover, and let steep until the tomatoes are soft and fully rehydrated, about 30 minutes. Meanwhile, heat the peanut oil in a small skillet and sauté the capers over medium-high heat until crispy. Drain on paper towels, patting off any excess oil. Place in a mixing bowl and add the remaining ingredients. Strain the rehydrated tomatoes, finely dice, and add to the bowl. Toss all the ingredients well to thoroughly combine. Store in the refrigerator.

Ripening mangoes.

Roasted Tomato Salsa

I was inspired to create this spicy salsa after listening to a two-hour discourse on chiles given by my friend Mark Miller, of Coyote Cafe in Santa Fe. The addition of chile pepper water (look for it in gourmet stores) gives an otherwise basic salsa plenty of heat. Serve chilled with pork or chicken.

6 tablespoons canola oil
2 or 3 ripe beefsteak tomatoes
6 to 8 cloves garlic

¼ cup chopped fresh cilantro
½ cup diced Maui onion
Salt and freshly ground pepper
   to taste

¼ cup red wine vinegar
Juice of 3 limes
¼ cup chile pepper water

Heat 4 tablespoons of the canola oil in a large cast-iron skillet and blacken the tomatoes over medium heat, turning to blacken evenly. Heat the remaining 2 tablespoons of the oil in a separate skillet and sauté the garlic over medium heat until soft and lightly browned. Put the blackened tomatoes and garlic in a blender, add the remaining ingredients, and blend until smooth. Store in the refrigerator.

Tropical Island Salsa

This fruity salsa contains a delicious array of tropical flavors. It goes best with tuna or pork.

½ cup peeled, cored, and diced fresh
   pineapple
½ cup peeled, cored, and diced
   Granny Smith apple
½ cup peeled, pitted, and diced ripe,
   firm mango

2 tablespoons minced red onion
¼ cup chopped fresh cilantro
1 tablespoon finely minced ginger
1 jalapeño chile, roasted, seeded,
   and minced (page 220)

1 ripe tomato, peeled, seeded and
   diced
2 tablespoons fresh passion fruit juice
Juice of 2 limes

Gently combine all the ingredients in a mixing bowl. Chill before serving.

Opposite page: Guava harvesters, Kilauea Agronomics, Kau

Brunch

Brunch is an American institution that I became aware of only after I'd graduated from culinary school. My first brunch was at Bruce Marder's West Beach Cafe in Los Angeles. I ordered huevos rancheros with chorizo (the fact that I remember exactly what I ate proves that it made an impression on me), and it was to be the first of many brunches I enjoyed while I was living in California.

One theory is that brunch originated in New Orleans; another (supported by H.L. Mencken) asserts that it was imported from England at the turn of the century. While brunch is a popular weekend meal in many parts of the country, it's not such a big deal in Hawaii. This is probably because there's so much to do here, so many beaches to enjoy, and so little time to fit it all in.

Many of the recipes in this chapter are the creation of Gordon Hopkins, my chef de cuisine and partner at Roy's in Honolulu. We serve brunch on special occasions, such as Mother's Day, on some weekends during the holiday season, and year-round at Roy's in Tokyo.

Whether you're making these recipes on the East Coast, in the Midwest, on the West Coast, in Hawaii, or perhaps even further afield, and whether you're celebrating or not, Gordon's dishes are the best way imaginable to ease into the day ahead.

Hawaiian Sweet Bread

❯❯ YIELD: 2 LOAVES ❮❮

In the late 1800s, large numbers of Portuguese came to the islands to work on the sugar plantations. One of the foods they introduced to Hawaii was their pao doce, a soft, sweet, egg-rich bread. It has since become a staple here (you'll find it in every grocery store and bakery), and it's usually labeled Hawaiian sweet bread, even though it's really Portuguese. Here is my own version of this bread. Not only is it delicious on its own (try it toasted), but it makes a good beginning for the French toast recipe that follows and for Johnny's Griddle-Top Bread Pudding (page 174).

½ cup evaporated milk, at room temperature

1 package (1 tablespoon) active dry yeast

6 cups bread flour, unsifted

1½ cups hot water

2 eggs

4 tablespoons unsalted butter

¼ cup instant potato flakes

½ cup sugar

¼ teaspoon salt

1 teaspoon lemon extract

1 teaspoon pure vanilla extract

Place the evaporated milk in a bowl and sprinkle the yeast over the milk; let sit for 5 minutes, or until the yeast has dissolved. Transfer to the bowl of an electric mixer together with the flour, water, eggs, butter, and potato flakes. Using the dough hook, knead at low speed for about 7 minutes; the dough should be fairly soft. Cover the bowl with plastic wrap and let the dough rise in a warm place for 1 hour, or until doubled in bulk. (You may mix and knead the dough by hand, if you prefer, in which case you should knead the dough on a floured surface until the dough is smooth and elastic. Use additional flour to keep it from sticking, but keep extra flour to a minimum. Put the dough in a lightly greased bowl, cover, and let rise as above.)

Add the sugar, salt, and lemon and vanilla extracts to the dough and knead again at low speed for 7 minutes (or by hand for about 10 minutes). Divide the dough in half and form into two balls. Place in greased 8-inch round cake pans, cover, and let the dough rise again for 1 hour.

Preheat the oven to 375 degrees and bake the loaves for about 1 hour, or until the bread is dark brown and sounds hollow when tapped on the bottom. Cool in the pans for 15 minutes, then remove and cool on a wire rack.

French Toast with Caramelized Apples, Strawberries, Star Fruit, and Plums

This recipe gives a distinctively Hawaiian, tropical accent to the classic brunch dish.

6 eggs, beaten

1 cup milk

¼ teaspoon pure vanilla extract

6 tablespoons packed brown sugar, plus additional for the apples

1½ teaspoons ground cinnamon

8 thick, triangular slices Hawaiian Sweet Bread (see preceding recipe), or your favorite bread

1 large apple, peeled, cored, and cut into 12 slices

4 tablespoons unsalted butter

¼ cup whipped cream

4 sprigs fresh mint

4 plums, pitted and each cut into 7 slices

2 star fruit (carambolas), each cut into 8 slices

8 strawberries, diced

4 tablespoons toasted macadamia nuts, chopped (page 220)

1 cup pure maple syrup, warmed

*I*n a mixing bowl, whisk together the eggs, milk, vanilla extract, brown sugar, and cinnamon with a wire whisk. Soak the bread in the batter, giving it a little time to completely absorb all the liquid.

Lightly coat the apple slices in brown sugar. Heat 1 tablespoon of the butter in a nonstick pan, and sear the apples until the sugar caramelizes. Reserve and keep warm. Using the remaining 3 tablespoons of the butter, cook the bread slices until evenly brown on both sides. (You can use the same nonstick pan or a griddle, if you wish.)

Transfer two pieces of French toast to each serving plate, and top with 3 slices of apple, a dollop of whipped cream, and a mint sprig. Arrange a circle of the plum slices around the French toast, with the 4 slices of the star fruit evenly spaced about. Sprinkle with the strawberries and macadamia nuts, and serve with the maple syrup.

Pictured on opposite page

Strawberries at the Hilo open market.

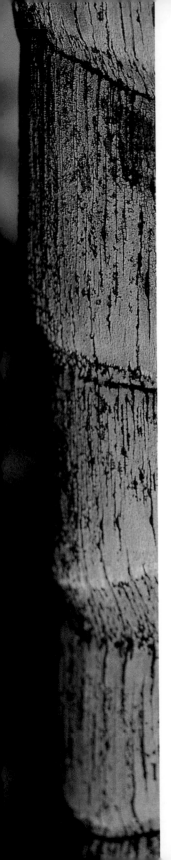

Johnny's Griddle-Top Bread Pudding with Fresh Fruit Coulis

⟫ SERVES 12 ⟪

This brunch dish should be cooked the previous day so it can chill overnight. It is named for one of my former managers who adored this dish. The recipe makes quite a lot, but leftovers freeze well—unless, of course, Johnny is around and gets to them first! Just cut into serving-sized portions, and freeze in an airtight bag.

Bread Pudding:

4 cups milk

8 eggs

1 cup sugar

½ tablespoon pure vanilla extract

¾ teaspoon salt

1 loaf day-old Hawaiian Sweet Bread (page 171), or your favorite bread, cut into ¾-inch cubes

⅔ cup raisins

½ tablespoon ground cinnamon

½ tablespoon ground nutmeg

Garnishes:

¾ cup Raspberry Coulis (page 175)

¾ cup Papaya Coulis (page 175)

12 strawberries, cut in half

6 kiwifruit, peeled and cut into wedges

½ cup confectioners' sugar

12 fresh mint leaves

...

1 cup pure maple syrup, warmed

*B*lend the milk, eggs, sugar, vanilla extract, and salt together in a blender and chill. Preheat the oven to 250 degrees. Place the bread in an 8 x 12-inch baking pan and add the chilled milk and egg mixture; allow 10 to 15 minutes for the bread to absorb all the liquid (a little stirring may help this along). Stir in the raisins, cinnamon, and nutmeg. Bake in the oven for 2 hours, or until the bread pudding is firm and cooked. Let cool, and refrigerate overnight.

Cut the bread pudding into 3-inch squares, place on a hot griddle or in a large skillet, and brown evenly on both sides over medium heat. Drizzle 1 tablespoon of both fruit coulis on each serving plate and then spoon the cooked bread pudding on top. Garnish each plate with 1 strawberry and the kiwifruit, sprinkle with the confectioners' sugar, and place a mint leaf on top of the bread pudding. Serve with the maple syrup.

Papaya grove, Big Island.

Roy's Feasts from Hawaii

Banana Pancakes with Raspberry Coulis and Candied Pecans

SERVES 4 (12 PANCAKES)

I created this recipe for a Mother's Day brunch. They're a far cry from the pancakes Thomas Jefferson served at Monticello.

¼ cup Raspberry Coulis (recipe follows)

1½ cups flour

1 tablespoon sugar

1 tablespoon baking powder

Pinch of salt

1 egg plus 1 egg white, beaten

1½ cups whole milk

3 tablespoons canola oil

5 firm, ripe bananas, peeled

2 to 3 teaspoons granulated sugar

4 sprigs fresh mint

2 kiwifruit, peeled and cut in quarters

4 strawberries, cut in half

¼ cup confectioners' sugar

4 teaspoons chopped Candied Pecans (page 219)

1 cup pure maple syrup, warmed

Prepare the Raspberry Coulis and set aside. Place the flour, sugar, baking powder, and salt in a mixing bowl, stir together, and form a well in the center. Pour in the eggs, milk, and canola oil, and mix until blended but still a little lumpy. Avoid overmixing or the pancakes will be less light and fluffy.

Cut 4 of the bananas into 9 slices each, and the remaining banana into 8 spears. Sprinkle the spears with a little sugar, and grill or broil until browned.

Heat a lightly oiled griddle to 350 degrees, or a large sauté pan until just smoking. With a ¼-cup measure, ladle 3 circles of batter onto the griddle or pan. When bubbles start to form, place 3 banana slices on each pancake. Flip over and cook the other side. Stack the 3 pancakes on a serving plate, keep warm and repeat for the other 3 servings.

Place two banana spears and a mint sprig on top of each stack of pancakes. Drizzle a tablespoon of the Raspberry Coulis around each plate, and garnish the coulis with 2 kiwifruit quarters and 2 strawberry halves. Sprinkle with the confectioners' sugar and Candied Pecans, and serve with the warm maple syrup.

Raspberry Coulis

This coulis recipe can be made with other fruits, such as strawberries, papayas, or mangoes. Just substitute the same amount of fruit for the raspberries.

4 ounces fresh raspberries   3 tablespoons Simple Syrup (page 216)

Purée the raspberries with the syrup in a blender, and strain through cheesecloth. Adjust the consistency of the coulis by adding more puréed fruit or more syrup if desired.

Japanese-Style Seafood Frittata with Sautéed Spinach and Shrimp Butter Sauce

❧ SERVES 4 ❧

This brunch favorite is inspired by okonomiyaki, *the Japanese dish eaten at any time of day that's a cross between a pancake and an omelet. It's also reputed to be an infallible hangover cure!*

4 teaspoons sesame oil	4 teaspoons grated ginger	Garnish:
4 ounces scallops, diced	8 eggs	4 tablespoons red pickled ginger, well drained
4 ounces shrimp, peeled, deveined, and diced	2 to 3 teaspoons canola oil or unsalted butter	20 fresh chives
8 ounces shiitake mushrooms, sliced	4 teaspoons sliced scallions	4 tablespoons *rayu* (spicy sesame oil)
4 Roma tomatoes, diced	Salt and freshly ground pepper to taste	Shrimp Butter Sauce (recipe follows)
½ onion, diced	Garlic Spinach (page 157)	1 teaspoon *shichimi*
		2 teaspoons black sesame seeds

Heat the sesame oil in a sauté pan and sauté the scallops and shrimp over medium-high heat until barely cooked through, about 30 seconds. Add the mushrooms, tomatoes, onion, and ginger, and sauté for 30 seconds longer. Set aside.

Make a mold to shape the frittatas, using a strip of aluminum foil about 12 inches wide and 18 inches long. Fold the strip in half lengthwise first, then form a ring by overlapping the ends of the strip. (You can mold the aluminum into a circle or square, or whatever shape you like.) For each frittata, beat 2 eggs in a small bowl. Heat an ovenproof sauté pan over medium-high heat, place the foil mold in the middle of the pan, and put a little of the canola oil or butter in the center. Spread one-quarter of the mushroom-seafood mixture inside the mold, pour in the eggs, and sprinkle in 1 teaspoon of scallions. Season to taste with salt and pepper. When the bottom is cooked to a golden brown, place the pan under the broiler and cook until done, about 1 to 2 minutes. Repeat for the remaining frittatas.

Arrange a bed of the Garlic Spinach on each serving plate, and top with a frittata. To garnish, put 1 tablespoon of the pickled ginger mounded in the center of each frittata, with 5 chives stuck upright in the ginger. Drizzle a little *rayu* around the plate, followed by a drizzle of Shrimp Butter Sauce, and sprinkle with the *shichimi* and sesame seeds.

Pictured on opposite page

Shrimp Butter Sauce

1 to 2 cups Shrimp Stock (page 214)	½ cup *Beurre Blanc* (page 216)	Salt and freshly ground pepper to taste

Place the Shrimp Stock in a saucepan and reduce it over medium-high heat to a thick paste (about 1 to 2 tablespoons). Warm the *Beurre Blanc* in a double boiler. Whisk in the Shrimp Stock until well blended, and season with salt and pepper. Serve immediately, or keep warm in a double boiler.

Roy's Feasts from Hawaii

Fresh Mushroom Frittata with Potatoes, Onions, Cheese, and Pancetta

This frittata (or open-face omelet) is made differently than the previous recipe, and it's easier to prepare. My preference is to cook it until the edges become slightly charred.

1 potato (about 6 ounces), unpeeled, diced

2 teaspoons clarified butter

8 ounces mixed mushrooms, cut into quarters

4 teaspoons finely diced pancetta

½ large red bell pepper, seeded and diced

½ large green bell pepper, seeded and diced

1 onion, diced

2 Roma tomatoes, diced

8 eggs

4 teaspoons canola oil

4 teaspoons scallions, angle-cut

Salt and freshly ground pepper to taste

4 to 8 ounces mozzarella cheese, grated

Garnish:

1 onion, thinly sliced and sautéed in clarified butter until golden brown

4 teaspoons Basic Tomato Sauce (page 215)

4 sprigs fresh parsley

4 teaspoons Pesto (page 214)

Bring a pan of salted water to a boil, and cook the potato for 5 minutes. Drain and set aside.

Heat the clarified butter in a large sauté pan and sauté the mushrooms, pancetta, bell peppers, onion, and boiled potato over medium-high heat for about 1 minute. Add the tomatoes, cook briefly, and remove from the heat. Divide the mixture into 4 portions.

For each frittata, beat 2 eggs in a small bowl. Heat 1 teaspoon of the canola oil in an omelet pan or small skillet, and add one-quarter of the sautéed vegetables. Add the eggs and 1 teaspoon of the scallions, and season with salt and pepper. When the eggs have set, flip the frittata and cook until the underside is golden yellow. Flip again, sprinkle a quarter of the cheese over the top and cook until the cheese melts. Remove to a serving plate and keep warm. Repeat for the remaining frittatas.

To garnish, place some of the sautéed onions in the center of each frittata. Add a teaspoon of the Basic Tomato Sauce to the onions and top with a sprig of parsley. Drizzle 1 teaspoon of the Pesto around each frittata.

Louisiana Crab Cakes Benedict with Andouille and Tarragon-Mustard Sauce

This recipe was inspired by popular demand—and our customers are always right. Make the crab cakes the same way as you would make the Kona Crab Cakes (page 121), but omit the basil. If you form the crab cakes ahead of time, you can fry them as the eggs are poaching. Just remember that the vegetables and seasonings for the crab cakes have to be sautéed first and then allowed to chill for an hour before you can make the crab cakes.

8 crab cakes (see note above)

Tarragon-Mustard Sauce:

1 teaspoon clarified butter

1 teaspoon minced red bell pepper

1 teaspoon minced green bell pepper

1 teaspoon minced yellow bell pepper

½ cup *Beurre Blanc* (page 216)

2 teaspoons whole-grain mustard

2 teaspoons minced fresh tarragon

. . .

1 quart water

¼ cup white vinegar

8 eggs

¼ cup diced andouille sausage

2 teaspoons minced fresh parsley for garnish

Heat the clarified butter in a sauté pan and sauté the bell peppers over medium-high heat for about 1 minute, or until soft; drain any excess butter. Warm the *Beurre Blanc* in a double boiler. Whisk in the mustard and sautéed bell peppers. Stir in the tarragon and keep warm.

Bring the water and vinegar to a boil in a saucepan, lower the heat, and simmer for 2 minutes. Carefully crack 1 egg at a time into the water and cook for 3 to 4 minutes. Heat a dry sauté pan or skillet over medium-high heat and sauté the andouille for about 1 minute.

Place 2 crab cakes on each serving plate. Remove the eggs from the water with a slotted spoon, drain excess water on paper towels, and place 1 egg on top of each crab cake. Place the andouille next to the crab cakes and pour a little sauce over the eggs. Sprinkle with the parsley and serve.

Volcanic crater, Haleakala National Park, Maui.

Roy's Homemade Corned Beef Hash with Poached Eggs

I love corned beef hash, but all too often what you get looks like, tastes like, and probably is canned. With its strands of home-cooked corned beef, this recipe is a Sunday brunch treat that will appeal to everyone. Plan ahead: the corned beef needs to cook for four or five hours. If you have leftover corned beef, have another round of corned beef hash, or use it for sandwiches.

Corned Beef:

2 teaspoons canola oil

1 small onion, diced

1 small carrot, diced

1 stalk celery, diced

1½ to 2½ pounds corned beef

1 to 2 tablespoons chopped fresh basil

1 to 2 tablespoons chopped fresh thyme

1 to 2 tablespoons chopped fresh tarragon

...

½ cup clarified butter

½ red bell pepper, seeded and julienned

½ green bell pepper, seeded and julienned

½ yellow bell pepper, seeded and julienned

1 Maui onion, diced

1½ tablespoons minced garlic

4 ounces mushrooms, sliced

2 ounces fresh spinach, chopped

1 teaspoon mixed chopped fresh herbs (such as basil, thyme, and rosemary)

1 cup Chianti Sauce (recipe follows)

1 cup Basic Tomato Sauce (page 215)

8 eggs

¼ cup warm *Beurre Blanc* (page 216)

1½ tablespoons chopped fresh parsley, for garnish

1½ tablespoons mixed finely diced red, green, and yellow bell peppers, for garnish

$\mathcal{H}$eat the canola oil in a large saucepan and sauté the onion, carrot, and celery for 30 seconds over high heat. Add the corned beef, herbs, and enough water to cover. Simmer for 4 or 5 hours, or until the meat is soft enough to fall apart (add more water as needed). Strain and let cool. Shred the meat (you need about 1 pound for this recipe).

Heat the clarified butter in a pan and sauté the bell peppers, onion, garlic, mushrooms, and spinach over medium-high heat until well cooked. Add the shredded corned beef and mixed herbs and continue to sauté until slightly crispy. Add ¾ cup of the Chianti Sauce and the Basic Tomato Sauce, and reduce until the saauce has thickened and most of the liquid has evaporated.

Meanwhile, poach the eggs to the desired doneness (see preceding recipe). Make two "nests" of corned beef on each serving plate, and place 2 poached eggs in each. Drizzle 1 tablespoon of the *Beurre Blanc* over the eggs and around the hash. Drizzle the remaining Chianti Sauce around the hash. To garnish, sprinkle the parsley and bell pepper confetti over the plate.

Chianti Sauce

¼ cups chianti wine

½ cup sugar

¾ cup *Beurre Blanc* (page 216)

$\mathcal{C}$ombine the chianti and sugar in a heavy-bottomed saucepan and reduce over medium-high heat to about ¼ cup. Remove from the heat and let cool until just warm, then whisk in the *Beurre Blanc*. Keep warm in a double boiler.

Oriental Gravlax

✤ SERVES 4 ✤

This recipe gives the traditional Swedish gravlax, or cured salmon, an Oriental twist. To make the transformation, I coat the fish with white miso, which is mild and rather sweet, then cure it in a mixture that contains a number of highly aromatic Asian ingredients.

1 pound fresh salmon fillet, skin on
½ cup (*shiro miso*) white miso
1 cup brown sugar
1 cup white sugar

1 cup kosher salt
½ cup minced ginger
1 tablespoon minced garlic
⅓ cup minced lemon grass

4 kaffir lime leaves, chopped
1 tablespoon *shichimi togarashi*
1 cup chopped fresh cilantro

With a sharp knife, lightly score the skin of the salmon lengthwise with three parallel cuts, just breaking the skin. Rub the miso over the entire salmon.

Combine the remaining ingredients in a large stainless steel bowl. Lay out a piece of plastic wrap that's big enough to wrap up the fish. Spread with half of the curing mixture in roughly the shape of the piece of salmon. Place the salmon on top and spread it with the remainder of the curing mixture. Wrap the salmon carefully, making sure the package does not leak, and set on a platter. Refrigerate for 6 hours.

Remove the plastic wrap and rinse off all of the seasoning. Slice the salmon thinly and arrange on serving plates. Serve with triangle-shaped pieces of toast, or with a light salad.

SUGARCANE (Ko) IS A GIANT GRASS that was originally introduced to the Hawaiian islands by the South Pacific Polynesians who first settled the archipelago. They would cut the cane and chew on the sweet juice.

Once the first commercial sugar plantations were established on Kauai in 1835 (and then on the other islands), all aspects of Hawaiian life changed irrevocably. Plantation owners began to import foreign labor, and successive waves of immigration from China, Japan, Portugal, Puerto Rico, the Philippines, and Korea (among many other countries) laid the foundation for the multicultural population that makes up today's Hawaii.

The major sugar companies—Alexander and Baldwin, C. Brewer and Co. Ltd., Castle & Cook, Theo H. Davies, and Amfac—not only formed the economic backbone of Hawaii until recent years, but molded the islands' political history. Tourism and the federal government have now surpassed the sugar industry in economic importance, and although acreage has continued to decline, sugar still accounts for more than 15,000 jobs statewide, directly or indirectly. Pictured here is Maui's Puunene Sugar Mill.

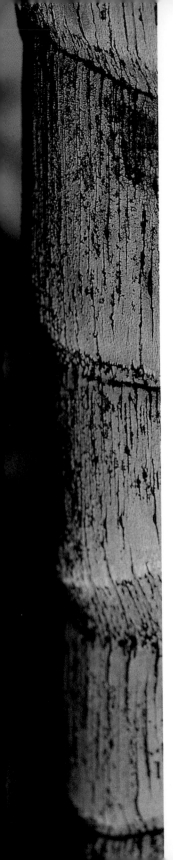

Loco Moco Bistro-Style

⟫⟫ SERVES 4 ⟪⟪

Loco Moco is a hefty local dish consisting of rice, a hamburger, and a couple of fried eggs all piled up on top of each other, with plenty of brown gravy to give it the final touch. It's really delicious—but so is this slightly more elegant version. The cucumber salad we serve it with needs at least an hour to marinate and chill.

Cucumber Salad (recipe follows)

4 cups hot Japanese White Rice (page 151)

¼ cup *furikake*

2 tablespoons pickled red ginger, sliced

4 salmon fillets, about 3 ounces each

¼ cup Szechwan Marinade (page 36) or teriyaki sauce

4 eggs

2 tablespoons sesame or canola oil

1 cup Sweet Ponzu Sauce (page 217)

Garnish:

4 teaspoons black sesame seeds

2 tablespoons scallions, angle-cut

*P*repare the Cucumber Salad.

Prepare the hibachi or barbecue grill. Press the hot rice into cups and turn upside down to unmold onto serving plates. Sprinkle with half the *furikake*, half the pickled ginger, and all the Cucumber Salad.

Brush the salmon fillets with the Szechwan Marinade or Teriyaki Sauce and grill for about 2 minutes per side for medium-rare. Place the salmon on top of the Cucumber Salad and rice.

Fry the eggs in the sesame or canola oil to the desired doneness and place on top of the salmon. Ladle ¼ cup of the Sweet Ponzu Sauce over each egg, letting the sauce run down onto the plate. Garnish with the remaining *furikake* and pickled ginger, the sesame seeds, and scallions.

Cucumber Salad

12 ounces Japanese cucumber, seeded and finely julienned, or firm regular cucumbers

¾ cup peeled, seeded, and diced tomatoes

1 teaspoon dried red chile flakes

2 tablespoons minced anchovies

¼ cup fish sauce

1 tablespoon fresh lemon juice

2 cups water

*C*ombine the cucumber, tomatoes, and red chile flakes in a mixing bowl. Set aside in the refrigerator. In a saucepan, bring the anchovies, fish sauce, lemon juice, and water to a boil, and reduce to about ¼ cup. Refrigerate. When chilled, add to the cucumbers and tomatoes, and marinate for 1 hour before serving.

Shrimp Spring Rolls with Orange-Chile Sauce

⋙ SERVES 4 ⋘

I created this recipe because I wanted a healthy, fresh brunch dish with clean, strong flavors. I decided on Vietnamese-style spring rolls, which are quite light because, unlike Chinese spring rolls, they are not fried. One of the filling ingredients is harusame, or "spring rain" noodles, which are thin, translucent noodles made from rice or potato flour. Harusame is sold in Asian stores as Japanese saifun. If you can't get it, you can substitute Chinese bean thread noodles.

Orange-Chile Sauce (page 217)

16 to 20 extra-large shrimp (about 1 pound), peeled and deveined

3 ounces *harusame* or bean thread noodles

1 cup warm water

1 teaspoon sugar

4 sheets round rice paper wrappers

8 avocados, peeled, pitted, and cut into 16 strips about ¼ inch wide

4 cucumbers, peeled, seeded, and cut into 8 strips about ¼ inch wide

1 small carrot, finely julienned

2 ounces bean sprouts

1 ounce Japanese spice sprouts

20 fresh mint leaves

Garnish:

1 teaspoon black sesame seeds

8 chives, about 5 inches long

Prepare the Orange-Chile Sauce and keep warm.

Steam the shrimp in simmering water for 1 minute, or until pink and cooked through. Let cool. Cook the *harusame* or bean thread noodles in boiling water for 7 to 10 minutes, until soft but still firm.

Place 1 cup of water in a shallow dish and dissolve the sugar in it. Soften a wrapper by dipping the rice paper into the sweetened warm water for 5 to 10 seconds. Pat dry with a clean kitchen towel and lay out on a flat work surface. About an inch up from the bottom of the wrapper, place a band of avocado, cucumber, carrot, bean sprouts, spice sprouts, and mint leaves across the wrapper (leave a 1-inch margin on either side). Add a layer of *harusame* or bean thread noodles, and place 4 or 5 shrimp side by side on top of the noodles. Roll the wrapper up from the bottom, tucking in the sides to form a neat cylinder. Repeat for the remaining wrappers. Slice each roll into 4 pieces.

Stand 4 pieces upright next to each other in the center of each plate. Pour some of the reserved sauce around the spring rolls, and garnish with the sesame seeds. Arrange the chives so they stick out of the center of the arrangement.

Pictured on page 185 (lower right)

Shrimp Hash with Spicy Lobster Sesame Sauce

⋙ SERVES 8 ⋘

I created this popular brunch item as an alternative to corned beef hash (page 180) when some of our customers requested a hash made with mashed potatoes.

Spicy Lobster Sauce:
1 cup *Beurre Blanc* (page 216)
2 to 3 tablespoons Lobster Paste (page 215)
1 teaspoon *shichimi*
2 tablespoons *rayu* (spicy sesame oil)
2 tablespoons unseasoned rice vinegar
...

16 to 20 extra-large shrimp (about 1 pound)
½ cup canola oil
1 teaspoon minced garlic
Salt and freshly ground pepper to taste
1 tablespoon finely diced onion
1 tablespoon seeded and finely diced red bell pepper

1 tablespoon seeded and finely diced green bell pepper
1 tablespoon sliced scallions
¼ cup diced shiitake mushrooms
1½ tablespoons finely chopped fresh basil
1½ cups Roy's Mashed Potatoes (page 153)
Hot milk, as necessary

Combine all the sauce ingredients in a double boiler and keep warm.

Set aside 8 whole shrimp, with their heads on. Peel, devein, and coarsely chop the remaining shrimp. Heat 2 tablespoons of the canola oil in a sauté pan and sauté ½ teaspoon of the garlic and the chopped shrimp over high heat for about 15 seconds (it should not be cooked through). Season with salt and pepper. Finely dice the shrimp mixture and reserve in a mixing bowl.

Heat another 2 tablespoons of the canola oil and sauté the remaining ½ teaspoon of garlic over medium-high heat for about 5 seconds. Add the onion, bell peppers, scallions, mushrooms, and basil, and sauté for 2 minutes. Season with salt and pepper. Add the vegetables to the diced shrimp, along with the mashed potatoes, and thoroughly combine. Adjust the seasonings, and soften with a little hot milk, if necessary. Form into 16 patties.

Heat 2 more tablespoons of the canola oil in a sauté pan or skillet and sauté the patties over medium heat until nicely browned, about 1½ minutes per side. In a separate skillet, heat the remaining 2 tablespoons of the canola oil and sauté the 8 whole shrimp until cooked through. Remove from the heat and let cool slightly. Remove and reserve the shrimp heads, and peel the tails of the shrimp.

To arrange each serving, place 1 peeled shrimp in the center of the serving plate with a shrimp hash patty on either side. Place a shrimp head in front of the tail and a pool of the sauce on the opposite side.

Pictured on opposite page (upper left)

Roy's Feasts from Hawaii

Kona Coffee: Only from Hawaii!

The unique growing conditions and altitude of the Kona region in the southwestern part of the Big Island support the only commercial coffee industry in the United States. Coffee beans (coffee "cherries") are the fruit of small tropical trees that prosper at an elevation of one to two thousand feet, in a dry climate with seasonal rainfall, as long as they have shade to protect them from scorching, and protection from the wind.

Most of the coffee in Kona is grown on small farms of less than five acres; many growers belong to the Kona Growers Co-operative. Coffee trees take three years before producing their first crop, and two additional years to reach full maturity and maximum production. Each year, a coffee tree will produce about five pounds of coffee cherries, which is enough to yield about three-quarters of a pound of roasted coffee. Think about *that* ratio when you sip your next cup!

A lot has to happen before the hand-harvested cherries become drinkable. The fruit ripens in waves between August and February; they are taken to a mill and passed through a pulper, which removes the covering from the bean (the pulp is used for mulching). The beans are spread on large decks and dried in the sun for about five or six days, after which the tough outer parchmentlike skin (rather like the covering of peanuts) can be removed mechanically. The beans are then graded by size and roasted for about 15 minutes to a rich, dark brown color. Each batch is custom-roasted to allow for differences in quality, moisture content, and the desired darkness of the roast.

Coffee trees, originally native to the highlands of Ethiopia, were brought to Oahu from Brazil in the early 1800s. Cuttings were then brought to the Kona region for propagation as ornamental trees in 1828. Shortly thereafter, coffee began to be grown commercially in Kona at suitable elevations. In 1875, *A Hawaiian Guide Book* commented, "Respecting coffee, we must say that there is no more delicious coffee in the world than that grown in Kona, Hawaii."

Since the late 1800s, when Kona coffee was first grown in substantial amounts, world coffee prices determined a cyclical trend of boom and bust for Kona coffee growers. Then,

Coffee cherries and flowers, Greenwell Farms, Kealakekua, Big Island.

in the late 1960s and early 1970s, stringent quality control of the Kona crop was introduced and improved marketing further upgraded the reputation of Kona coffee. The boom in coffee drinking since the mid-1980s has arrested the decline in production, brought about by increasingly high labor costs, and prospects for the future are bright.

Opposite: Raking coffee beans as they dry in the sun, Bayview Farms, Kealakekua, Big Is

Desserts

One of Hawaii's great natural resources is its vast array of tropical fruits. Many of these, including bananas, coconuts, and breadfruits, were brought here by the first Polynesian settlers. Others, like the mango, papaya, pineapple, watermelon, and guava, were introduced by more recent settlers from other regions.

Fruit was used extensively by the ancient Hawaiians. Bananas were considered a delicacy, and were eaten both fresh and cooked in the imu (underground oven). Mashed, cooked bananas were used for a version of poi if taro was unavailable. Likewise, coconut milk was mixed with arrowroot and made into Haupia Cake (see page 196).

The recipes that follow give these distinctly Hawaiian ingredients a modern twist, sometimes with the help of techniques or ingredients from Europe or Asia. You'll also find our popular chocolate desserts—we'd invite hate mail if we didn't include them.

With one or two exceptions, the recipes in this chapter are simple to make and straightforward; all of them will bring a little of the tropics and their spirit to your dinner table. Most were created or perfected by Casey Logsdon, our talented pastry chef at Roy's Kahana Bar and Grill on Maui.

A few words of advice: Do not underestimate the impression a wonderful dessert can make. After all, it's the parting indulgence you can offer your guests, and who doesn't enjoy a creamy, rich, delicious finale to a meal? Use the freshest, best-quality ingredients you can find. These desserts tend to require exact quantities of ingredients, so I recommend that you follow the recipes the first time around before you experiment or substitute different ingredients.

Coconut Mousse with Hana Bay Rum-Soaked Pineapple and Coconut Tuiles

❯❯ SERVES 4 ❮❮

We like to use Hana Bay Premium Gold Rum in this recipe, but any premium light rum will give you the same rich flavor. Tuiles (pronounced tweels) are crispy curved cookies, perfect for serving with mousses.

¼ cup peeled, cored, and diced fresh
    pineapple

¼ cup Hana Bay rum

Mousse:

¼ cup Hana Bay rum

1 tablespoon unflavored gelatin

1½ cups milk

⅓ cup sugar

½ vanilla bean, split lengthwise

2 tablespoons cornstarch

2 eggs, beaten

2 cups heavy cream

1 cup shredded coconut

Coconut Tuiles:

2 tablespoons unsalted butter,
    at room temperature

¼ cup sugar

1 egg white

¼ cup flour

1½ tablespoons shredded coconut

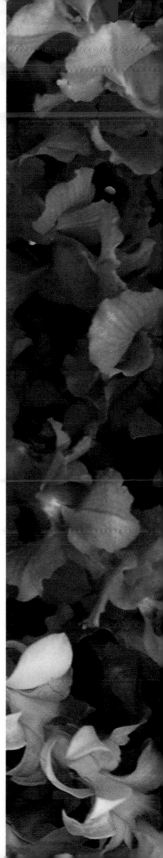

Place the pineapple in a small bowl, add the rum, and chill.

To prepare the mousse, combine the rum and gelatin in a small bowl. Let stand to allow the gelatin to soften. Meanwhile, prepare a custard by bringing the milk, half of the sugar (2 tablespoons and 2 teaspoons), and the vanilla bean to a boil in a saucepan. Remove from the heat and discard the vanilla bean. In a mixing bowl, whisk the cornstarch and remaining sugar lightly to remove any lumps. Whisk in ¼ cup of the hot milk mixture and the eggs, and continue to whisk until incorporated. Bring the remaining milk mixture back to a boil, and whisk in the egg mixture. Reduce the heat to medium, and continue stirring until the custard has thickened. Remove from the heat.

Whip the heavy cream until it forms soft peaks and set aside.

Transfer the rum and gelatin mixture to a saucepan and warm over medium heat until all of the gelatin dissolves. Remove from the heat. Add 3 tablespoons of the custard and return the pan to the heat, stirring with a wire whisk until the custard is incorporated. Stir in the remaining custard and the coconut, then gently but quickly fold in the reserved whipped cream with a rubber spatula. Remove from the heat and set aside. When cool, chill this mousse in the refrigerator for 2 hours.

To prepare the tuiles, preheat the oven to 350 degrees and line a baking sheet with parchment paper. Cream the butter and sugar together with an electric mixer or by hand. Add the egg whites and flour, and beat until smooth. Using a rubber spatula, spread the dough into 4 circles on the parchment paper, sprinkle with 2 tablespoons of the shredded coconut, and bake in the preheated oven for 15 minutes, or until golden brown. Remove from the oven and immediately mold the wafers around inverted large ramekins to form the tuiles. (You may find it easier to bake and mold the tuiles in two separate batches.)

To serve, thoroughly drain the rum-soaked pineapple. To serve, place a scoop of the mousse inside each tuile, and scatter the pineapple around the mousse and tuile. Garnish with remaining coconut.

Strawberry Petals

※ SERVES 4 ※

This is a simple dish that looks stunning. Be sure to plan ahead when you wish to make it because the custard has to chill overnight. There are some great strawberry farms in "up-country" Maui, on the slopes of Mount Haleakala, the island's imposing volcano. We'd travel from Tokyo to visit my grandfather when I was a kid, and one of my strongest childhood food memories is of gorging on plump, ripe Maui strawberries.

2 cups whole milk
¾ cup sugar
½ vanilla bean, split lengthwise

3 tablespoons cornstarch
3 eggs, beaten

1 pint fresh strawberries, stems and crowns removed

Place the milk, ¼ cup of the sugar, and the vanilla bean in a saucepan, bring to a boil, and remove from the heat. Discard the vanilla bean. In a mixing bowl, whisk the cornstarch and ¼ cup of the sugar together lightly to remove any lumps. Whisk in ¼ cup of the hot milk mixture, then add the eggs and continue to whisk until incorporated. Bring the remaining milk mixture to a boil and whisk in the egg mixture. Reduce the heat to medium and continue stirring, until thickened. Strain into a bowl, cover with plastic wrap, and chill in the refrigerator overnight.

When ready to serve, whisk the custard until smooth, and spread on a large serving platter. Slice the strawberries and arrange in a flower pattern or circle over the custard, working from the outside in. Sprinkle with the remaining ¼ cup of the sugar and place the dish under the broiler briefly to caramelize to a golden brown. If you prefer, you can use a handheld propane torch to caramelize the sugar.

Taro and Coconut Pudding

❋ SERVES 4 ❋

Poi, which is simply a mash of cooked taro, is an important staple in the Hawaiian diet. It's so common in the islands that all the grocery stores carry it (it comes packed in plastic bags). Mixed with coconut milk, sweet fresh poi makes a delicious, creamy tropical pudding. There's no substitute so, unfortunately, if you can't get fresh poi where you live, then you'll have to skip this recipe.

3 cups unsweetened coconut milk
1 cup whole milk
1½ cups sugar

2 tablespoons cornstarch
3 eggs, beaten
¼ cup fresh poi

Garnish:
1 papaya, peeled, seeded, and quartered
Whipped cream (optional)

Place 2 cups of the coconut milk in a saucepan and reduce over medium heat to 1 cup; it should be as thick as heavy cream. Add some whole milk to thin slightly, if necessary. Keep warm or refrigerate, depending on whether you are serving the pudding warm or cold (see serving methods below).

In a saucepan, heat the remaining 1 cup coconut milk, the whole milk, and 1 cup of the sugar over medium heat, stirring frequently until it almost comes to a boil. Remove from the heat. In a mixing bowl, lightly whisk the cornstarch and the remaining ½ cup of sugar, to remove any lumps. Add the eggs, and whisk until smooth. Whisk in ½ cup of the hot milk mixture and continue to whisk until incorporated. Bring the remaining milk mixture back to a boil and whisk in the egg mixture. Reduce the heat to medium and continue stirring, until thickened. Remove the custard from the heat.

Briefly stir in the poi (it should not be completely incorporated) and pour into 4 large soup bowls. Serve the pudding hot with the cold coconut milk poured over, or chill the pudding and serve with hot coconut milk. Thinly slice each papaya quarter, fan out the slices, and garnish the pudding. Add a dollop of whipped cream, if desired.

Harvesting taro at Haraguchi Farm, Hanalei, Kauai.

Big Island Cheesecake with Coconut Crust and Macadamia Nut Praline

The texture of the coconut crust makes a perfect contrast with the smooth, silky goat cheese that Karin and Steve Sayre supply us from their farm in Puna (see page 15).

Crust:
4 tablespoons unsalted butter
2 cups grated fresh coconut

Filling:
4 ounces goat cheese
4 ounces cream cheese
1 cup sour cream
½ cup sugar

Zest and juice of 1 lemon
1 papaya or mango, peeled, seeded (or pitted) and very thinly sliced
…
Macadamia Nut Praline, for garnish (recipe follows)

Preheat the oven to 300 degrees.

To prepare the crust, melt the butter in a saucepan and stir in the coconut until is has absorbed the butter. Press the coconut into the bottom of a generously buttered 8-inch springform pan, gradually increasing the thickness to about ¼ inch. Bake in the oven for about 15 minutes, until lightly browned. Set aside to cool, and lower the oven temperature to 275 degrees.

Using an electric mixer fitted with a paddle attachment, prepare the filling by beating the goat cheese, cream cheese, and sour cream together until well blended and creamy. Add the sugar and beat another 3 minutes. Add the lemon juice and zest, and beat for 3 minutes more. Set aside.

Arrange the sliced papaya or mango over the cooled crust, then spread the filling evenly over the fruit. Bake in the oven for 45 minutes, or until slightly firm but still a little soft. Garnish with chunks of the Macadamia Nut Praline.

Macadamia Nut Praline

1½ cups water

¾ cup sugar

4 ounces macadamia nuts, toasted and chopped (page 220)

To prepare the praline, bring the water and sugar to a boil in a saucepan. Keep the heat on high, and when the sugar begins to caramelize, stir to even the caramelization process. When the sugar is a clear golden brown, add the macadamia nuts immediately. Stir with a wooden spoon to coat the nuts thoroughly with the sugar mixture. Spread out evenly on a baking sheet to cool. When the praline has set completely, break it into the desired shapes, or coarsely chop.

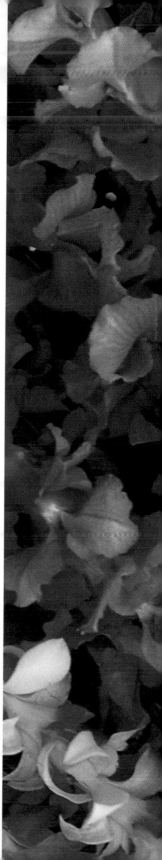

Lemon Tart

❊ SERVES 8 TO 10 ❊

I particularly like to make this simple recipe when juicy Meyer lemons are in season, from October through December. Because they are less acidic than regular lemons, you can use less sugar.

1 prebaked 9-inch Sweet Tart Shell (page 198)
2 eggs plus 3 yolks
Zest of 1 lemon

⅔ cup fresh lemon juice
1 cup sugar
½ cup unsalted butter, at room temperature

Brown sugar (optional)
16 to 20 fresh raspberries, for garnish

Make the tart shell, using a 9-inch tart pan with a removable bottom. (There will be excess dough, which you can save for another purpose.)

In a mixing bowl, whisk together the eggs, egg yolks, lemon zest, lemon juice, and sugar until smooth. Transfer to a double boiler and whisk continuously, until very thick, about 10 minutes. Add the softened butter and continue to whisk. When incorporated, immediately pour the custard into the tart shell. (The custard will set immediately after you stop whisking. If you need to soften it, place in a double boiler again and whisk.) If desired, sprinkle the custard liberally with brown sugar and place under the broiler to caramelize, until browned. If you prefer, you can use a handheld propane torch to caramelize the sugar. Refrigerate for 1 hour before serving. Garnish with raspberries or other fruit of your choice.

Variation: For **Lemon Custard Brûlée**, omit the tart shell. Pour the lemon custard into deep soup bowls (there should be enough for 4 to 6 servings). Top each serving with two peeled lemon segments. Glaze with brown sugar, if desired, as described above.

Macadamia Nuts, Mauna Loa Macadamia Nut Corporation.

Haupia Cake

Haupia is a coconut pudding, usually made firm enough so that after it has set, it can be cut into small squares and eaten out of hand. It's a traditional Hawaiian dessert that's commonly served at parties and luaus. It was even served at an official state luau held for the Emperor and Empress of Japan when they visited Honolulu recently. In this recipe, the haupia is used as a filling and frosting for a cake. For best results, make the cake the day before you plan to serve it (or even several days). If you want to dress it up even more, serve it with a fresh tropical fruit salad.

Sponge Cake:
1 cup cake flour
1 teaspoon baking powder
2 eggs plus 2 yolks
1 cup sugar

½ cup water
2 tablespoons unsalted butter
Haupia:
4 cups unsweetened coconut milk
2 cups water

1 cup sugar
½ cup cornstarch
…
1 tablespoon shredded coconut, for garnish

Preheat the oven to 350 degrees and grease a 9-inch round cake pan. To prepare the sponge cake, sift the flour and baking powder into a small mixing bowl. Using an electric mixer, beat the eggs and yolks at high speed for about 4 minutes, or until thick. Gradually add the sugar to the eggs and beat at medium speed for 4 or 5 minutes, until light and fluffy. Add the flour mixture to the eggs and beat at medium-low speed until just combined. Put the water and butter in a saucepan and stir over medium heat until the butter melts. Add to the batter and beat until combined.

Pour the batter into the prepared baking pan. Bake in the oven for 20 to 25 minutes, or until an inserted toothpick comes out clean. Let the cake cool in the pan briefly, then remove and cool on a wire rack. Cover with plastic wrap or foil and place in the freezer, preferably overnight.

To prepare the haupia, place the coconut milk, 1 cup of the water, and the sugar in a saucepan and bring to a boil. Mix the cornstarch and the remaining 1 cup of water together in a bowl, add to the pan, and stir until the mixture returns to a boil and thickens. Remove from the heat and keep warm in a double boiler.

Remove the sponge cake from the freezer and cut a thin slice off the top to level off the cake. Slice the cake in half horizontally to make two even layers. Pour the haupia over the bottom layer, to a thickness of about ½ inch. Place the top layer of cake over the haupia, gently pressing down. Pour more of the haupia over the top of the cake, using a spatula to spread it around evenly. Any remaining haupia can be spread over the sides with a spatula (or chill it in a small shallow pan, cut it into squares, and serve with the cake—or eat it before your company arrives!). Refrigerate the cake for 3 to 4 hours. When ready to serve, garnish with the shredded coconut.

Roy's Feasts from Hawaii

Tropical Island Tart

I was lucky enough to have learned how to make tart shells from the late Jean Bertranou at L'Ermitage. This dessert combines some of the bounty of locally grown fruits, all with their own distinct flavors and textures.

Flaky Tart Shell:

1¼ cups pastry flour

10 tablespoons chilled unsalted butter, chopped

⅓ cup sugar

1 egg yolk

Filling:

½ cup peeled, cored, and diced fresh pineapple

3 eggs

1 cup sugar

¼ cup flour

¾ cup unsalted butter

1 teaspoon pure vanilla extract (or to taste)

½ cup fresh raspberries

1 mango, peeled, pitted, and cubed

½ cup fresh blueberries

½ cup toasted macadamia nuts (page 220)

…

20 to 24 fresh raspberries, for garnish

Place all the tart shell ingredients in a food processor and blend until they stick together. Form into a ball, cover with plastic wrap, and chill in the refrigerator for 30 minutes.

Remove the dough from the refrigerator and roll out on a lightly floured work surface into a circle at least 13 inches in diameter and about ⅛ inch thick. Ease the dough into an 11-inch tart pan with a removable bottom, running the dough up the sides of the pan with the excess lapping over the edge. Trim the excess off with a knife or by running a rolling pin along the rim of the tart pan. Place the tart shell in the freezer for 15 minutes.

Preheat the oven to 350 degrees. Line the tart shell with foil and place some dried beans or pie weights on top. Bake in the oven for 15 minutes. Remove the foil and beans or weights and bake another 5 to 10 minutes, until a pale golden brown. Place the tart pan on a wire rack to cool.

To prepare the filling, place the pineapple in a sauté pan and cook over medium heat until the juice has evaporated. Set aside. In an electric mixer, beat together the eggs, sugar, and flour until well blended. Heat the butter in a sauté pan over medium-high heat until it turns golden brown and has a nutty flavor, about 3 minutes; take care not to burn it. Immediately pour the butter into the flour mixture, add the vanilla, and beat well. Gently fold in the sautéed pineapple, the remaining fruit (except the berries for garnish), and the macadamia nuts.

Pour the filling into the prepared tart shell. Bake in the oven for about 30 minutes, or until the filling is set. Remove and cool on a rack. When cool, remove the sides of the pan and cut the tart into slices. Serve garnished with the raspberries.

Caramelized Pineapple Tart

Until just recently, more pineapples were grown in Hawaii than anywhere else in the world.

2 cups peeled, cored, and diced fresh
   pineapple

Sweet Tart Shell:

¾ cup confectioners' sugar

½ cup unsalted butter, at room
   temperature

½ tablespoon pure vanilla extract

1 egg

2 cups flour

1 cup sugar

3 tablespoons cornstarch

¼ cup water

Place the diced pineapple in a strainer and let it drain for 2 to 3 hours, reserving the juice.

Using an electric mixer, prepare the tart shell by creaming the confectioners' sugar, butter, and vanilla together until just incorporated. Add the egg and beat for 1 minute. Add the flour and mix just until smooth; be careful not to overmix. Cover with plastic wrap and refrigerate overnight.

When ready to make the tart, preheat the oven to 350 degrees. Unwrap the dough and knead gently on a lightly floured work surface to soften slightly. Roll the dough out to a ⅛-inch thickness and trim to fit an 8- or 9-inch tart pan. Gently place the dough in the pan, line with foil, and weight the foil down with dried beans or pie weights. Bake in the oven about 15 minutes. Remove the foil and beans or weights and bake another 5 to 10 minutes, until a pale golden brown. Place the tart pan on a rack to cool.

Place the drained pineapple in a sauté pan with the sugar and sauté over medium heat, stirring constantly with a wooden spoon until the mixture becomes caramelized and syrupy and the pineapple is well glazed, about 5 to 8 minutes. Pour the caramelized pineapple back into the strainer and let it drain for about 1 hour, again reserving the juice.

Place all the reserved pineapple juice in a sauté pan and bring to a boil. In a bowl, mix together the cornstarch and water, add to the pan, and stir until the mixture returns to a boil and thickens. Add the drained caramelized pineapple, stir for 1 minute, and remove from the heat. Pour the pineapple filling into the tart shell, spreading it evenly with a spatula. Refrigerate for 2 hours before serving. Serve with whipped cream or Vanilla Ice Cream (page 208).

PINEAPPLE IS THE HAWAIIAN SYMBOL of hospitality. Native to Central and South America, pineapples were first grown in Hawaii in the early 1800s. It was one hundred years later that the first successful pineapple plantation and cannery was established by James B. Dole. For years, the Dole Honolulu pineapple cannery was the largest fruit cannery in the world.

In the 1920s, much of Lanai was given over to pineapple, and big pineapple plantations were on all of the main islands. For decades, pineapple was the second-largest industry in hawaii (after sugar), employing over 200,000 workers when sales were at their peak. In recent years, most of the pineapple industry, like sugar, has shifted to Southeast Asia, where production costs are lower. However, pineapples are still a major Hawaiian crop and a popular gift many visitors take back with them to the mainland.

Roy's Feasts from Hawaii

Banana Mousse with Mac' Nut Cream

Not only are the flavors of this dessert deliciously rich, but the contrast between the cold mousse and the warm cream is almost addictive.

6 ripe bananas, unpeeled

...

Mac' Nut Cream:

¾ cup unsalted butter

2 cups sugar

1½ cups coarsely chopped
  macadamia nuts

1 cup heavy cream

Whipped Sweet Cream Garnish:

1 cup heavy cream

½ teaspoon sugar

Preheat the oven to 400 degrees.

Place the bananas on a baking sheet, and bake until they turn black and the skins split, about 10 minutes. Let cool a little and then peel the bananas and purée in a food processor or blender. Line six 2-inch ramekins with parchment paper. Pour the purée into the ramekins and refrigerate for 2 hours.

To prepare the Mac' Nut Cream, melt the butter in a saucepan, add the sugar and macadamia nuts, and bring to a boil. Continue boiling until the mixtures turns a dark golden brown. Stirs in the cream until incorporated, remove the pan from the heat and cool to room temperature. When ready to serve, warm the Mac' Nut Cream gently. For the garnish, whip the cream with the sugar until soft peaks form.

To serve, place a chilled banana mousse on each serving plate and remove the parchment paper. Top with the whipped cream and pour the warm Mac' Nut Cream around.

Richard Ha at the Keeau banana plantation, Big Island.

Banana-Macadamia Nut Bread

≫ YIELD: 1 LOAF ≪

This rich and delicious bread makes an excellent dessert served plain or topped with whipped cream or a scoop of homemade ice cream (page 208). It also makes good toast and terrific bread pudding (see recipe page 202). You can even serve it with turkey, as an alternative to corn bread.

½ cup unsalted butter, at room temperature

¾ cup sugar

½ cup brown sugar

1 pound overripe bananas, peeled and mashed

2 teaspoons baking powder

2 teaspoons baking soda

3⅓ cups flour

2 eggs

⅓ cup water

½ cup chopped macadamia nuts (reserve 2 tablespoons for the topping)

¼ cup raisins (optional)

¼ cup shredded coconut (optional)

Preheat the oven to 350 degrees. Grease and flour a 9-inch round cake pan or loaf pan.

In the bowl of an electric mixer, cream together the butter and sugars until smooth. Add the bananas and beat for 1 minute. Sift the baking powder and baking soda into the flour, and stir into the banana-butter mixture. Add the eggs and water, and beat for 1 minute. Stir in the nuts, and the raisins and coconut, if desired.

Pour the batter into the prepared pan and sprinkle with the reserved nuts. Bake on the middle rack of the oven for 35 to 45 minutes, or until a toothpick inserted in the middle comes out clean. Remove from the oven and let cool on a wire rack.

Hand-gathering macadamia nuts in the Mauna Loa Corporation's orchards, Keaau, Big Island.

Roy's Feasts from Hawaii

Macadamia Nuts: A Favorite Way to Savor Hawaii

Rich, buttery macadamia nuts are synonymous with Hawaii, where 90 percent of the world's commercial crop is grown. The evergreen macadamia tree was first brought from its native Australia to Hawaii around 1880 by a sugar plantation owner who admired the tree for its ornamental quality. However, he happened to import the variety of macadamia that yields bitter-tasting nuts, and it wasn't until the 1920s that orchards were planted with the edible variety of macadamia. The nuts were first pioneered as a cash crop in the 1930s, which was when macadamia nuts began to reach the Hawaiian market.

Several Hawaiian sugar and pineapple companies recognized the potential for growing macadamia nuts on marginally profitable plantations, and several large orchards were planted on the Big Island in the 1940s and 1950s. The combination of the rich but porous volcanic soil, the abundant rainfall, and the tropical climate proved ideal for the macadamias. Among the early large-scale growers was the C. Brewer and Co. Ltd. and when it bought Castle & Cooke's Keaau orchard in 1974, it became the largest grower of macadamia nuts in the world, marketing the nuts under the Mauna Loa label. Mauna Loa's main orchard and processing factory is located just outside Hilo (the "Macadamia Nut Capital of the World").

Growing macadamias is a labor-intensive operation: each tree must be grafted to ensure quality, and is planted two months later. The trees

Here I am with Mauna Loa Macadamia Nut Corporation's chairman and CEO, Doc Buyers, at the C. Brewer and Co. Ltd. headquarters in downtown Honolulu.

only start to bear nuts at five years old, and reach full-bearing potential at fifteen years of age. The trees blossom periodically and yield nuts in waves, requiring five or six harvests annually. Mechanical harvesters collect half the fallen nuts, but crews of hand-pickers are needed to harvest those in less accessible locations. The nuts are then shelled, dried, and processed, which in itself is an extensive operation.

The Mauna Loa plantation employs about five hundred people—one hundred to tend the orchards and pick the nuts, and the rest in the processing and packaging plant on three shifts every day. There are close to one million trees on ten thousand acres, which are divided into sections by rows of tall Norfolk pines, which act as windbreaks. This is a necessary precaution—a severe windstorm in 1986 destroyed fifteen thousand trees.

About half of the macadamia nut crop is consumed in Hawaii, either by residents or visitors. The bulk of sales is made up of the whole, roasted, lightly salted nuts, but other tasty macadamia nut products include brittle, Kona coffee-glazed nuts, honey-roasted nuts, and chocolate-covered nuts.

Roy's Bread Pudding
❧ SERVES 4 TO 6 ❧

Although you can make this recipe with any bread, it's best made with Hawaiian Sweet Bread (page 171). In fact, I was inspired to add this dessert to our menu after munching on some of the wonderful Hawaiian Sweet Bread that our pastry chef Casey Logsdon makes at our restaurant on Maui. Another option is to use the Banana-Macadamia Nut Bread from the preceding recipe.

1 loaf Hawaiian Sweet Bread (page 171) or Banana-Macadamia Nut Bread (page 200), cut into 1-inch dice

1½ cups diced mixed dried fruit, (such as banana, pineapple, apricot, apple, and papaya)

1 quart whole milk

1 cup sugar

9 eggs

Preheat the oven to 250 degrees. Spread the diced bread on a baking sheet, and place in the oven to dry. (Alternatively, slice and toast the bread, then dice it.) Increase the oven temperature to 350 degrees. Place the bread in two 9-inch cake pans or a large casserole (the pans or dish should only be filled to about three-quarters capacity). Sprinkle the dried fruit on top of the bread and set aside.

Warm the milk and ½ cup of the sugar in a large saucepan over medium heat (do not allow it to come to a boil). Remove from the heat. In a mixing bowl, beat the eggs together with the remaining ½ cup sugar, and stir into the warm milk. Strain through a fine sieve over the bread in the cake pans or casserole. Place in a water bath on the bottom rack of the oven, and bake for 1 hour, until firm. Serve hot or warm.

THESE CACAO BEANS are grown by Jim Walsh's Hawaiian Vintage Chocolate company in the Kona and Keaau regions of the Big Island. What makes Jim's chocolate special is that it's the only brand that uses beans grown in the United States (it also tastes terrific!). After harvesting, the beans are roasted and then shipped to San Francisco, where they are ground and refined into premium-quality bittersweet and white chocolate.

The name of the company refers to Jim's practice of aging the beans for a year and marketing the chocolate by vintage, or the year the beans were picked. Hawaiian Vintage Chocolate is available by mail in one-pound quantities (808-735-8494).

Roy's Feasts from Hawaii

Chocolate Kona Coffee Mousse

⁂ SERVES 4 TO 6 ⁂

Most people are surprised to learn that cocoa beans are now grown on the Big Island. The beans are processed in California for the Hawaiian Vintage Chocolate company, which means it's the only chocolate made from beans grown in the United States. Likewise, Kona, on the Big Island, is the only coffee-growing region in the country.

10 ounces semi-sweet chocolate

4 egg yolks

2 tablespoons sugar

2½ cups heavy cream

2 tablespoons finely ground Kona coffee beans

Garnish:

Whipped cream

Finely ground Kona coffee beans, (optional)

*B*reak the chocolate into chunks and place in a double boiler set over hot, but not boiling, water. Allow the chocolate to melt and then remove from the heat.

Place the egg yolks in a separate stainless steel bowl, again over hot but not boiling water. Whisk until the yolks turn pale in color and are hot to the touch. Add the sugar and continue whisking until incorporated. Set aside.

In a mixing bowl, whisk the cream until stiff peaks form. Fold ½ cup of the cream into the yolks, and then fold in the melted chocolate until smooth. Add the remaining whisked cream and coffee, and mix until well blended.

Transfer to a pastry bag and pipe into wine glasses. Chill in the refrigerator for at least 3 hours before serving. Garnish with additional whipped cream and a dusting of the finely ground coffee beans, if desired.

Freshly roasted Kona coffee beans, ready for grinding.

Chocolate Coconut Macadamia Nut Tart

There's nothing like the combination of nuts and chocolate, as is evidenced by this recipe. Rich macadamia nuts make a particularly popular partner for chocolate, and, if you need proof, you'll find boxes of chocolate-covered macadamia nuts in just about every food and convenience store in Honolulu.

1 prebaked 9-inch tart shell (page 198)

Filling:

½ cup unsalted butter

½ cup sugar

1½ cups heavy cream

1 cup chopped macadamia nuts

½ cup freshly grated coconut

1 cup sour cream

3 eggs

2 tablespoons cornstarch

6 ounces semi-sweet chocolate chips

Garnish:

1 cup Whipped Sweet Cream (page 199)

¼ cup lightly toasted macadamia nuts (page 220)

¼ cup fresh raspberries (optional)

Melt the butter in a saucepan and add the sugar. Raise the heat to high and boil the mixture until it caramelizes, about 2 to 3 minutes. Remove from the heat and add ½ cup of the cream, the toasted nuts, and the grated coconut to the caramel. Mix together thoroughly and pour into the tart shell. Chill in the refrigerator for 1 hour.

To prepare the second layer of filling, heat the remaining 1 cup of heavy cream and the sour cream in a heavy saucepan over medium heat, but do not boil. In a mixing bowl, combine the eggs and corn-starch. Add a little of the hot cream mixture to the mixing bowl to temper the cornstarch mixture, and return this mixture to the saucepan. Stir until thickened, remove from the heat, and add the chocolate chips. Mix well until the chips are completely melted, and then pour the mixture over the chilled caramel layer in the tart shell. Chill the tart in the refrigerator for 1 hour. Garnish with the whipped cream, macadamia nuts, and raspberries.

Roy's Chocolate Soufflé

This is the all-time, absolute favorite of my daughter, Nicole. Casey Logsdon, our pastry chef at Roy's Kahana Bar and Grill on Maui, has perfected this recipe to the point where frequent visitors to the island claim they return just for this soufflé. We've made things easier for them now, by also serving this dessert in Honolulu. This recipe is best when started the day before so the chocolate mixture can rest overnight in the refrigerator. If you prefer, you can bake the whole recipe in a small casserole dish and serve it at the table, or make the individual soufflés in ramekins. We make our individual chocolate soufflés in metal rings that are available from J.B. Prince Co. in New York (212-683-3553).

6 tablespoons unsalted butter	¾ cup sugar	2 eggs plus 2 egg yolks
4 ounces semi-sweet chocolate	1¾ tablespoons cornstarch	

*I*n a saucepan over low heat, melt the butter and chocolate together. Set aside.

In a mixing bowl, combine the sugar and cornstarch. In a separate bowl, whisk the eggs and yolks together. Add the melted butter-chocolate mixture to the sugar mixture and combine thoroughly with a wire whisk. Stir in the eggs and whisk just until smooth. Place in the refrigerator overnight.

Preheat the oven to 400 degrees. Line 4 metal rings (about 2¾ inches across and 2 inches high) with greased parchment paper. (Alternatively, use 6 smaller molds.) Line a baking sheet with parchment paper and set the molds on the sheet. Scoop the mixture into the molds so they are two-thirds full, and make sure the molds are not leaking.

Bake on the top oven rack for 20 minutes. Remove the baking sheet from the oven, and, while holding each mold with tongs, slide a metal spatula underneath, carefully lift, and transfer to a serving plate. Gently lift off the mold and remove the parchment paper. Serve immediately.

Pictured on page 207 (lower left)

Winter surf crashing on Oahu's North Shore.

Tropical Ratatouille Fruit Gyoza with Passion Fruit Cream and Macadamia Nut Praline

West meets East once more as I use my fruit version of the Provençal vegetable dish to fill potsticker wrappers.

Tropical Fruit Filling:

3 tablespoons diced orange

3 tablespoons peeled and diced banana

3 tablespoons peeled, pitted, and diced mango

3 tablespoons peeled, seeded, and diced papaya

2 tablespoons peeled, cored, and diced fresh pineapple

2 tablespoons dried cherries

½ tablespoon julienned fresh mint

¼ teaspoon ground cinnamon

Pinch of ground allspice

2 tablespoons chopped Macadamia Nut Praline (page 194), (optional)

1 tablespoon sugar

¼ teaspoon fresh lemon juice

Ratatouille Fruit Gyoza:

1 tablespoon cornstarch

1 tablespoon cold water

16 gyoza wrappers

3 tablespoons vegetable oil

Passion Fruit Cream:

1 quart whole milk

1 vanilla bean, split lengthwise

8 egg yolks

¾ cup plus 1 tablespoon sugar

½ cup passion fruit syrup

Juice of 2 fresh passion fruits

…

½ cup diced pineapple

¼ cup fresh raspberries

¼ cup diced mango

1 kiwifruit, sliced

¼ cup cranberries

2 tablespoons chopped candied ginger, for garnish (optional)

To prepare the Tropical Fruit Filling, combine the fruit, mint, cinnamon, allspice, and chopped praline (if desired) in a large mixing bowl. Refrigerate for 1 hour.

In a saucepan, heat the tablespoon of sugar over medium heat until it caramelizes and becomes a clear golden brown. Add the refrigerated fruit mixture to the saucepan and cook, stirring, for 1 minute longer. Stir in the lemon juice and remove from the heat. Set aside to cool.

To prepare the Ratatouille Fruit Gyoza, combine the cornstarch and cold water and set aside. Lay out the wrappers on a work surface and place 1½ tablespoons of the fruit filling on each wrapper. Fold into half-moon shapes and seal the edges with the cornstarch mixture.

In a skillet, heat the vegetable oil. Fry the gyozas until lightly browned on one side only and gently add just enough water (about ¼ cup) to cover the oil. Cover and cook until the liquid has completely evaporated, about 1 minute. Remove from the pan and pat dry with paper towels. (Note: only one side of the gyoza will be crispy.)

To prepare the Passion Fruit Cream, cream together the egg yolks and sugar in a mixing bowl. In a saucepan, bring the milk and vanilla bean to a boil. Add the boiling milk to the egg mixture while whisking. Return the mixture to the saucepan and heat while stirring continuously with a wooden spoon, until it begins to thicken; do not let the mixture boil. Immediately strain the mixture into a stainless steel bowl set over ice. Add the passion fruit syrup and the passion fruit juice, mix together, and let cool.

To serve, pour 3 tablespoons of the Passion Fruit Cream onto serving plates. Stack the pineapple, raspberries, mango, kiwifruit, and cranberries in the center of each plate. Place 4 gyozas (crispy side up) on top of the sauce on each plate. Garnish with the candied ginger, if desired.

Pictured on opposite page

Vanilla Ice Cream

※ YIELD: ABOUT 1½ QUARTS ※

The best vanilla in the world comes from Tahiti, in French Polynesia. Buy vanilla pods that are supple and aromatic—sure signs of freshness.

4 vanilla beans, split lengthwise   8 egg yolks   2 cups heavy cream
2 cups whole milk   ½ cup sugar

Heat the vanilla beans and milk in a saucepan to just below boiling. Remove the pan from the heat and let sit for 1 hour to steep. Remove the vanilla beans and discard.

In a stainless steel bowl, whisk the egg yolks and sugar until creamy and pale yellow in color, about 2 minutes. Whisk in the steeped milk, and transfer to a clean saucepan. Over low heat, stir the mixture for about 15 minutes with a wooden spoon or spatula, continuously scraping the bottom and sides of the pan to prevent the mixture from sticking. When the mixture thickens enough to coat the back of a spoon, add the cream. Return to a simmer, and remove from the heat.

Strain the mixture into an ice cream maker and freeze according to the manufacturer's directions.

Kona Coffee Ice Cream

※ YIELD: ABOUT 1½ QUARTS ※

Follow the recipe for Vanilla Ice Cream (above), but steep 1 cup very coarsely ground Kona coffee beans in the milk, along with the vanilla beans. Strain the mixture before whisking into the eggs. Stir in 2 tablespoons coffee liqueur (such as Kahlúa) just before freezing.

Passion Fruit Ice Cream

※ YIELD: ABOUT 1½ to 2 QUARTS ※

Follow the recipe for Vanilla Ice Cream (above), adding ¾ cup passion fruit nectar or syrup to the vanilla beans and milk.

SHAVE ICE IS THE EVER-POPULAR Hawaiian treat. The best versions are found in family-run groceries or general stores. On Oahu's North Shore, for example, you'll find shave ice stands by the beach or the roadside. Even in the more remote areas of the state, where there's no gas station or telephone for miles, chances are there's a shave ice stand.

The authentic method of making it involves shaving or scraping ice from a large block, placing it in a paper cone, and dousing it liberally with a fruit-flavored colored syrup. You can choose from a long list of syrups, such as strawberry, banana, coconut, passion fruit, pineapple (which for some mysterious reason is usually colored blue), and guava. Rainbow-colored shave ice is a favorite with the *keikis*.

Basic Recipes

The recipes in this chapter are the foundations of my cooking, and many of them appear as components in other recipes. Stocks are particularly important building blocks, and while it's possible to use the premade, commercial variety (especially chicken stock), homemade stocks are invariably superior, healthier, and well worth the effort. Stocks freeze well, so if you expect to be cooking with them frequently, you might want to consider making up a double batch and keeping the reserve in the freezer.

I use a lot of sauces in my Euro-Asian cuisine. Although many appear with their respective recipes in earlier chapters the sauces in this chapter are the ones that I use most frequently throughout the book. For example, the Basic Tomato Sauce and Napoletana Sauce appear with different pizzas, pastas, and other dishes; and the Pesto works well as a garnish with numerous recipes. I use the Beurre Blanc, or white butter sauce, both on its own and as a foundation for other flavored sauces. Invaluable "pantry" items in this chapter like the Pesto, Candied Pecans, and Pickled Ginger can also be made ahead of time and refrigerated or frozen for future use.

Be creative with these recipes—they're multipurpose, and you'll find you can use them with many different styles of food.

Chicken Stock

1 to 2 chicken carcasses, broken up
2 tablespoons olive oil
1 stalk celery, coarsely chopped
½ cup coarsely chopped onion

½ cup coarsely chopped carrot
4 quarts water
¼ cup fresh basil leaves
¼ cup fresh thyme leaves

5 black peppercorns
2 bay leaves
Salt and freshly ground pepper
    to taste

*P*reheat the oven to 350 degrees. Place the chicken bones in a roasting pan and sprinkle with 1½ tablespoons of the oil. Roast in the oven until brown, about 15 to 20 minutes. Heat the remaining ½ tablespoon of olive oil in a large stockpot and sauté the celery, onion, and carrot over medium-high heat until tender. Add the water, basil, thyme, peppercorns, bay leaves, and roasted bones, and bring to a boil. Lower the heat and simmer until reduced by three-quarters (to about 1 quart), about 45 minutes, periodically skimming the surface of the stock to remove any impurities. Strain, discarding the solids, and season with salt and pepper.

Variation: For **Duck Stock,** follow the recipe for Chicken Stock, substituting 1 to 2 duck carcasses for the chicken carcasses.

Veal Stock

1 to 2 pounds veal bones
¼ cup coarsely chopped celery
¼ cup coarsely chopped carrot
½ cup coarsely chopped onion
½ cup coarsely chopped tomatoes

2 tablespoons coarsely chopped
    mushroom stems
2 cloves garlic
1 tablespoon tomato purée
½ cup fresh basil leaves
½ teaspoon minced fresh thyme

1 bay leaf, julienned
3 black peppercorns
4 quarts water
Salt and freshly ground pepper
    to taste

*P*reheat the oven to 350 degrees. Place the veal bones, celery, carrot, onion, tomatoes, mushroom stems, garlic, tomato purée, basil, thyme, bay leaf, and peppercorns in a roasting pan, mix together, and roast in the oven until dark brown, about 20 to 30 minutes. Transfer to a stockpot, add the water, and bring to a boil. Lower the heat and simmer until reduced by half (to about 2 quarts), periodically skimming the surface of the stock to remove any impurities. Strain, discarding the solids, and season with salt and pepper.

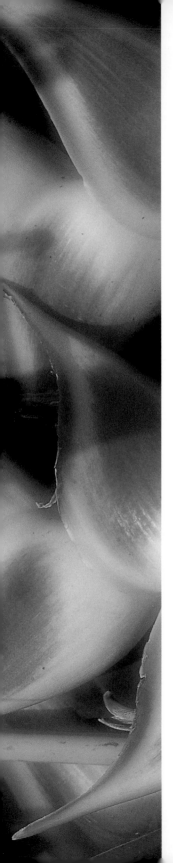

Vegetable Stock

1 onion, sliced
1 carrot, sliced
1 stalk celery, sliced

2 cloves garlic
3 sprigs fresh thyme
4 black peppercorns

3 bay leaves
2 quarts water
Salt and freshly ground pepper to taste

Place the onion, carrot, celery, garlic, thyme, peppercorns, bay leaves, and water in a stockpot and bring to a boil. Lower the heat and simmer for 45 minutes to 1 hour, or until reduced by half (to about 1 quart). Strain, discarding the solids, and season with salt and pepper.

Shrimp Stock

2 pounds shrimp shells
1 small onion, sliced
1 carrot, sliced
1 stalk celery, sliced

3 cloves garlic
1 teaspoon chopped fresh thyme
1 bunch fresh parsley, tied
6 black peppercorns

2 bay leaves
2 quarts water

Preheat the oven to 350 degrees. Place the shrimp shells in a roasting pan and heat in the oven until dried, about 15 to 20 minutes. Place the shells in a stockpot along with all the remaining ingredients, and bring to a boil. Lower the heat and simmer for about 1 hour, or until the liquid has reduced by half (to about 1 quart), periodically skimming the surface of the stock to remove any impurities. Strain, discarding the solids, and season with salt and pepper.

Variation: For **Shrimp Paste**, place the Shrimp Stock in a saucepan and reduce to a thick paste (1 cup of stock will yield approximately 1 tablespoon Shrimp Paste).

Variation: For **Fish Stock**, substitute 2 pounds of fish bones or scraps for the shrimp shells. Rinse the bones and scraps under cold running water, but do not roast. Season the finished stock with salt and pepper to taste.

Pesto

4 ounces fresh basil, julienned
¼ cup extra virgin olive oil

1 tablespoon pine nuts
1 clove garlic

1 ounce grated parmesan cheese
Salt and freshly ground pepper to taste

Place all the ingredients in a blender or food processor and purée until smooth.

Lobster Paste

≫ YIELD: ABOUT ½ CUP ≪

1 tablespoon peanut oil
½ onion, chopped
½ carrot, chopped
½ stalk celery, chopped

8 ounces lobster shells, or 2 Maine lobster heads
2 cloves garlic, minced
1 small tomato, chopped

2 or 3 sprigs fresh parsley
½ teaspoon chopped fresh tarragon
½ cup white wine
6 cups water

Heat the peanut oil in a large saucepan and sauté the onion, carrot, and celery over medium heat for about 2 minutes, until semi-soft. Add the lobster shells or heads, garlic, tomato, parsley, and tarragon, and stir briefly. Deglaze with the wine, and simmer for 5 minutes. Add the water and simmer for 30 minutes longer over medium-low heat. Strain into a clean saucepan, discarding the vegetables. Pulverize the lobster shells or heads in a blender, or with a wooden mallet, and strain the liquid back into the pan through a fine sieve. Reduce the strained liquid to the consistency of a runny paste.

Note: To prepare live lobster for cooking, place it right side up on a cutting board and sever the spinal cord by cutting the lobster at the neck where the tail meets the body shell. This will kill it immediately. Once this is done, you can break off the head and claws and remove the tail meat. Use the heads to make lobster paste.

Basic Tomato Sauce

≫ YIELD: ABOUT 2 CUPS ≪

¼ cup extra virgin olive oil
4 cloves garlic, minced
1 small onion, coarsely chopped
1 small carrot, coarsely chopped

1 stalk celery, coarsely chopped
1 large can (28 ounces) Italian-style Roma tomatoes in their juice, preferably with basil

Salt and freshly ground pepper to taste
1 tablespoon sugar
½ cup packed fresh basil leaves

Heat the oil in a large saucepan and sauté the garlic, onion, carrot, and celery over medium-high heat until golden brown, about 1 minute. Place the tomatoes in a large bowl, crush with your hands, and add to the saucepan. Add the salt, pepper, and sugar, and cook the sauce over low heat for 20 to 30 minutes, until reduced by about one-third. Add the basil leaves and cook for another 5 minutes, stirring frequently. If you prefer a smoother consistency, pulse the sauce in a food processor for about 10 seconds.

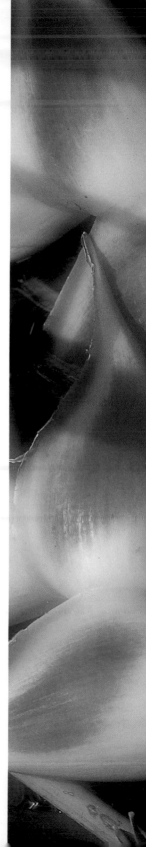

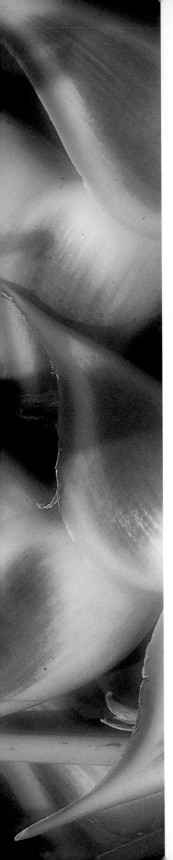

Beurre Blanc

≫ YIELD: ABOUT 1½ CUPS ≪

The foundation for many of my sauces is this wonderfully adaptable sauce, otherwise known as White Butter Sauce.

½ cup white wine

2 teaspoons white wine vinegar

1 teaspoon fresh lemon juice

1 tablespoon minced shallot

2 tablespoons heavy cream

½ cup unsalted butter, chopped

¼ teaspoon salt

Freshly ground white pepper to taste

Combine the wine, wine vinegar, lemon juice, and shallot in a saucepan and bring to a boil over medium-high heat. Reduce the liquid until it becomes syrupy. Add the cream, and reduce by half. Turn the heat to low and gradually add the butter, stirring slowly (do not whisk) until it is all incorporated. Be careful not to let the mixture boil, or it will break and separate. Season with salt and pepper and strain through a fine sieve. Transfer to a double boiler and keep warm.

Cabernet Sauce

≫ YIELD: 2½ CUPS ≪

¼ cup olive oil

1 onion, chopped

1 carrot, chopped

1 stalk celery, chopped

8 cloves garlic, chopped

4 bay leaves

5 black peppercorns

2 tablespoons sugar

4 cups cabernet sauvignon, or other red wine

4 cups Veal Stock (page 213)

Heat the olive oil in a saucepan, and sauté the onion, carrot, celery, garlic, bay leaves, and peppercorns for about 5 minutes over medium heat, or until the vegetables are golden brown. Add the sugar and caramelize for about 2 minutes, while stirring. Deglaze with the wine, and reduce the liquid by two-thirds (to about 1½ cups). Add the Veal Stock and again reduce by two-thirds. Strain through a fine sieve into a clean pan, and continue to reduce until the sauce is thick enough to coat the back of a spoon.

Simple Syrup

≫ YIELD: 3 CUPS ≪

For whatever quantity you need, make it in the following proportions.

2 cups sugar

1¾ cups water

Place the sugar and water in a saucepan. Dissolve the sugar, stirring continuously, and bring to a boil. Remove from the heat and reserve.

Orange-Chile Sauce

½ cup sake

Zest of ½ orange

1 cup sweet chile sauce (preferably Lingham's brand)

¼ cup fresh orange juice

¼ cup water

1 teaspoon minced shallot

¼ teaspoon minced ginger

¼ teaspoon minced garlic

In a saucepan, bring the sake and orange zest to a boil (take care as the alcohol may ignite as it is boiling off). Reduce the liquid by half. Lower the heat to medium, stir in the remaining ingredients, and continue to reduce until the sauce reaches a syrupy consistency and is thick enough to coat the back of a spoon. Strain and use as a dipping sauce.

Variation: For **Orange-Chile-Plum Sauce**, omit the orange zest. Combine all the other ingredients in a saucepan, bring to a boil, reduce the heat to low, and simmer for 10 to 15 minutes until thickened. Strain and return to a clean saucepan. Add 4 fresh plums that have been pitted and cut into 5 or 6 slices each, and simmer for 5 minutes over very low heat. Strain before serving (if suitable, the plum slices can be used as garnish).

Basic Ponzu Sauce

Ponzu is a Japanese soy-and-citrus dipping sauce that is commonly served with fish. Bottled ponzu sauces are available in Asian markets, but it's much better to prepare your own. There are two versions below: the first is somewhat stronger and goes well with chicken and heavier fish; the second is sweeter, and is better with mild-flavored fish. Proportions in either can be adjusted to your taste.

1 cup mirin

¾ cup light soy sauce (preferably Yamasa brand)

1 teaspoon dried red chile flakes, or to taste

2 tablespoons fresh lemon juice

Bring the mirin to a boil in a saucepan, and reduce to ⅓ cup, about 5 minutes. Remove from the heat and allow to cool. Whisk in the soy sauce, chile flakes, and lemon juice. Cool to room temperature.

Variation: For **Sweet Ponzu Sauce**, use only ¼ cup of the soy sauce, and ¼ teaspoon of the chile flakes. Prepare as described above for Basic Ponzu Sauce.

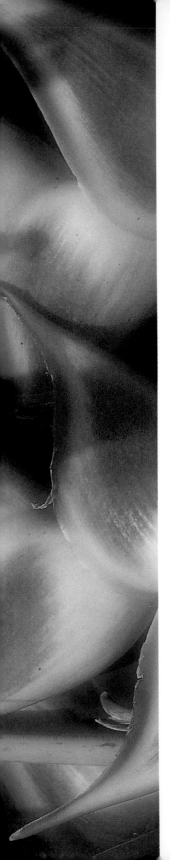

Napoletana Sauce

¼ cup olive oil

4 cloves garlic, thinly sliced

½ small Maui onion, quartered and thinly sliced

5 tomatoes, peeled and seeded

½ cup julienned fresh basil

½ teaspoon minced fresh thyme

½ teaspoon sugar

½ teaspoon salt, or to taste

½ teaspoon freshly ground pepper

Heat the olive oil in a large saucepan and sauté the garlic and onion over medium heat until translucent, about 2 or 3 minutes. Reduce the heat to low. By hand, gently squeeze the tomatoes of their juice, reserving the juice. Chop the tomatoes and add to the pan together with their juice and all the remaining ingredients. Simmer for about 30 minutes, or until slightly thickened.

Sun-Dried Tomato Sauce

4 cloves garlic, sliced to ⅛-inch thickness

2 tablespoons olive oil

1 teaspoon minced garlic

6 oil-packed sun-dried tomatoes, drained and chopped

½ cup Napoletana Sauce (see preceding recipe)

1 tablespoon minced fresh basil

Salt and freshly ground pepper to taste

Put the sliced garlic in a small saucepan of water and bring to a boil. Drain off the water, add fresh water, and simmer for about 3 minutes, or until the garlic is al dente. Drain and reserve the garlic. (This "double-blanching" process will eliminate the pungent smell and strong taste of the garlic.)

Heat the olive oil in a skillet and sauté the minced garlic and sun-dried tomatoes until the garlic is lightly browned. Quickly stir in the Napoletana Sauce, basil, and double-blanched garlic. Season with salt and pepper.

Black sand beach, Big Island.

Roy's Feasts from Hawaii

Candied Pecans

※ YIELD: 1 CUP ※

4 tablespoons unsalted butter   4 ounces pecans   1 tablespoon honey

*H*eat the butter in a saucepan and sauté the pecans over low heat, stirring occasionally. Gradually add the honey and cook for about 2 or 3 minutes, stirring continuously, until the honey binds to the pecans and any liquid has evaporated.

Pink Pickled Ginger

※ YIELD: 1 CUP ※

It is important to use young, pliable ginger for this recipe rather than older, harder ginger. Kombu is a dried sea kelp used in Japanese cuisine for flavoring stocks and soups; it's available in most Asian markets.

1½ cups unseasoned rice vinegar
6 tablespoons sugar

8 ounces very finely sliced young ginger
10 black peppercorns

1 piece *kombu* (kelp), about 6 inches long

*C*ombine the vinegar and sugar in a mixing bowl, stirring until the sugar dissolves. Add the ginger, peppercorns, and *kombu*, and place in an airtight container for 2 or 3 days, at which time it is ready for use. Stored in the refrigerator, it will keep for 2 weeks.

Kaunolu Bay, near the site of an ancient village, Lanai.

A Word About Cooking

STIR-FRYING Many of the recipes in this book call for stir-frying, which involves cooking food over very high heat, and tossing and turning the ingredients so that everything in the pan cooks very quickly. Whether you use a pan, skillet, or wok, it's essential to heat the oil in the pan almost to the smoking point before adding the ingredients. If you're cooking a combination of ingredients that require different cooking times, add them in the order of how long they take to cook, and/or keep the quicker-cooking foods to the edges of the pan, where the heat is less intense. Advance preparation is essential. This usually involves cutting and dicing the food into small, attractive pieces (to speed the cooking process), and organizing everything within reach so that you can cook without interruption.

GRILLING Many of our dishes are cooked on the grill. If you haven't got a grill, either indoor or outdoor, in most cases you can improvise by using the oven broiler or by pan-frying the food, instead. You may have to make some adjustments in timing.

ROASTING BELL PEPPERS AND CHILES Roasting bell peppers and chiles gives them a smoky flavor and concentrates the natural sugars, and also facilitates peeling the tough, bitter skin. Place the peppers or chiles on a grill, under a broiler, or on a rack over an open flame on top of the stove. Turn them quickly and often so they blacken evenly and do not burn. Put them in a paper or plastic bag and twist the bag shut, or put them in a covered bowl. Let them sweat for 15 to 20 minutes or until cool, then peel with a knife or pull off the skin by hand, and remove the stem, seeds, and interior ribs.

ROASTING GARLIC Roasted garlic loses much of its bitterness and instead tastes very sweet and mellow. To roast, place unpeeled cloves of garlic in a lightly oiled baking pan and roast at 350 degrees for about 30 minutes. Shake the pan occasionally or stir the cloves around with a wooden spoon. Remove from the oven and squeeze the garlic from each clove.

TOASTING SEEDS AND NUTS In most cases, this is an optional step, and you can skip it if time is short. But toasting does bring out the full flavors and aromas of seeds and nuts, and is pretty simple. To toast sesame seeds, heat a dry cast-iron skillet over medium-high heat. When hot, add the seeds in a single layer and toss continuously for 45 seconds to 1 minute, until golden brown and shiny. To reduce the risk of burning and to better control the process, start with a cold pan, add the seeds, and heat over medium-high until toasted. Other seeds can be toasted the same way, and should take 1 to 2 minutes. To toast macadamia nuts, spread the nuts in a single layer in a baking pan and place in a 400-degree oven for 5 to 7 minutes or until golden brown, shaking the pan occasionally. Smaller nuts take about 3 to 5 minutes. For both seeds and nuts, watch carefully to be sure they don't burn.

Roy's Feasts from Hawaii

Glossary

Ahi Hawaiian name for bigeye or yellowfin tuna. Often served as sashimi.

Bamboo shoots Cream-colored, cone-shaped young shoots of the bamboo plant. Canned shoots are fine to use.

Basil Common sweet basil has a green leaf; opal basil is purple-leaved; Thai basil has green and maroon leaves, and is slightly spicy. These varieties can be used interchangeably.

Bean thread noodles Also called glass noodles, cellophane noodles, or *saifun*. A thin, clear noodle made from the starch of the mung bean. Bean noodles have very little flavor of their own but soak up the flavors of whatever they're cooked with.

Beni shoga Also called *gari*. Pickled ginger sometimes dyed bright red.

Big Island The island of Hawaii, the largest in the chain of Hawaiian islands. Also known as the Orchid Island.

Bok choy Also known as baby bok choy or Chinese white cabbage. Has dark green leaves and a long white stem. *See also* **choy sum**. [Note: Many Asian vegetables are very similar in look and taste, and are easily confused. They may go by different names in different locales—or even from market to market—which adds to the confusion. Most of the cabbage-type vegetables can be used interchangeably, with the exception of *gai choy*, which is fairly bitter.]

Carambola (star fruit) A yellow-orange fruit, about 5 inches long, with waxy skin and juicy, tart flesh. When cut crosswise, the slices are an almost perfect star shape. Peeling is unnecessary, and there are few seeds to bother with. Good in fruit salads.

Char siu Cantonese-style barbecued pork.

Chile pastes and sauces There is a bewildering variety on the market, each slightly different from the other. All contain chiles, salt, and oil. In addition, there may be vinegar, sugar, garlic, black beans, or other seasonings in varying combinations and amounts. My two favorite brands are Lan Chi, a Chinese product that contains a good measure of garlic, and the Malaysian Lingham's Chilli Sauce. Both come in jars. *See also* **sambal sekera; sriracha.**

Choy sum Or bok choy sum. Cabbage similiar to bok choy, but slightly smaller with yellow flowers. *See also* **bok choy.**

Cilantro Also known as Chinese parsley, fresh coriander, or Mexican parsley. Has a flat, lacy leaf, somewhat like Italian parsley. Very aromatic, with its own distinct flavor. There is not a good substitute, but this herb is widely available.

Coconut milk Rich liquid made from grated fresh coconut meat combined with hot water and squeezed through a filter. Can be made fresh but is readily available canned.

Curry pastes A blend of chiles and spices, often categorized as red, green, or yellow. (The color varies depending on the type of chiles used to make the curry paste.) An essential ingredient in Thai cooking. I particularly recommend the Matsaman curry paste, which is a blend of red chiles, garlic, salt, onion, and spices.

Daikon A large white radish with a crisp, juicy flesh and fairly mild taste. Used often in Japanese cuisine.

Egg roll wrappers Also known as spring roll wrappers. Rectangular wrappers made of flour and egg, available in different thicknesses and sizes. The typical egg roll wrapper measures about 6 inches square. After the filling is wrapped, the egg roll is fried. Chinese egg rolls and spring rolls are basically the same (both are fried), but the Vietnamese spring roll is not. *See also* **lumpia wrappers; rice paper.**

Enoki mushrooms Also called *enokitake*. Tiny, whitish mushrooms sold in clumps. Their spongy roots should be cut off before they're used.

Fish sauce A strong-smelling, salty, brown liquid, typically made from anchovies or other small fish fermented in brine. A basic ingredient in Southeast Asian cooking. Keeps indefinitely unrefrigerated. Thai and Filipino versions are milder than the Vietnamese or Burmese types. One of my favorites is the Tiparos brand.

Furikake A prepackaged blend of dried seasonings such as dried bonito flakes, ground sesame seeds, crumbled dried seaweed, and salt.

Gai choy (Chinese) mustard cabbage. Has a thick, curvy stem, and a slightly bitter flavor.

Gari ginger Pickled ginger, usually a light pink color. A common accompaniment to sushi dishes.

Ginger root A fibrous, peppery rhizome (in other words, it is technically not a root). Not native to Hawaii, but grows well here. Hawaiian ginger is sweet and juicy.

Glass noodles *See* **bean thread noodles.**

Gyoza wrappers Japanese potstickers or potsticker wrappers. *See also* **potsticker wrappers.**

Hamachi Japanese for yellowtail tuna; a type of jackfish related to pompano.

Harusame Japanese cellophane or bean thread noodles made from rice or potato starch. Substitute with bean thread noodles made from mung beans.

Hawaiian red chiles Small, red-orange, extremely hot Hawaiian peppers. Substitute with red jalapeños, Fiesta chiles, or red serranos.

Hawaiian Vintage Chocolate High-quality chocolate made from cocoa beans grown on the Big Island.

Hibachi A small grill ("fire bowl" in Japanese). Hibachi cooking is popular in Hawaii.

Hoisin sauce A sweet, spicy, garlicky sauce made from fermented soybean paste.

Japanese cucumber Smaller and thinner-skinned than cucumbers generally found in the United States. Substitute with the youngest American cucumbers available, peeled and seeded.

Japanese eggplant A long, narrow variety with deep-purple skin and white flesh.

Japanese plum paste Also known as *bainiku*. Made from puréed *umeboshi*, salt-pickled unripe plums. Not to be confused with *umeboshi paste*, which is also made from pickled plums. Available canned or bottled.

Japanese spice sprouts (kaiware sprouts) Easily grown from daikon seeds, these sprouts have a sharp, spicy flavor. To use, cut off the root ends.

Kabocha Pumpkin-like winter squash. Turban shaped with light green skin and bright yellow to medium-orange flesh. Substitute with acorn squash or pumpkin.

Kaffir lime leaves The leaves from the kaffir lime tree have a strong floral-lemon fragrance. If using dried leaves, soak in warm water for about 20 minutes before using. There is no substitute.

Kaiware sprouts *See* **Japanese spice sprouts.**

Kiawe Fragrant wood from a tree that grows abundantly in Hawaii. Hawaii's mesquite. Used for grilling foods.

Kimchee Korean pickled cabbage, usually made with napa cabbage. Can be very hot and spicy.

Kona coffee Rich coffee made from beans grown in the Kona district on the Big Island. (See page 186.)

Kona crab These crabs are fished throughout Hawaiian waters and are sweeter and more moist than Maryland or Louisiana crab, but not as firm. They are in season May through August. Any other kind of crab may be substituted.

Lemon grass Fragrant stalk frequently used in Thai cooking. Use the lower part of the stalk, peeling off the tough outer leaves. There is no good substitute.

Lumpia wrappers Wrappers for Philippine egg rolls or spring rolls, about 8 inches square. *See also* **egg roll wrappers; rice paper.**

Mahimahi Also called dolphinfish, but not related to the marine mammal. Substitute with a firm-fleshed fish.

Mandoline A versatile vegetable slicer and shredder.

Maui onions Sweet, moist, mild-tasting onion grown in Kula, the up-country region of Maui. Substitute with other sweet onions, such as Vidalia or Walla Walla onions. (See page 60.)

Mirin Sweet, syrupy Japanese rice wine used in sauces and marinades.

Miso Thick soybean paste made by salting and fermenting soybeans and rice or barley. Comes in a variety of colors and textures. White miso *(shiro miso)* is sweet and fine-textured, good for use in soups and dressings, and for grilled foods. Red miso *(aka miso)* is saltier. It is also good in soups.

Mustard cabbage *See* **gai choy.**

Nage A flavored broth.

Napa cabbage Also known as celery cabbage, Chinese cabbage, or *won bok*. Pale green at the top to white at the stem with crinkly leaves.

Nori Also called purple laver. Dried, thin sheets of black-green seaweed, frequently used in Japanese cooking, often for wrapping sushi.

Ono Also called *wahoo*. A member of the mackerel family, often used for sashimi. Substitute with grouper, snapper, or sea bass. *Ono* also means "delicious" in Hawaiian.

Opah Also called moonfish. Has pinkish flesh. Substitute with swordfish or tuna.

Opakapaka Hawaiian pink snapper. Substitute with red snapper or grouper.

Oyster sauce Concentrated brown sauce made from oysters, water, and salt. Keeps indefinitely in the refrigerator.

Palm sugar Coarse, raw, honey-colored sugar made from palm sap. Used in Thai cooking. Substitute with dark brown sugar.

Panko Crispy Japanese-style bread crumbs, coarser than regular bread crumbs. Substitute with regular unseasoned bread crumbs.

Passion fruit Also know by its Hawaiian name, *lilikoi*. A highly aromatic egg-sized fruit, yellowish, brownish, or purplish in color with a very intense flavor. Used to flavor drinks, ice creams, dressings, and sauces. To prepare, scoop the yellow-orange teardrop-shaped pulp from the shell and force through a nonaluminum sieve.

Pickled ginger A common Japanese condiment. May be labeled *beni shoga* or *gari shoga*. Can be found in the produce or dairy section in many markets, either packed in small plastic tubs or jars. You can make your own pink pickled ginger (see page 219). Commercial red pickled ginger is artificially colored.

Ponzu A Japanese sauce primarily of citrus juice, soy sauce, and vinegar. Some versions are sweet, others are more acidic.

Potsticker wrappers Thin, round pastry dough made from flour and water, used to wrap certain kinds of Chinese dumplings. May also be sold as *gyoza* wrappers or *shiu mai* wrappers. If none of these are available, use wonton wrappers trimmed into circles.

Puna goat cheese Rich, creamy cheese made from the milk of goats raised in the eastern Big Island region of Puna. (See page 15.)

Ramen noodles One of the main varieties of Asian noodles made from wheat. Available fresh and dried.

Rayu Spicy sesame oil.

Rice paper Made from rice flour, water,

and salt. Usually soaked or brushed with water to soften before using to wrap foods. Used to make Vietnamese-style spring rolls. More delicate than lumpia wrappers or egg roll wrappers.

Rice vinegar Light vinegar made from fermented rice wine.

Saifun *See* **bean thread noodles.**

Sake Also known as Japanese rice wine. A clear, fragrant wine made from fermented rice.

Sambal sekera Spicy chile paste from Malaysia or Indonesia. *See also* **chile pastes and sauces.**

Sashimi Thinly sliced raw fish.

Shichimi Translates from Japanese as "seven spices" or "seven flavors." A mixture of *sansho*, orange peel, poppy seeds, white and black sesame seeds, chile pepper, and seaweed. If the bottle says *shichimi togarashi*, it's probably very spicy.

Shiitake mushrooms Brown Japanese mushrooms with meaty caps and woody stems. Available both fresh and dried. Dried mushrooms need to be rehydrated before use.

Shiu mai Round steamed wontons, usually filled with a pork or shrimp mixture. Also, any appetizer-sized dumpling that has been steamed, boiled, or fried.

Shiu mai wrappers The thin round wrappers used to make *shiu mai*. Can be used interchangeably with *gyoza* and potsticker wrappers.

Shutome Broadbill swordfish, which is caught in Hawaiian waters. Substitute with other swordfish.

Soy sauce A salty brown sauce made of soybeans, flour, salt, and water. Available in many varieties, with different levels of saltiness and different flavors. *Light soy*

does not necessarily contain less salt; different brands of light soy may be saltier than regular soy sauces. Yamasa is a particularly good brand. *Dark soy* is aged longer than other soy sauces, and is slightly thicker and sweeter, with added caramel or molasses. *Mushroom soy* is a dark soy sauce flavored with straw mushrooms. *Shoyu* is a Japanese variety, frequently used in Hawaii. It is slightly sweeter and less salty than Chinese versions.

Spiny lobster A small, colorful lobster without the large front claws of other varieties of lobster. Has a sweeter tasting meat and a firmer texture than Maine lobster.

Spring rolls Vietnamese spring rolls are wrapped in rice paper. They are not fried, like the Chinese spring rolls.

Sriracha A sweet and spicy condiment commonly set out on the tables of Vietnamese and Thai restaurants. Made of chiles, vinegar, salt, and sugar. *See also* **chile pastes and sauces.**

Star anise A distinctive looking pod shaped like a star with eight points. Licorice-flavored. One of the components of Chinese five-spices mixtures.

Star fruit *See* **carambola.**

Szechwan peppercorns Pungent, dried reddish-brown berries not actually related to peppercorns or chile peppers. Commonly used to add a spicy-woodsy flavor to roasts.

Szechwan-style cooking This style, from the Szechwan province of China, can be characterized as relatively spicy.

Tamarind Sweet/sour fruit from the pods of the tamarind tree. Sold in pods, powder, and pulp. Most recipes use the liquid from the soaked pulp. Sometimes

whole immature pods are used in soups and stews.

Taro A nutritious tuber and staple food of ancient Hawaiian culture. Traditionally used to make *poi*. The leaves can be used to wrap foods for cooking. Do not eat taro or its leaves raw as it may irritate the skin and throat. Hawaiian taro roots are large (anywhere from ½ to 2 pounds). The variety commonly used in Chinese and Japanese cooking is about the size of a new potato.

Thai basil *See* **basil.**

Tobiko caviar Orange-red flying fish roe with a mild, sweet fishy flavor.

Udon noodles Round or flat white Japanese noodle made of wheat flour, salt, and water. Available fresh and dried.

Wasabi Also called Japanese horseradish. A hot, spicy paste that usually accompanies Japanese sashimi. Available as a powder or as a less flavorful ready-made paste (the paste comes in a tube like toothpaste). Occasionally, fresh wasabi roots are available and can be prepared by paring off the brown-green skin and finely grating.

Water chestnuts Resemble chestnuts but are actually a kind of water grass. The flesh is white and crunchy. Available fresh or canned, whole or sliced, fresh water chestnuts must be peeled before they can be used.

Won bok *See* **napa cabbage.**

Wonton wrappers Very thin, square sheets of wheat flour and egg dough typically used to make dumplings of different types. The dough can be cut into strips and fried for garnishes.

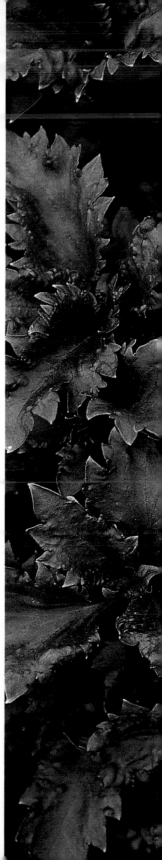

What Food Lovers Say About Chef Roy Yamaguchi

"Every year I vacation in Hawaii for two reasons: because it's Hawaii and because it's where I get to eat Roy Yamaguchi's food. His cookbook will provide an invaluable service by making it possible for us 'mainlanders' to enjoy the unique experience of eating Roy's cooking all year long."

Jeffrey Katzenberg, partner, Dreamworks SKG

"It was love at first taste with Roy's cooking . . . I wouldn't fly through Honolulu without visiting Roy's for his meals of magic. In fact, the one time I couldn't get off the plane en route to New Zealand, I had his fabulous food delivered to the jet for the flight down under!"

Robin Leach, *Lifestyles*

"What Roy does with food is simply magic. His delicious Euro-Asian creations have done for fine dining what Monet did for fine art."

John Waihee, former governor of Hawaii

"When Roy Yamaguchi was a teaching chef for our Great Chef's program at the Robert Mondavi Winery, he not only showed us [how] to combine the seafood, fish, meat, vegetables, and fruit of Hawaii for his delicious dishes, which are traditional and exotic, he also proved that our wines complement his genial cuisine very well!"

Margrit Biever Mondavi

"I am very happy to hear Roy is publishing a cookbook. I have always wanted to be able to make his dishes for my friends who can't visit his restaurants."

Shep Gordon, president, Alive (Beverly Hills)

"Roy is the kind of chef who defines originality while never wandering into the bizarre or trivial. Understanding fresh materials, finding nuance, creating harmony of flavor. That's Roy!"

Jamie and Jack Davies, Schramsberg Vineyards and Cellars, Calistoga, CA

"The first time I experienced Roy Yamaguchi's food was at 385 North in Los Angeles about ten years ago. Although I was a bit taken aback by the waiters' uniforms (they wore fitted jumpsuits with large industrial zippers in strategic places—I didn't know whether they were going to take my order or service my BMW), I quickly realized I was in the presence of a kitchen master. This assessment has been borne out by Roy's well-deserved success in Hawaii, where he has taken part in no less than the founding and establishment of a completely new cuisine. I would have expected no less from him."

Anthony Dias Blue, *Bon Appétit* **wine & spirits editor and book author**

"What a joy to have this maestro's might available to us all! Roy is a magician and a talent to be honored!"

William Tomicki, author of the syndicated column "Entree," *New York Times*

"Roy Yamaguchi is *the* 'Main Man' of Pacific Rim cooking. He cooks with his heart and soul . . . and it shows!"

Drew Nieporent, owner Rubicon, Montrachet, Nobu, and Tribeca Grill restaurants

"That Roy is a master in the kitchen goes without saying. But to me, what's truly unique and wonderful about Roy, is the unabashed joy and wit he brings to his cooking. Roy is clearly having a great time creating his dishes—and the dishes reflect that in every bite."

Merrill Shindler, restaurant critic, KABC (Los Angeles)

"Roy is a wonderful chef as well as being one of the nicest I know."

Jeremiah Tower, chef/owner, Stars (San Francisco)

"I have great admiration for Roy. He is the foremost practitioner of Hawaiian Regional cooking—and I feel that it is *very* important that all the regional cuisines of the U.S. are kept alive and vibrant. It seems Roy has done more than his share for his region."

Jasper White, chef/owner, Jasper's (Boston)

"Roy Yamaguchi has proved that Hawaiian cuisine is within reach of everyone . . ."

Jean Joho, chef/owner, Everest (Chicago)

"Roy and his colleagues successfully combine the exotic flavors of Hawaii and the light, healthy cuisine of the '90s."

Martin Yan, *Yan Can Cook*

"No one has gone so far yet, at least with success, in blending French, Italian, Thai, Japanese, and Chinese cuisines."

Alain Gayot, publisher, *Gault Millau,* **André Gayot Publications**

"I have had the pleasure of cooking with Roy on several occasions. His quality of excellence, creative and innovative design of food make him a winner. This book will inspire you to cook as though you are on the islands . . ."

Bradley M. Ogden, chef and co-owner, The Lark Creek Inn (Larkspur, CA) and One Market restaurant

"Roy Yamaguchi is without a doubt, one of America's most promising new chefs. His blending of East and West and creative style with food has certainly paved a new path in the evolving American culinary map."

Ken Hom, author of eight cookbooks, chef, and consultant

"Roy could rightly be called the father of East-West cooking, although that sounds much too stuffy for the least pretentious of chefs. I will never forget the excitement of eating his food for the first time in the early 1980s. It was in an obscure restaurant in LAX [Los Angeles International Airport], and here was this young French-trained chef searing fish on a teppan-style grill, turning out impeccable sauces seasoned with seaweeds and Asian spices many people had never heard of, and creating spicy-sparkly dishes that were seductive and completely original. Today a great many chefs are playing around with similar ideas, but it is a borrowed cooking style. Roy's springs from his roots and his unerring sense of how to put ingredients together."

Caroline Bates, *Gourmet*

"His dishes are imaginative, but also soundly based—the stumbling block of many experimenters. If there is an emphasis, it would be Hawaiian, modified by French, inspired and interpreted by Roy . . ."

Lois Dwan, former restaurant editor for the *Los Angeles Times*

Roy's Feasts from Hawaii

"My first visit to Roy's was an exciting adventure and culinary event. The menu, blends of taste, and artful presentation were long remembered. *Nation's Restaurant News* was honored to name Roy Yamaguchi to its Fine Dining Hall of Fame in 1992, one of only ten restaurants selected. This well-deserved recognition emphasizes the true professional and culinary contributions to the restaurant industry by Mr. Yamaguchi."

James C. Doherty, publisher, *Nation's Restaurant News*

"I've been writing about Roy Yamaguchi for the past decade, watching his career blossom. His cooking has flourished to embrace the best of the East and the West in a dynamic and irresistible style. Roy is one of the nation's preeminent talents, a chef who continually tests the boundaries of the cutting edge, with culinary reason wisely prevailing."

Janice Wald Henderson, food writer

Index

Roy's Feasts from Hawaii